JFK Case 'NOT' Closed:

Key Evidence Dismissed, Ignored, Altered or Suppressed to Frame Lee Harvey Oswald as the 'Lone' Assassin!

by Dave O'Brien
Author of
Through The Oswald Window

with JFK Assassination Researcher Johnny Cairns

"The torch has been passed to a new generation..."

President John F. Kennedy
Inaugural Address
January 20, 1961

This book is dedicated to the next generation of JFK assassination researchers and seekers of the truth.

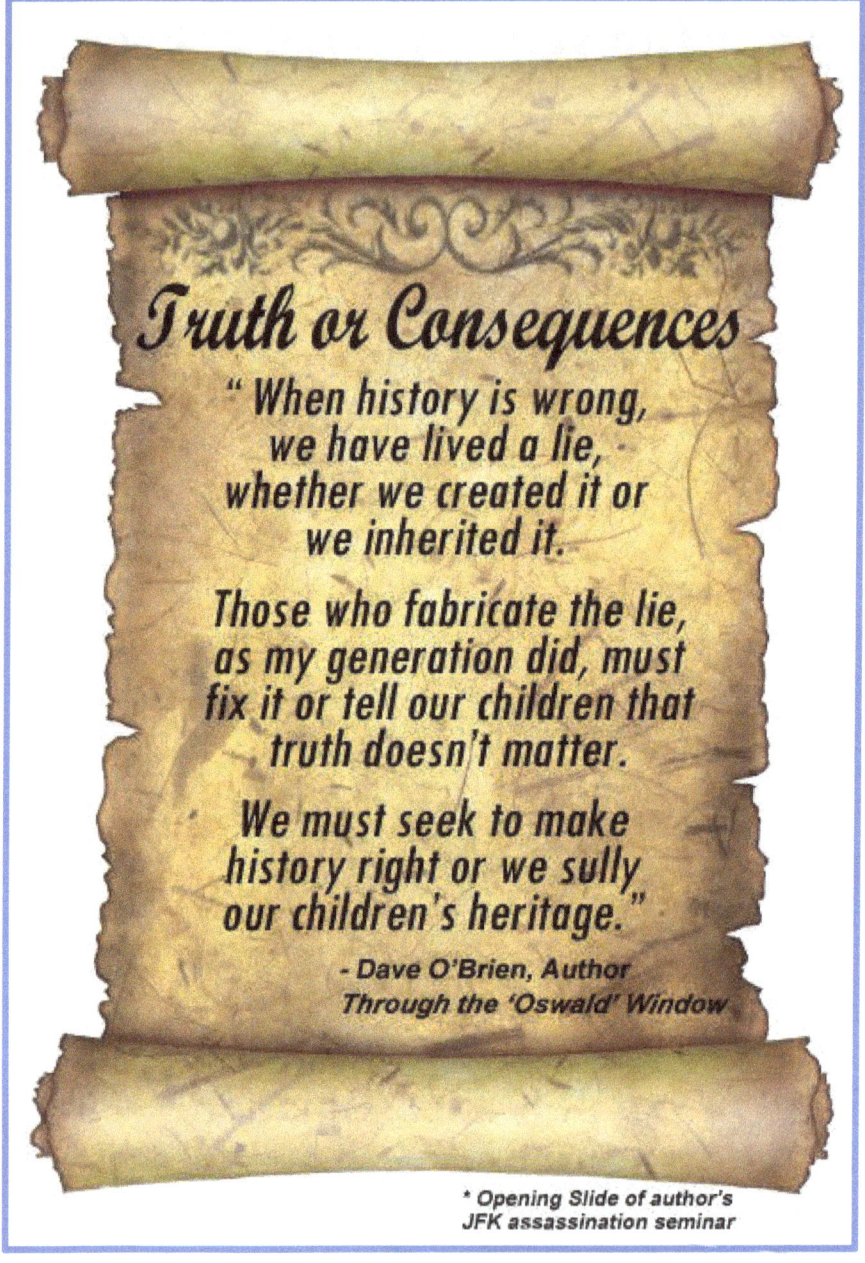

Table of Contents

Introduction – Correcting History by Giving Accused JFK Assassin Lee Harvey Oswald the Defense He Never Received in Life or Death!

Chapter 1 – Views of Conspiracy from the 'Oswald' Window

Chapter 2 – The Ignored Warren Commission Ballistic Tests that Disprove its Own 'Single Bullet' and 'Lone Gunman' Theories!

Chapter 3 – Recently Discovered Film Oddity that Indicates JFK Fatal Head Shot Fired by Second Gunman Now Backed by Modern Technologies!

Introduction to Chapters 4,5,6 & 7

    A Circumstantial Case:
    A Defense of Lee Harvey Oswald by JFK Assassination Researcher Johnny Cairns

Chapter 4 – Debunking the Circumstantial Evidence Used by the Warren Commission to Name Lee Oswald as the 'Lone' Assassin of JFK!

    Part 1 – The 'Lone' Assassin Rifle

Chapter 5 – Debunking the Circumstantial Evidence Used by the Warren Commission to Name Lee Oswald as the 'Lone' Assassin of JFK!

Part 2 – The Problematic Paper Bag

Chapter 6 – Debunking the Circumstantial Evidence Used by the Warren Commission to Name Lee Oswald as the 'Lone' Assassin of JFK!

Part 3 – The Ammunition Linked to Oswald

Chapter 7 – Debunking the Circumstantial Evidence Used by the Warren Commission to Name Lee Oswald as the 'Lone' Assassin of JFK!

Part 4 – CE 399 (The Magic Bullet)

Chapter 8 – Seeing **ISN'T** Believing? Putting the Film and Photo Myths to Rest Once and For All

Chapter 9 – The Natural, Instinctive Physical Reactions of Three Key People in Dealey Plaza that Prove a Second Gunman!

Chapter 10 – The 'Magic' Bullet May be Less Magical than We Thought but Still Not Possible!

Chapter 11 – Altering Vital Photographic Evidence to Declare Oswald as the 'Lone' Assassin of JFK!

Chapter 12 – Why the 'Military' Autopsy Alone Would Have Acquitted Lee Harvey Oswald at Trial!

Chapter 13 – Shocking Discoveries by Two Experts Who Reviewed the JFK Medical Evidence and Found Conspiracy and Cover-Up!

Chapter 14 – How Two Medical Illustrators Were Duped into Falsifying Autopsy Photos in Support of a 'Lone' Assassin!

Chapter 15 – Ghosts of Witnesses Passed: They May Be Deceased but the Many Ignored Witnesses of 11/22/63 Can Still Tell Us How JFK Was Assassinated!

Chapter 16 – How Advancement in Imaging Proves JFK Autopsy Photos and X-Rays Were Altered to Frame Oswald as a '**Lone**' Assassin!

Chapter 17 – From Cartoons to Modern 3D Realism: These Evolving Technologies Seek to Finally Tell Us How JFK Was Assassinated!

Chapter 18 – Top Researchers Weigh In on How Best to Formally Re-Investigate the JFK Assassination and the Key Evidence that Needs to be Examined

Appendices
Resources
Index
About Johnny Cairns
About Dave O'Brien

JFK Case 'NOT' Closed

* JFK Case NOT Closed: Key Evidence Dismissed, Ignored, Altered or Suppressed to Frame Lee Harvey Oswald as the 'Lone' Assassin – © 2022 by Dave O'Brien and Paul O'Brien
* All Rights Reserved by the Publishers
* Book ISBN: 978-0-9880187-7-8
* Author – Dave O'Brien
* Book Cover Design – Paul O'Brien
* Book Design – Paul O'Brien
* Printed and Distributed by IngramSpark, La Vergne, TN

This book (JFK Case NOT Closed) may not be copied, whole or in part, reproduced or e-mailed, whole or in part without the written permission of the publishers.

You may not modify or prepare derivative works based upon this book or any element thereof, and you may not redistribute, sell, de-compile, or disassemble any and/or all text contained in this book without the expressed written permission of the publishers.

You may not redistribute, sell, de-compile, or disassemble four specific images presented in this book including one animated video. The four images are identified via a watermark displayed as www.ThroughTheOswaldWindow.com as follows:

1. Photograph of Dave O'Brien at the 'Oswald' Window.
2. Photograph of Oak Tree Taken from the 'Oswald' Window by book author.
3. Layout image of the sixth floor in the Texas School Book Depository Building.

4. Animated Video of alleged JFK kill shot from the 6th floor Book Depository window.

This book may contain references to websites or blogs as resource materials. These sites are not under the control of the Publishers. Dave O'Brien and Paul O'Brien are not responsible for the content of any site referenced in this book, including without limitation any link contained in a recommended site and up-dates to a Linked Site within that recommended site.

The Publishers are not responsible for webcasting or any other form of transmission received from any sites referred to in this book. The (JFK Case NOT Closed) book is providing these sites to you only as secondary information sources and the inclusion of any site does not imply endorsement by the publishers, author or book designer. At the time of publication, any URLs displayed in this book were viable links on the Internet.

To obtain written permission from the publishers, make media inquiries, register a complaint or submit a comment to the publishers or author, write to:

dave@throughtheoswaldwindow.com

Facebook - Please Like us on Facebook - https://www.facebook.com/ThroughTheOswaldWindow/

Introduction

Challenging History by Giving Accused JFK Assassin Lee Harvey Oswald the Defense He Never Received in Life or Death!

> *"If the JFK assassination was a 'simple murder' as the Warren Commission concluded, why was evidence suppression and alteration required?"*
>
> Douglas Horne
> JFK assassination researcher

Although the focus here is entirely on the JFK assassination, a primary objective of this book is to support the Kennedy and King families in their unified call for new official investigations into the murders of John F. Kennedy, Malcolm X, Martin Luther King Jr. and Robert F. Kennedy.

A joint release by the Kennedy and King families states:

"We call for a major public inquest on the four major assassinations of the 1960s that together had a disastrous impact on the course of American history."

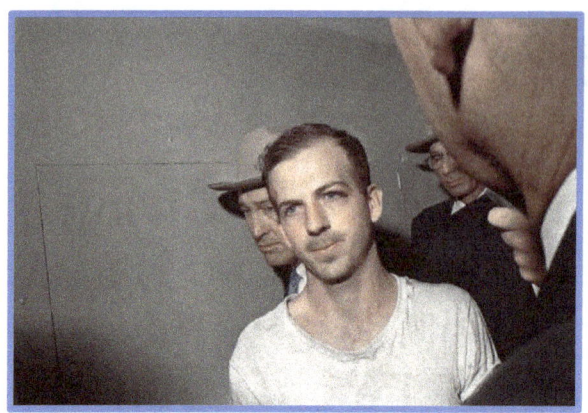

Lee Harvey Oswald was denied legal representation while in police custody when he was murdered before having his day in court and his rights as an accused was also denied by the Warren Commission.

Indeed, the assassination of President Kennedy started a decade of turbulence that continues to impact American history to this very day.

Had President Kennedy not been assassinated, would the Vietnam war have claimed more than 58,000 U.S. military lives and raged on for as long as it did? Would there have been a Robert F. Kennedy presidency in 1968 instead of another Kennedy mourned?

Would Dr. King have been murdered? Would Watergate have happened and therefore a Ford presidency? When we consider that the JFK assassination prompted three successive U.S. presidential elections to be impacted as much by bullets as ballots (1964, 1968, 1972), what affect did JFK's murder have on all presidencies from Lyndon Johnson in 1964 to Joe Biden in 2020?

It's not just the Kennedy, Little and King families who deserve justice, truth and closure. We all do.

For those of you who feel the government has kept the truth from the American public for all these decades, this book summons you to support Robert F. Kennedy Jr. and

Martin Luther King III in their call for a new public inquiry. How you can support this important endeavor is detailed in the concluding chapter.

This book rallies the JFK assassination research community to this purpose. No less than 15 top JFK researchers and authors participated in a brief two-question survey to discuss viable methods of conducting a new formal inquiry that:

- **A)** Avoids another Warren Commission.
- **B)** Presents specific key evidence a new inquiry ought to examine that was initially dismissed, ignored, altered or suppressed by the Warren Commission so it could name Lee Harvey Oswald as the '**lone**' assassin of President Kennedy.

JFK Case NOT Closed does not purport to solve the crime. That's the mandate for a new formal inquiry demanded by members of the Kennedy family, supporters, organized groups such as the Citizens Against Political Assassinations (CAPA) and several prominent independent researchers and authors, some of whom weigh in on the matter in chapter 18.

And for all you JFK assassination 'conspiracy theorists,' of which I am one, this is not the latest in an endless parade of 'Whodunit' books that have distorted the truth almost as much as the Warren Report itself. As top researcher Jefferson Morley points out:

"Suspicions of conspiracy did not originate with conspiracy theorists, they did not begin with Oliver Stone. Suspicions of a conspiracy originated in the circumstances of the crime…Some people say, 'the

President was shot and everyone knew what had happened, and then conspiracy theorists came along later and drummed up these theories.'

"In fact, what happened was when people saw and learned about what occurred in the assassination, they immediately came to the conclusion that one person couldn't have done this. So, it wasn't that someone later on wrote an article or a book or published a movie that put forth a conspiracy theory and the only motive was that these people were trying to sell something. Instead, it was the facts themselves. It was the facts of the events that made people question what happened.

"So, I'm trying to draw a distinction between when people say that Oliver Stone just conned people into believing a conspiracy theory. No, it doesn't work that way. It was the facts of the crime that made people think it happened in a different way than the way the Warren Report set forth."

Imagine the mind-numbing confusion of a person today who has become interested in the events of 11/22/63 and begins to read up on it.

How long does his or her interest or care last when the first dozen books he or she reads each persuasively present a different conspiracy theory about how and why JFK was assassinated?

JUST THE FACTS

The second objective of this book is to help steer a new generation of people interested in the JFK assassination, possible future influencers or top researchers, away from conspiracy theories.

Instead, JFK Case NOT Closed focuses on key *"facts of the crime"* as Morley cites above. The facts in this crime can be found in the evidence, much of which still exists today in the National Archives.

Beyond this moment, you will read nothing more about dime-a-dozen conspiracy theories in this book. There was no such thing as a JFK conspiracy theory when I first started reading the 26 volumes of the Warren Report in 1965 as a 13-year-old.

What enraged me and turned me into a JFK assassination researcher was that the Warren Commission named Lee Oswald as the 'lone nut' assassin despite blatantly dismissing, ignoring, altering or suppressing much of the exculpatory evidence in the case.

Even more alarming was the plentiful evidence of a second gunman in Dealey Plaza that would emerge thanks to reporters and researchers, little of which could be found in the expansive Warren Report.

Keep in mind that it was not conspiracy theories that began to erode public trust in the findings of the Warren Commission. It was the challenging of the evidence by pioneer researchers and authors like Mark Lane, Josiah Thompson, Harold Weisberg and my mentor Penn Jones Jr.

Pioneer researcher Mark Lane.

Conspiracy theories may be thought-provoking, but this book serves up examples of evidence that would have been problematic for prosecutors in a public courtroom had Oswald lived to stand trial.

Whether you have been a student of Kennedy's murder for some time or a newcomer to the shocking events in Dallas, by focusing on key evidence handled negligently by the Warren Commission, my hope is that you will become angry enough to join the growing groundswell of action demanding a new formal inquiry into John Kennedy's murder.

As researcher John Orr points out in chapter 17, every government inquiry into the events of 11/22/63 after the Warren Commission was born out of public outcry, not about conspiracy but about the evidence in this case.

In the interest of justice for Oswald, the Kennedy family and the American people, the evidence in this case must finally be given due process by a new official inquiry to approximate as much as possible the legal standard as required in a court of law. Justice delayed is preferable to justice denied.

THE NEXT GENERATION

Another objective of JFK Case NOT Closed is to pass the torch, so to speak, to the next generation of researchers.

While still blessed with a current crop of outstanding independent researchers and authors, many of whom participated in the short survey in chapter 18, as well as first generation legendary researchers like Mark Lane, Josiah Thompson, Harold Weisberg, Mary Ferrell, J. Gary Shaw and second generation researcher Robert Groden, their collective work provides the next generation with a roadmap to the truth.

Scotsman Johnny Cairns, now in his early 30's, has already established himself as a relentless researcher with these advantages:

1) Laser Beam Focus – Cairns is not a conspiracy theorist, per se, although he asserts that Lee Oswald is innocent of the crime. He does not obsess about the conspiracy to assassinate President Kennedy. Instead, his unbreakable focus is on the evidence cited by the Warren Commission in naming Oswald as the 'lone' assassin.

2) Youthful Relentlessness – The truth about America's ultimate cold case may not be discovered in my lifetime, but Johnny Cairns is positioned perfectly to lead the next generation of JFK assassination researchers in an era when the 'facts' of the events of 11/22/63 are more likely than ever to be revealed.

Fittingly, Johnny Cairns was asked to contribute significantly to JFK Case NOT Closed. The result is four chapters in which he methodically examines the key physical evidence the Commission cited in naming Oswald as the 'lone nut' assassin of Kennedy.

While in Dallas police custody for almost 45 hours as an accused double murderer, Lee Oswald was denied his right to legal representation. And when his right to a fair trial was denied by his killer Jack Ruby just two days later, his right to a legal defense died with him.

The Warren Commission had the opportunity to allow Oswald a limited posthumous defense but turned down the family's plea to have attorney Mark Lane represent his interests before it's hearings.

Accordingly, Cairns comes to the defense of the accused so thoroughly in chapters 4,5,6 & 7, he single-handedly turns much of the same circumstantial evidence used by the Commission to incriminate Oswald into evidence that exonerates him per the legal standard required in a U.S. court of law.

Contemporary JFK assassination researcher Johnny Cairns (right) meets iconic researcher and author Robert Groden during a 2018 visit to Dealey Plaza.

The totality of the Cairns chapters alone will anger you hopefully enough to want to be part of a movement to have the government finally release all remaining classified files and/or the growing call for a new official investigation into the public execution of President John F Kennedy.

NEW HOPE FOR A NEW ERA

Anger causes action, but after almost 60 years of deceit and governmental cover-up, is there really any hope that the truth about 11/22/63 will ever be known?

More than ever before, the answer is YES!

The truth about the JFK assassination that has been denied me for my 70 years of life, I predict, will no longer be able to withstand the relentless pursuit by today's top researchers or the Cairns generation of researchers.

Cairns is what each generation of researchers need – a Pit Bull who will not let up. My generation is putting a lot on him and his new era of researchers but if they persist, they inherit a promising age of hope.

This brings us to the other objective of JFK Case NOT Closed – embracing exciting new technology that can be applied to the evidence in this case that resides in the National Archives.

This book offers a history-changing example of technology not available in 1963 that has been applied to the JFK autopsy photos and evidence in the government archives.

Dr. David Mantik, a noted radiation oncologist, was the first specialist to administer new technology to Kennedy's autopsy x-rays.

The result? Stunning evidence that the Kennedy autopsy x-rays and photos were altered to incriminate Oswald as a 'lone' assassin.

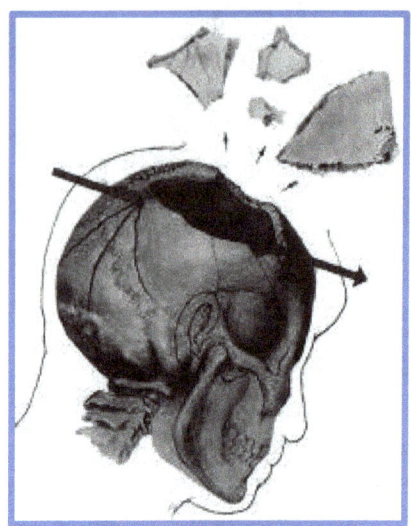

This medical illustration by Ida Dox for the HSCA was entirely based on altered JFK x-rays according to technology developed after 1963.

As detailed in chapter 16, Mantik and fellow medical experts Dr. Michael Chesser and Dr. Gary Aguilar agree that the original x-rays establish the President was struck in the head by more than one gunshot from different directions.

The scientists provide evidence that the Warren Commission's conclusion that Oswald was the 'lone' assassin was not arrived at mistakenly or incompetently. Dr. Mantik bluntly claims that the x-rays show clear proof of being altered to explicitly *"incriminate Oswald."*

As the science of x-ray imaging continues to advance, any new formal inquiry should apply new technologies to verify the stunning findings of the three experts.

NEW TECHNOLOGY BEFORE OUR EYES

This book also discusses technological advancements currently being applied to the JFK assassination that will reveal shocking revelations as early as 2023, the 60th anniversary.

Chapter 17 tells the story of DP3D, a project that utilizes the latest of three technologies to create a 3D visual model of the shots in Dealey Plaza that is painstakingly accurate to less than a few millimeters.

The end result of the DP3D project will be a stunning visual documentary that applies new technologies to existing evidence that finally tell us the number of shots fired at the Kennedy limousine, where each shot came from and the end result of each shot, all to a scientific certainty.

Project leader John Orr divulges one shocking revelation in chapter 17 with assurances that when the DP3D documentary is complete, the science involved will elevate it well beyond the many theories that have been fueled by pure conjecture.

NEW TECHNOLOGY, OLD EVIDENCE

It is shocking to learn that all technology of that era was not applied to the available evidence, especially in the field of ballistics.

Why weren't bullet fragments removed from Governor John Connally ballistically proven to have come from CE 399 to validate the 'Single Bullet Theory' presented by the Warren Commission in its claim that Oswald fired the shot that caused all the non-fatal wounds sustained by Kennedy and Connally?

Or why weren't the bullet fragments recovered in the Presidential limousine tested by FBI ballistics in an effort to match them to the alleged Oswald murder weapon or any of the specific wounds sustained by Kennedy or Connally seated in the car?

These are just two examples of how tests utilizing today's technology can be performed on existing evidence to help uncover the truth about how history was changed on 11/22/63.

UP TO YOU

JFK Case NOT Closed provides you with ample physical evidence grossly mishandled by the Warren Commission which, upon re-examination and subjected to modern technology, may finally tell us how President John F. Kennedy was assassinated on November 22, 1963.

This book chronicles an alarming number of witnesses and evidence blatantly dismissed, ignored, altered or even suppressed by the Warren Commission in order to affix the death of a President on a solitary whack-job.

Thanks to evolving technologies, time is shown to be a friend of the truth rather than the cause of its demise. Chapter 16 gives you an exciting example of how technology not available in 1963 has already exposed the fraud of the Warren Report.

Dr. Cyril Wecht once stood alone in daring to challenge the credibility of the JFK autopsy, putting his reputation and career on the line, but now due to modern technology and the three men in chapter 16 willing to apply it, the truth is closer than ever before.

This chapter gives promise and hope to the next generation of researchers and historians by demonstrating that advancements in technology, literally being applied to the JFK assassination as you read this, can rescue truth from the trash heap of lies.

The one common element in all of this is people like you, from the many witnesses at the crime scene who tried to tell us what they saw or heard to the relentless pursuit of the 'facts' of this case by researchers and scientists of today.

You can play an important role in helping to solve America's ultimate cold case. You don't have to be a brilliant scientist with cutting edge technology that can be applied to this case.

You don't even have to be the next Mark Lane or Oliver Stone or Johnny Cairns. But you can make a difference by supporting Larry Schnapf's efforts in chapter 18 to have the remaining sealed documents released and be part of the public outcry for a new formal inquiry into the murder of John F. Kennedy.

The conclusion of this book details some of the key efforts presently underway to achieve full disclosure of government files and calls for a new public investigation.

When you have read the last page and close the cover of JFK Case NOT Closed, it doesn't have to be the end, but an opportunity for you to possibly help change the historical record of a murdered President.

Chapter 1

Views of Conspiracy from the 'Oswald' Window

The author at the 'Oswald' window demonstrates the awkward posture needed by an assassin to shoot down onto the kill site on Elm Street.

Had Lee Harvey Oswald lived to stand public trial, it is likely the presiding judge would have directed the jurors to tour the crime scene in Dealey Plaza.

The jurors, like millions of people since that tragic day in Dallas, would have traced the motorcade along Houston Street and imagined it making that fateful 90-degree left turn onto Elm Street where the vibrant President's life would end in a matter of seconds.

From Elm Street, they would no doubt have looked up to the southeast sixth floor corner window of the Texas School Book Depository Building where the State claims all the shots were fired by the accused 'lone' assassin Lee Oswald. From down on Elm Street, it looks so painfully possible.

Minutes later, once the freight elevator stopped at the sixth floor inside the empty Book Depository building, the jurors would get a perspective of the assassination that very few people have ever had even to this day – a view of the JFK assassination through the eyes of the assassin at that notorious window!

Just as I experienced first-hand on February 11, 1979, per the photo above, the jurors would have been caught off-guard as they approached the infamous 'Oswald' window from which the accused was alleged to have fired the shots that wounded Texas Governor John Connally and took the life of the nation's 35th President.

As you see me having to crouch at the window in order to point down toward the kill site as the assassin would have had to do with his rifle, the awkwardness of needing to kneel or crouch to fire from that window surprises you when you see it.

The window is open to the max in the photo and sits no more than 18 inches from the floor, forcing the sniper to assume an awkward posture while firing at his moving target.

Expert marksmen will tell you that this posture is not all that difficult, but when taking into account the target is moving away from the shooter at 11 mph, the oak tree as shown below quickly becomes an obstacle and his timing is very limited due to the bridge just yards ahead, I submit that Oswald's mediocre marksman's scores in the Marines makes this a difficult task for him specifically.

And none of this takes into account the added pressure of him taking aim at the President of the United States!

Government re-enactments of the motorcade route through Dealey Plaza have done little more than document what it believes happened that day in Dallas.

With today's advanced technology in many aspects of forensics, 3D imaging, laser targeting and the improving science of acoustics, a new formal investigation can and needs to re-enact every frame of the Zapruder and Nix films to prove or disprove the precision claimed to have been executed by Oswald. Here are other reasons why:

1. THE BEST SHOT NEVER TAKEN

When you arrive at the window and assume the position of the actual assassin, you are immediately stunned by an observation not adequately addressed in the Warren Report.

As this picture (below) shows, the sniper at this window would have watched the President's limousine approach him on Houston Street and slow from 11 mph to less than 5 mph to make the 90-degree left turn onto Elm Street directly below the window.

Once the turn is made, the target President stops approaching the sniper and begins to move away from him. Does this matter?

If the gunman at this window was a '**lone**' assassin as would have been claimed by the state prosecutor at a public trial of Oswald, it matters greatly.

A '**lone**' assassin, hellbent on murdering the POTUS, would not have passed on his best opportunity to execute his mission.

When standing at that 6th floor southeast corner window, it becomes clear that the easiest shots available to a '**lone**' assassin to guarantee success was while the President's car was approaching him on Houston Street.

From the so-called 'Oswald' window, the view of the oncoming target (JFK) is clear, but the sniper declined this shot. Why?

This observation, apparently insignificant to the Warren Commission, may have been perplexing to jurors deciding the guilt or innocence of the accused Oswald.

As you are about to discover, a '**lone**' assassin allowing the President to turn left onto Elm Street unharmed is fraught with obstacles, a significant increase in difficulty and diminishing time to execute his mission to kill the President. Here's why:

2. THE MENACING OAK TREE

As this photo taken by me shows, a mature oak tree on Elm Street comes into play just as the '**lone**' assassin readies himself to gun down President Kennedy.

This Elm Street view from the 'Oswald' window shows the obstacles the sniper faced. Now compare this shooting scenario with the photo of Houston Street above. – Photo by Dave O'Brien

During the entire time JFK is obstructed by this oak tree, a '**lone**' assassin at this window cannot take aim at his target. He must either shoot *before* Kennedy disappears under the foliage, for which there is no definitive evidence of happening, or the sniper must wait until *after* Kennedy emerges from behind the leaves and branches.

The oak tree obstruction creates a timing problem for a '**lone**' assassin at this window:

3. A BRIDGE TO SAFETY

Tragically, had President Kennedy made it safely to the protection of the bridge just yards away, his limousine would have taken an on-ramp to Stemmons Freeway to the Dallas Trade Mart for a luncheon speech.

The presidential target is accessible to a '**lone**' gunman at the 6th floor Book Depository window only from the time he clears the brush of the oak tree until he disappears under the bridge at the top of the photo.

With JFK moving farther away from the crouched assassin at 11 mph, the '**lone**' assassin has left himself the most difficult scenario possible to successfully complete his mission.

There is only one possible reason why this situation would pose no problem for a shooter positioned at the 6th floor, southeast corner window:

NOT A 'LONE' ASSASSIN!

As I looked from that window down into the kill site through the eyes of the assassin, I found myself asking: *"Why didn't Warren Commission investigators see what I am seeing?"*

A '**lone**' assassin would have scouted his sniper's nest for days, if not longer, to select the best possible vantage point to carry out his horrendous act.

And yet he chose this southeast corner window that gave him his best opportunity to kill the President while on Houston Street but declined that shot.

He let his famous target turn left onto Elm Street directly beneath him, allowing the limousine to move away from him at 11 mph as if to give the President a chance to escape.

Even more puzzling about the assassin choosing the southeast corner window is that during my visit, it took mere minutes to discover a much better sniper's nest for a 'lone' assassin that would have:

- Removed the oak tree as an obstacle.

- Placed the President directly beneath him just like the corner of Houston and Elm.
- Given him unimpeded access to his target until the car went under the bridge.
- Provided the assassin with a more direct, quicker and unimpeded escape from the sixth floor.

The 'smarter' sniper's nest is the southwest corner window on the same floor. The assassin had days or weeks to plan his nest, yet I found a better option for a 'lone' assassin within minutes of scanning the sixth floor! Oswald had worked in that building for several weeks whereas I had the same access for mere minutes!

Yet, he chose the southeast corner window and allowed the left-hand turn onto Elm Street knowing that the fully-blossomed Oak Tree protected his target for valuable seconds and that once clear of the foliage, his target was mere seconds from safety under the bridge just yards away.

WHY?

It's because the sniper at that window was **NOT** a '**lone**' assassin!

He could **NOT** shoot at the President while the car was on Houston Street because the target was not yet in position for the triangulation of crossfire that awaited him on Elm Street.

A fellow gunman stationed in the Dal-Tex Records building at Houston and Elm Streets had a clear shot at President Kennedy without the oak tree being an obstacle.

A sniper at the third floor stairwell of the Dal-Tex building could have fired the first shot that hit JFK whereas the same shot was obstructed by the oak tree in front of the Book Depository building.

More importantly, a fellow gunman positioned behind the picket fence on the grassy knoll had the ultimate close, clear and direct shot at the target with no obstacles of any kind.

In concluding that Lee Oswald fired all the shots from the southeast 6th floor Book Depository building window and acted alone in doing so, the Warren Commission literally never investigated any evidence or indication of multiple gunmen.

Unlike a public trial, the Commission never even had to consider other possibilities, such as the stupidity of the 6th floor southeast corner Book Depository window being the sniper's nest of choice for a '**lone**' assassin for the reasons cited here.

The Commission didn't have to consider such inconvenient questions or scenarios of possible conspiracy, but a new formal inquiry into the events of 11/22/63 would do well to make sense of the kill site in Dealey Plaza, especially the alleged sniper's nest of a 'lone' assassin.

Even if a new panel of investigators cannot answer the

many questions of conspiracy raised by researchers over the years, it needs to better explain why we should accept that it was possible for one man to have executed America's President.

Chapter 2

The Failed Warren Commission Ballistic Tests that Disprove its Own 'Single Bullet' and 'Lone Gunman' Theories!

Of all the areas of expertise that Dr. Cyril Wecht is qualified to address about the assassination of John F. Kennedy, it is the Warren Commission and House Select Committee on Assassination's (HSCA) own ballistic tests that the board certified lawyer and forensic pathologist cites most often as proof of multiple gunmen in Dealey Plaza.

At issue is the Warren Commission's failure to prove that a bullet found at Parkland Hospital (CE 399) caused all the non-lethal damage attributed to it.

CE 399

This matter is so paramount to solving the controversy of one assassin or multiple gunmen, any new official investigation needs to make this evidence a primary focus of attention.

The Commission concluded that one bullet (CE 399) caused two survivable wounds to President Kennedy and five non-fatal wounds to Governor Connally, including two major broken bones, emerging in the pristine condition you see above.

This has become known as the 'Single Bullet Theory.'

This 'single bullet' conclusion by the Commission was necessary to be able to also conclude that Oswald acted alone and that no conspiracy existed. Why?

Zapruder frame 225 shows JFK reacting to the first shot to his upper back while Connally appears unhurt. The Commission says that Connally, indeed, has been hit by the same bullet that first struck the President.

Zapruder frames 225-236 expose the dilemma faced by the Warren Commission. These 11 frames represent just over ½ second of elapsed time, which would prove to be problematic for government investigators.

Zapruder frame 225 (above) shows President Kennedy emerging from behind the Stemmons Freeway traffic sign. His hands are ascending to his throat in reaction to the first shot that struck him in the upper back, causing a winded effect.

In frame 225, Connally does not appear to be hit by the shot that first struck Kennedy even though this bullet is said to rip through the Governor's chest, breaking off his fifth right rib and then shatters the distal radius bone in his right wrist before ending its flight in Connally's left thigh. The Commission says, in fact, that Connally has been hit by the CE 399 bullet at this moment.

Approximately ¼ of one second later, Zapruder frame 230 clearly shows JFK reacting to his upper back wound, yet Connally, seated only some three feet in front of Kennedy, still appears to not be hit.

Even if both men were injured by the same first shot as early as Zapruder frame 202 when JFK disappears behind the highway sign appearing unhurt, the Commission does not explain how the Governor could still be holding on to his white 10-gallon Stetson cowboy hat in frame 230 despite the bullet blowing a hole through the distal radius bone in his right wrist!

Although the Governor shows no signs of reacting to a bone shattering bullet through two separate parts of his body in frame 230, Mrs. Kennedy begins to notice that something is wrong with her husband.

It isn't until frame 236, just over ½ of a second after JFK is first seen reacting to his upper back wound that Connally is seen reacting to his wounds. His right shoulder buckles, his mouth flies open and he cries out in pain.

Until his death in 1993, Governor Connally steadfastly maintained that he was **NOT** hit by any shot that first struck President Kennedy.

These collective 11 frames of the Zapruder film left the Warren Commission with only two possibilities:

1. **'Lone' Gunman'** – Kennedy and Connally were both hit by the same bullet (CE 399), thus enabling the 'Single Bullet Theory' and the conclusion that Oswald was the '**lone**' assassin.

2. **A Second Gunman** – Connally was hit by a second shot fired by a second sniper almost simultaneously to the first shot, thus disproving the 'Single Bullet Theory.'

The Warren Commission adopted point number one, which was necessary for it to also conclude that Lee Oswald was the '**lone**' assassin of President Kennedy.

Keep in mind that regardless of all other evidence in this case, if the Single Bullet Theory can be proven false, it becomes a certainty that more than one gunman in Dealey Plaza fired at President Kennedy that day. Why?

Because the Oswald Mannlicher-Carcano rifle, as determined by the FBI, could not be manually fired twice in less than 2.3 seconds.

Yet, Connally is seen reacting to his wounds prior to the time it would take a '**lone**' assassin to fire a second shot.

As you will read in chapter 17, technology is available today to a new formal inquiry that can remove human interpretation of the film footage of JFK's death and give us a precise accounting of the timing of the shots, the bullet trajectories and possibly the corresponding entry wounds on the two men.

THE UNCOOPERATIVE FBI BALLISTIC TEST

Knowing that it was essential to its lone assassin conclusion that this bullet (CE 399) did cause all seven non-lethal wounds on the two men, the Warren Commission ordered a ballistic test to prove exactly that.

According to Dr. Wecht, this experiment went terribly wrong for the government panel.

Using Oswald's rifle and an identical copper-jacketed 6.5 mm bullet, a test bullet was fired into the right wrist of a human cadaver to simulate Governor Connally's wrist.

It was reasoned that if such a ballistic test could replicate the most severe non-fatal wound suffered by Governor

Connally, leaving the test bullet in near pristine condition, it could reasonably assert that CE 399 caused all the other lesser wounds on the two men.

While the test shot into the wrist of a cadaver (CE 854) showed an eerily similar wrist wound as that sustained by the Governor, the test bullet (below) emerged with considerably more damage than CE 399.

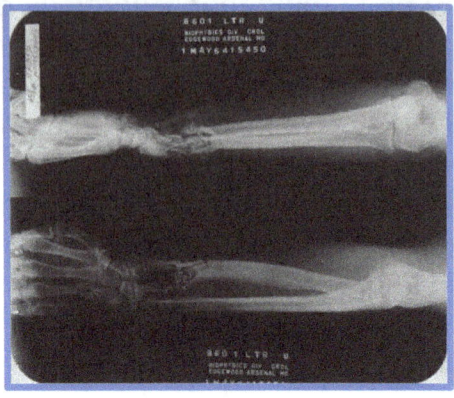

CE 854 is the wrist of a cadaver used for a ballistic test. The hole through the distal radius bone is remarkably identical to the wound sustained by Governor Connally.

While this test bullet (CE 856) establishes that it is highly unlikely that CE 399 caused even the Governor's wrist wound, never mind six additional wounds in two men and another broken rib bone in Connally, the Warren Commission ignored the finding of its own ballistic test in concluding that CE 399 did all the damage ascribed to it.

MORE FAILED TESTS

Using his vast experience in forensics and the application of ballistic science in criminal cases, Dr. Cyril Wecht dug deeper into the Commission's efforts to substantiate CE 399 as the solitary bullet that inflicted seven wounds on the two men.

Like other JFK assassination researchers, Dr. Wecht knows that if the Warren Commission's 'Single Bullet

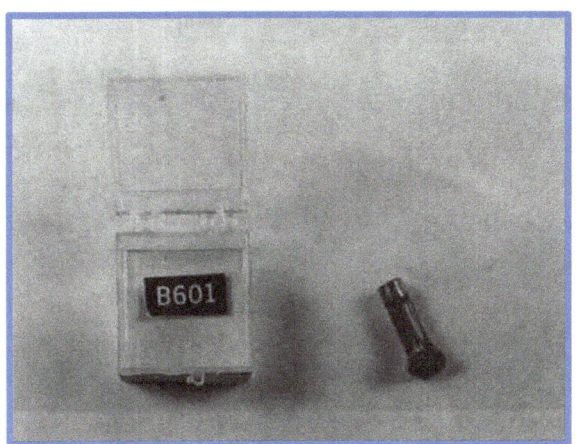

CE 856 is a test bullet fired into the wrist of a cadaver. While it caused identical damage to that sustained by Governor Connally, the test bullet emerged far more damaged than CE 399, which fails to support the Single Bullet Theory.

Theory' is proven false, then there had to be more than one gunman in Dealey Plaza and hence a conspiracy.

As he has said at his public speaking engagements, he would have loved to have presented the following evidence in a courtroom had Oswald lived to stand trial:

Dr. Wecht likes to point out that the test using the wrist of a cadaver (CE 856) wasn't the only ballistic experiment the Commission conducted in its efforts to support its claim that CE 399 could have caused all seven non-life-threatening wounds on Kennedy and Connally.

Other FBI ballistic tests were conducted in the Commission's hopeful effort to establish that Oswald carried out the assassination on his own.

In its attempt to come up with a test-fired bullet that looked like the barely damaged CE 399, the FBI used Oswald's rifle and identical bullets to fire into targets other than a human cadaver as shown in HSCA exhibit 294 on page 33.

Dr. Wecht, who served on the HSCA's medical committee that reviewed the JFK autopsy photos and x-rays, takes delight in noting that the collection of test bullets in exhibit 294 were not his doing.

As he told his audience at the 54th anniversary event hosted by the Sixth Floor Museum at Dealey Plaza, "The government put this picture together (exhibit 294), not Wecht or his associates," in pointing out both panel's blatant disregard of its own physical evidence. In his own words, Dr. Wecht explains these tests this way:

O'Brien and Dr. Wecht at the CAPA conference in Dallas on the 55th anniversary of JFK's assassination.

"In science, we try to prove or disprove something, so what do you do with bullets?

"You fire bullets into water or cotton wadding to see what the bullet will look like having struck nothing of substance. They did that," notes Dr. Wecht.

"A second set of targets consisted of a goat carcass, which was lined up for a shot through the chest to break a rib to simulate Connally's comminuted fracture."

For comparative purposes, Dr. Wecht notes that the bullet found on a stretcher at Parkland Hospital (CE 399) weighed 158.6 grains compared to 161 grains in its original state.

JFK Case NOT Closed

Therefore, the total metallic loss of substance to CE 399 was 2.4 grains or exactly 1.5% of the original weight of the bullet.

The question becomes: How does the damage to the test bullets after firing compare to what CE 399 experienced after allegedly causing seven wounds in two men and destroying two bones?

In his presentations, Dr. Wecht describes the test bullets as shown in the picture here as follows:

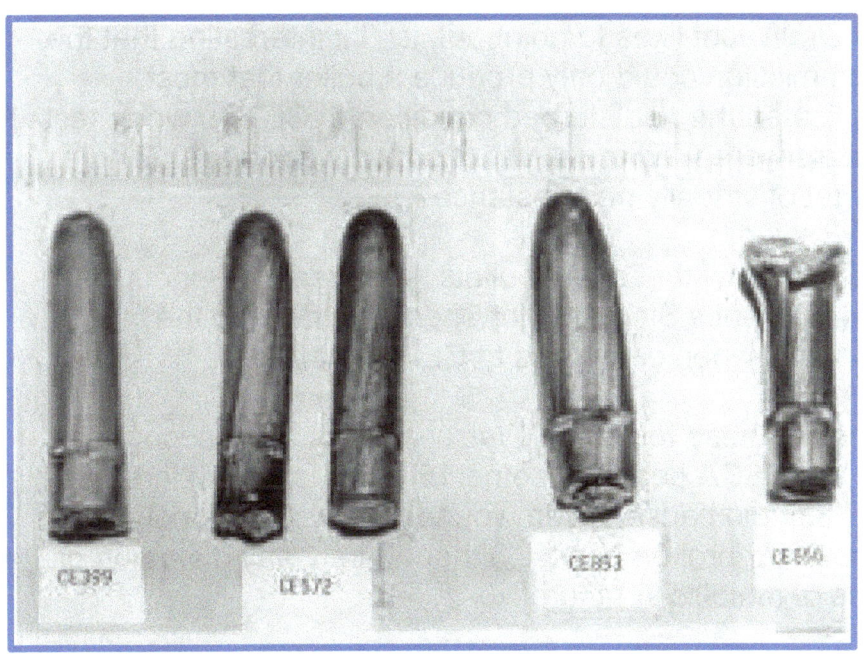

"The bullet at far right (CE 856) was fired into the distal radius section (wrist) of a human cadaver."

As you can see, the test bullet fired only into the wrist of a cadaver shows much more damage and loss of metal than CE 399 at far left that went through Connally chest

33

and severed a rib before causing identical damage to his wrist.

"The second bullet from the right (CE 853) is a bullet fired into the rib of a goat, emerging only slightly more misshapen than the bullets shot into a vat of cotton wadding.

"The second and third bullets to the left (CE 572) were fired into vats of cotton wadding, striking nothing," he notes.

As Dr. Wecht likes to point out, isn't it interesting that the Commission could only produce a bullet that most replicated the undisturbed condition of CE 399 when test bullets were fired into a vat of cotton wadding, striking a target of virtually no substance?

Remarkably, these test bullets, intended to support the government's Single Bullet Theory, in fact, do the opposite when compared to CE 399 at far left.

Despite these tests, the Warren Report, later seconded by the HSCA hearings some 15 years later, declared that CE 399 did cause seven wounds on two men, including two major broken bones, without barely any distortion or loss of metallic structure!

TESTING OUR BELIEF SYSTEM

Were there other ballistic tests by the FBI that were ignored or suppressed because they didn't help to establish Oswald as solely responsible for this crime?

Was there really no way to test the bullet fragments

removed from Connally's body to match them to CE 399 to show the Single Bullet Theory to be viable? With modern technology applied, surely ballistic tests could assist a new inquiry.

And what about Dr. Robert Shaw who operated on Connally's wrist? He has stated his belief that it is possible the fragments he extracted from the Governor's wrist, as well as the fragments left in Connally's wrist and chest, may add up more than the 2.4 grains of metal CE 399 is missing.

Given how critical the Single Bullet Theory is to whether one or more gunmen murdered President Kennedy, a new formal investigation needs to apply any ballistic or other scientific advances to this physical evidence in the National Archives.

Laser and 3D technology is presently being applied to study the viability of the alleged flightpath of CE 399 from the 'Oswald' window to see if it is possible to align all the non-lethal wounds sustained by Kennedy and Connally.

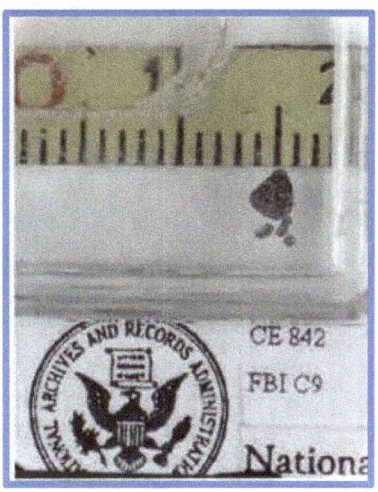

Fragments removed from Connally's wrist and given to the FBI went untested for link to CE 399.

Resolving the Single Bullet Theory as fact or fiction is so important, it could change the history books and bring new perspective to other evidence of controversy in this case.

All the physical evidence is still there to be examined, this time in search of the truth instead of a cover-up.

Chapter 3

Recently Discovered Film Oddity that Indicates JFK Fatal Head Shot Fired by Second Gunman Now Backed by Modern Technologies!

When people are asked what makes them believe JFK died as a result of a conspiracy, a high number of them site the violent backward movement of Kennedy's head immediately after the bullet's impact.

From almost touching Jackie's head with his head, the involuntary reaction of JFK from the fatal bullet impact was him being slammed back against the car seat.

The Zapruder film graphically shows the lethal bullet impact at frame 313 and the resulting instantaneous slamming of the President's head and upper body against the backrest of his car seat (see frame 323 on this page).

From the opposite side of Elm Street where Abraham Zapruder filmed history, the Orville Nix film affirms JFK's violent rearward head and upper body movement instantly after receiving a shot to the head.

However, these two stunning film recordings of President Kennedy's murder did not convince the Warren Commission that Kennedy's reaction was the result of the 'kill' shot coming from the right-front of the car as our eyes reasonably tell us.

After all, that's not where Lee Harvey Oswald was positioned in Dealey Plaza on that tragic day.

Film footage of Kennedy's death tops the list of evidence the Commission dismissed or ignored in considering the possibility of more than one gunman and hence a conspiracy to kill the 35th President of the United States.

Despite the multitude of questionable circumstantial evidence documented by fellow JFK assassination researcher Johnny Cairns in the following four chapters, the Commission concluded that Oswald was perched as the '**lone**' assassin at the 6th floor southeast corner window of the Texas School Book Depository Building.

This places Oswald 60 feet above and approximately 270 feet behind Kennedy at the time of the fatal head shot.

Further, the Commission concluded that:

- **Multiple Shots** – A total of three shots were fired from the so-called 'Oswald' window and no other location.

- **Two of Three Hits** – Of the three shots fired from that window, two shots struck President Kennedy and one shot missed the limousine and its occupants completely.
- **One Assassin** – Lee Harvey Oswald was the '**lone**' assassin of his target, President Kennedy. No conspiracy existed, foreign or domestic.

In explaining the violent backward movement of President Kennedy's head instantly following the bullet impact to his skull, the Warren Commission, as well as the House Select Committee on Assassinations (HSCA) 15 years later, decided to disregard Sir Isaac Newton's Second Law of Motion, which states:

"When a force acts on an object, the object accelerates in the direction of the force."

Instead, Commission counsel David Belin and Commission member Gerald Ford came up with a much lesser known science to account for Kennedy's reaction to the kill shot, to be discussed momentarily and in greater detail in Chapter 9.

Apparently, nothing would get in the way of attributing two precision hits to Oswald in a restricted period of time while the same sniper could also miss the limousine and its occupants completely with one of his three shots.

This becomes even more improbable to fellow researcher and contributor to this book Johnny Cairns who discusses the poor condition of the assassination rifle and Oswald's mediocre capability as a marksman in Chapter 4.

STUNNING FILM ODDITY

As a veteran JFK assassination researcher, when I examined the Zapruder film for what seemed to be the thousandth time, I detected an oddity on the eve of the 55th anniversary that I hadn't noticed before.

The Commission never explained why Mrs. Kennedy would jump onto the 'trunk' of the car if the fatal head shot came from above and behind.

It occurred to me that if the fatal head shot had come from above and behind, the natural, instinctive physical reaction of Jack Kennedy that resulted appeared to defy Newton's Second Law of Motion, not to mention the affirming instinctive physical reaction of the First Lady as well as what our own eyes were telling us.

The Commission insists that the kill shot came from above and behind the target, yet Kennedy's head snaps 'back' toward where the shot was fired, not forward as science dictates should have happened.

And Jackie Kennedy instinctively jumps onto the trunk of the car 'aback' of where she and her husband were sitting to retrieve a piece of her husband's skull, not forward into the jump seats occupied by Nellie and John Connally as would be a natural occurrence had the shot come from the rear.

Both the Governor and his wife would reasonably explain Jackie's movement to the 'rear' of the car when they both testified before the Warren Commission that only a light mist of blood and brain matter showered them in the jump seats, not sizeable pieces of brain matter or skull fragments.

NO HEAD ON COLLISION?

The physical reactions of Jackie and Jack Kennedy at odds with the Second Law of Motion became even more stunning when I noticed the positions of their heads in relation to each other at Zapruder frame 312, a mere $1/18^{th}$ of a second 'before' the deadly head impact of the bullet.

When Zapruder's camera captured the gruesome moment that took Kennedy's life, the President and Mrs. Kennedy were almost directly in front of Abraham Zapruder standing on a concrete pergola on the grassy knoll.

This establishes that there is no distortion of what the Zapruder film shows us, which is quite remarkable in its potential implications.

We see in frame 312 on the next page that JFK's forehead and Jackie's right cheek are no more than a couple of inches apart from each other, if not closer, a nano-second before the bullet impact.

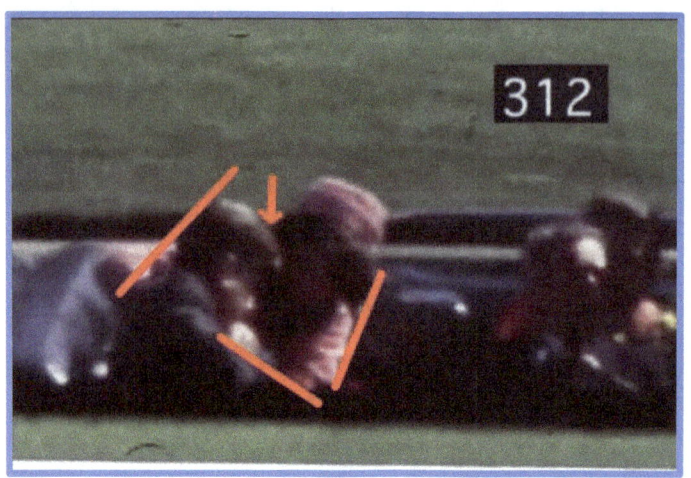

In fact, the Zapruder film shows that a slumping JFK is so close to his wife at that critical moment, the hair on his forehead very nearly touches the right cheek of Jackie's face.

Also, look at Jackie's left elbow and her white glove at her husband's chin. Her elbow is bent at a near full 90 degrees, proving that her head and left arm are almost directly in front of her husband at the moment of the fatal head shot.

If Jackie was seated further away from JFK at this critical moment as critics contend, her arm would appear to be reaching out to him rather than cocked at 90 degrees as she starts to realize that something is wrong with her husband.

Although not as obvious, the Nix film also shows the closeness of their heads when the bullet makes impact as well as the President's immediate corresponding snap backward away from Mrs. Kennedy's head.

As my short partially animated video below demonstrates, per the laws of physics by Sir Isaac Newton, if the kill shot had come from above and behind the limousine, striking the President in the rear crown area of his skull, why wasn't Mr. Kennedy's head driven forward the very short distance necessary to collide with Mrs. Kennedy's head?

How is it possible that a powerful impact of a high velocity, high energy-releasing bullet to Kennedy's skull failed to advance his head a maximum two inches or less to make contact with his wife's face?

To view video, type this link into your address bar
https://www.youtube.com/watch?v=qkobF6axwss&feature=youtu.be

To illustrate this oddity, the video asks you to participate in a harmless demonstration, which you can also do here as follows:

> *Gently tap the back of your own head with*
> *an open hand and observe the result.*

Notice that as a result of the gentle force of your hand to

the back of your head, your head moves in the same direction of the incoming object (your hand).

Isn't it remarkable at what little force it takes to advance your head one or two inches forward?

So again, if an intense energy-releasing projectile from above and behind impacted the back of JFK's head at approximately 2000 feet per second, could it really have caused no more frontal movement than a gentle tap to the back of your own head?

JACKIE'S INSTINCTIVE REACTION

Similarly, why didn't Jackie Kennedy sustain at least a minor injury to her face from being struck by her husband's head?

Instead, a completely uninjured Jackie jumps out onto the trunk of the car because she subconsciously saw a piece of her husband's skull fly 'back' in that direction in response to the bullet impact.

Even if she was not physically harmed by her husband's head striking her right cheek, it is reasonable to conclude that she may have been startled enough by the collision to have prevented her from reacting as we see on the Zapruder film after frame 313.

In this brief passage of time, the instinctive physical reactions of the President and First Lady obey the physics of motion and provide a natural and understandable reaction to what happened to them.

So, what happened to them?

The reason Jack and Jackie's heads did not collide is because the fatal head shot did **NOT** come from the 6th floor southeast corner Book Depository window above and behind them!

The reason the President's head was instead propelled back and to the left upon impact of the bullet was because the kill shot came from the grassy knoll to the right-front of the car!

And all these years later, when modern technologies such as those discussed in chapters 16 and 17 are applied to film and photo evidence or existing physical evidence, a frontal shot to JFK's head can now be established as fact.

A COUNTER SCIENCE TO EXPLAIN IT?

Counsel Belin and Commissioner Ford concluded: "*A massive neuromuscular reaction caused the President's head to move backward when struck from the rear by a bullet.*"

Could this lesser known science, Neuromuscular Reaction, actually explain the President's reaction to being shot in the head from the rear?

In other words, upon the bullet's impact, even if the President's head was propelled forward an inch or so, his contracting muscles (Neuromuscular Reaction), caused by the physical trauma of the moment, took control and forced his upper body 'back' toward the origin of the shot by the assassin in the 6th floor window.

The battle of these two sciences is examined more thoroughly in chapter 9 but when modern advancements in science and technology are applied to explain the wounds sustained by Kennedy in chapters 16 and 17, the clear cause of JFK's violent 'rearward' movement is one or possibly even two bullets struck his head a mere nano-second after the entry wound at the rear of the skull.

In making such a claim, Belin and Ford disregarded what causes a person to experience a neuromuscular reaction, which occurs when nerve centers in the brain sustain substantial damage.

While the nature of the President's head injury suggests the possibility of trauma to nerve centers in his brain, the autopsy report makes no such claim of such damage.

Oliver Stone, director of JFK Revisited: Through the Looking Glass, with screenplay by noted researcher James DiEugenio, points out that the nerve centers of the brain that would trigger a neuromuscular reaction are the medulla, the pons and the cerebellum, located in the left rear quadrant of the brain.

However, as more than a dozen doctors, nurses, technicians and trauma room attendants verified, there was no apparent damage to the left side of the President's head.

Instead, these expert medical witnesses observed massive damage to Kennedy's head at the right rear cerebral hemisphere where no nerve centers exist that might cause a forceful neuromuscular reaction of the magnitude required in this instance.

What happened to the occupants in the limousine is vital evidence, so let's use modern science to determine if the instinctive physical reactions of Mr. and Mrs. Kennedy are consistent with a shot coming from the right-front of the car, which would prove more than one gunman.

Can modern ballistic tests replicate the exact position of Mr. and Mrs. Kennedy's heads in Zapruder frame 312 to help determine the origin of the fatal head shot?

Surely, film analyses and modern science can allow us to ascertain the exact positions of the First Couple's heads in relation to each other 1/18th of a second before the deadly head shot.

And surely, since an adult male brain weighs on average 1370 grams and an adult female brain weighs on average 1200 grams with skin and skull thickness relatively the same for both, it would be possible today to replicate the Kennedy's with cadavers or compatible substances to position the two heads precisely as they appear in the Zapruder film.

Further, test firing Oswald's rifle and a similar bullet into the back of the simulated male head could ascertain the likeliness of their two heads colliding or not.

If a well-orchestrated test did produce a collision of the two heads, then reasonable doubt has been established, as necessary in a court of law, that the lethal head shot had to have come from a location other than above and behind.

Only trained scientists could tell us if such a demonstration is possible today and if it could shed light on the origin of the gunshot that killed JFK.

If there is any chance that the theory presented by the Warren Commission or the theory presented in this chapter can be verified by modern science and technology, I would be willing to be proven wrong in the pursuit of truth.

Would 'lone nut' believers be willing to do the same?

A Circumstantial Case:

A Defense of Lee Harvey Oswald by JFK Assassination Researcher Johnny Cairns

"I don't know what dispatches you people have been given but I emphatically deny these charges."

- Lee Oswald

Books by defense attorney Mark Lane indicate how he would have defended Lee Oswald at a public trial or the Warren Commission hearings. He got to do neither.

The evidentiary case against Lee Harvey Oswald was almost exclusively circumstantial, which would have been a focal point at a public trial.

The next four chapters in JFK Case NOT Closed documents key circumstantial evidence used by the Warren Commission in naming Oswald as the '**lone**' assassin of President Kennedy.

More importantly, chapters 4,5,6 & 7 offer up a defense of Oswald by citing the many flaws in the state's case as well as the egregious mishandling of the evidence against him.

While I firmly believe that these chapters reflect the challenges the prosecution would have faced in its case against Oswald at trial, I cannot present exculpatory evidence for Oswald as a defense attorney. Rather, as a JFK assassination researcher, I must wear the label of 'Conspiracy Theorist' in presenting this defense of Oswald to you.

Only 'Conspiracy Theorists' believe he has anything tantamount to a defense. That statement is false and is derived by those who charge Oswald as guilty as a sneer against those who proclaim he was innocent.

I offer no theory to this crime or why it transpired. I only offer the evidence in the public record and test the veracity of such evidence against the established legal standard as accepted in a U.S. court of law.

Accordingly, I will discuss much of the physical evidence which exists against Oswald in relation to the murder of President Kennedy.

Now, in any legal criminal proceeding, the onus is on the prosecution to prove 'beyond a reasonable doubt' the guilt of the accused. However, by virtue of his own murder, Oswald never stood trial in a court of law. Instead, Oswald's "guilt" was rubber-stamped by a Governmental Commission (Warren Commission) and their team of lawyers.

The Warren Commission and its 888-page report served as a prosecutorial brief and presented a weak circumstantial evidence case against the accused. The following passages are taken with regards to the Commission's conclusions in its report:

"The Commission has found no evidence that anyone assisted Oswald in planning or carrying out the assassination."

"The Commission has found no evidence that Oswald was involved with any person or group in a conspiracy to assassinate the President."

"The Commission has found no evidence to show that Oswald was employed, persuaded, or encouraged by any foreign government to assassinate President Kennedy or that he was an agent of any foreign government."

By the Commission's own admission here, if the assassination of President John F. Kennedy was concluded to be a conspiracy, then it is found that Lee Harvey Oswald would have no case to answer. This in itself must cause the physical evidence to be re-evaluated.

In this book's next four chapters, I will be dealing with the charge, as laid forth by the Commission, that Lee Harvey Oswald bore sole responsibility for the murder of President John F. Kennedy. That is the charge he would have faced had he been permitted to stand trial and it is the charge I will be defending him here against.

Remember that it is the sacred right of every person accused of committing a crime to the presumption of innocence. Oswald, regardless of the propaganda published or stated at his expense, is legally innocent of the charges brought against him.

In reference to those charges attorney Mark Lane, who was retained by Marguerite Oswald to represent her murdered son, proceeded to inform the Commission of his intention to act as council for Oswald. Mark Lane was denied his request citing a communication dated Jan 23rd, 1964, from Commission council J. Lee Rankin:

"The commission does not believe that it would be useful or desirable to permit an attorney representing Lee Harvey Oswald to have access to the investigatory materials within the possession of the commission or to participate in any hearings to be conducted by the commission."

However the decision not to permit council for the accused was met by widespread criticism. That criticism forced the Commission to relent on its previous decision and in doing so appointed Walter E. Craig, president of the American Bar Association *"to participate in the investigation and to advise the Commission whether in his opinion the proceedings conformed to the basic principles of American justice."*

But as pointed out by the late Sylvia Meagher... *"The Commission should not have required a reminder from the head of the ABA to recall that an accused person has a fundamental right to self-defense and the benefit of reasonable doubt - even posthumously."*

Contrary to the proclamations of the Commission, a defense of Oswald was sternly rejected by Craig who had stated *"He was not representing the interests of Lee H.*

Oswald... we are representing the interest of the American people."

Also, the belated nature of Craig's appointment was called into question and rightly so for several witnesses whom an independent lawyer (Mr. Lane) would have wanted to cross-examine had already testified before the Commission, including Marina Oswald.

In an act which would only compromise his own position, Craig attended only a handful of hearing dates before the Commission. This seeming lack of interest would explain why Craig was so inept to the basic facts of this case. These deficiencies are highlighted during the testimony of Secret Service agent William Greer:

Craig – "With respect to the position of the President's car that you were driving as it approached the underpass, you state now that you couldn't fix any specific distance (When the shots rang out). But would you say it was less than a mile that the car was from the overpass?"
Greer – *"Oh definitely. I couldn't say in feet or yards, but it was within – it was feet. I would say probably a hundred or 200 feet. It could be within that; it was definitely right up close to me..."*

Honestly? Craig's ignorance of the crime scene caused him to think the limousine was as much as a mile from the overpass when the shots rang out? A single viewing of the Zapruder film would have answered his own question.

Craig's negligence with respect to protecting Oswald's constitutional rights was compounded by the fact that he would not make a single solitary objection – to anything!

Oswald, an American citizen whose rights should have been protected as per the Constitution of the United States, received no defense in life or in death. He stated during his brief detention at the hands of the Dallas police:

"These people have given me a hearing without legal representation or anything."

Nowhere will you read in the Commission's report or accompanying 15 volumes of testimony, anyone representing Oswald's legal interests or rights. That includes, during the hearings, the choosing or calling of witnesses or the examination of witnesses inimitable to the pseudo-prosecution.

Nor was anyone available on Oswald's behalf to object to the many leading questions lobbed at prepped witnesses, to question the authenticity of the Commission's evidence or admit evidence into the proceedings which was exculpatory.

APPEAL TO A PUBLIC JURY

Had Lane been permitted to act as council for Oswald at trial or during the Commission hearings, I can guarantee that all of the above would have transpired.

Further, Lane would not have legally permitted all the circumstantial evidence I outline in chapters 4,5,6 and 7 to have been dismissed, ignored, altered or suppressed in either a courtroom or before the Commission hearings.

Thanks to Mark Lane doing video-recorded interviews,

dozens of witnesses in Dealey Plaza who were ignored by the Commission got to tell their story of what they saw or heard.

Is it a coincidence that almost all of the witnesses interviewed by Lane, as documented in Chapter 15, offer evidence that would have been exculpatory to Oswald in a court of law or before the Commission?

This defense of Oswald will comprise of rebutting these four key areas of physical evidence used by the Commission in naming Oswald the '**lone**' assassin in Dealey Plaza:

> Part 1 – The 'Lone' Assassin Rifle
> Part 2 – The Problematic Paper Bag
> Part 3 – The Ammunition Linked to Oswald
> Part 4 – CE 399 (The Magic Bullet)

Chapters 4, 5, 6, & 7 are dedicated to the memory of my late father Robert Mackenzie Cairns and President John Fitzgerald Kennedy

Chapter 4

Debunking the Circumstantial Evidence Used by the Warren Commission to Name Oswald as the 'Lone' Assassin of JFK!

Part 1 – The 'Lone' Assassin Rifle

by Johnny Cairns
JFK Assassination Researcher

A new official investigation ought to look into the following evidence about the alleged assassination rifle that the Warren Commission failed to examine or ignored:

MAIL ORDERED RIFLE?

The 6.5 Mannlicher-Carcano, serial number C2766, is the alleged murder weapon of President John F. Kennedy. We are told that the weapon was purchased by Lee Harvey Oswald through mail transaction, under the guise of an alias "A Hidell" on the 12th of March, 1963. But could Hidell receive mail at PO BOX 2915?

This question is crucial in determining if Oswald did in fact have in his possession the Mannlicher-Carcano prior to the assassination of President John F. Kennedy.

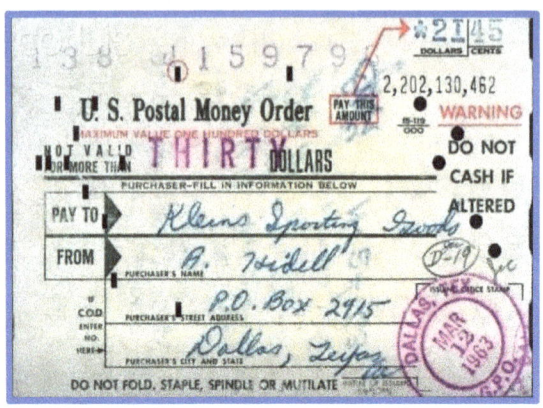

Using the alias A. Hidell, could Lee Oswald purchase the alleged JFK assassination rifle and have it sent to a PO Box in Dallas registered to his real name?

Lee Harvey Oswald had taken up the custodianship of PO Box 2915 in Dallas, on October 9th, 1962. He would naturally have completed an application form to rent this PO Box. Oswald's application for 2915 is available to view today, just not the complete form.

The most important part of the application form, in relation to the Hidell question, is unquestionably Part 3. This asks for 'Names of persons entitled to receive mail through box.' This part of the form is missing, presumed destroyed as testified to by Harry Holmes, Postal Inspector and FBI informant:

Holmes – "*Until he relinquishes the box. They pull this out and endorse it so the box has been closed and they tear off Part 3 and throw it away. It has no more purpose. That is what happened on box 2915.*"
Liebeler – "*They have thrown part 3 away?*"
Holmes – "*Yes, as it so happens, even though they closed the box in New Orleans, they still had part 3 and it showed that the mail for Marina Oswald and A. J. Hidell was good in the box. They hadn't complied with regulations. They still had it there.*"

Further from his testimony:

Liebeler – "Now is this regulation that says section 3 should be torn off and thrown away, is that a general regulation of the Post Office Department?"
Holmes – "*It is in the Post Office Manual instructions to employees, yes sir.*"

It is important to note here that Holmes never produced, nor was asked to produce by questioning council Liebeler, the regulation manual of the United States Post Office.

Contained within the Commission Report we find the following statement: "*In accordance with postal regulations, the portion of the application which lists names of persons, other than the applicant, entitled to receive mail was thrown away after the box was closed on May 14, 1963.*" (Warren Commission Report, Page 121).

In his article for JFK Lancer titled The Four Faces Of Harry D. Holmes, the late Ian Griggs stated that:

"*Members of Holmes' family have contacted JFK Lancer to say that their father should be remembered in the context of the times where it was considered a badge of honor to be an FBI informant and feel he did his duty in all areas of his responsibility in relation to the murder of President John F. Kennedy.*"

In 1966, researcher Stewart Galanor wrote to the United States Post Office regarding the postal regulations which were enforced in March of 1963. Ralph Rea, head of the Special Services Branch informed Galanor that in March of 1963, the following were the specific Postal Regulations in place:

Section 846.53h of the postal manual provides that the third portion of box rental applications, identifying persons other than the applicant authorized to receive mail, must be retained for two years after the box is closed. And...

Section 355.111b(4) prescribes that the mail addressed to a person at a post office box, who is not authorized to receive mail, shall be endorsed 'addressee unknown' and returned to sender where possible.

Rea's independent statement regarding the USPS regulations of March of 1963 is a direct challenge to the testimony of Harry Holmes. In a court of law, if Holmes had testified in the manner in which he did before the Commission, there is no doubt that defense council for Oswald would have impeached his testimony by using the United States Postal Regulations and the statements of Rea or another unbiased representative of the postal service.

Part three of Oswald's post office application for his box in New Orleans is still around today. Despite Holmes' assertion to the contrary, the New Orleans Post Office complied with postal regulation 846.53h and kept part 3 of the application form.

The retaining of such documentation is a direct challenge to the testimony of Holmes. The most convincing evidence we have that Oswald never authorized "Hidell" to receive mail at box 2915, is the apparent destruction of the specific portion of the postal application allegedly relating to a "A. Hidell."

The FBI Knew No Hidell

The Commission asserted that *"It is not known whether the application for post office box 2915 listed 'A Hidell' as a person entitled to receive mail at this box."*

However information printed in the Commission's own volumes indicate that the FBI knew that Oswald had not indicated that an "A Hidell" be permitted to receive mail through his box.

Commission Exhibit 2585, is a document from the FBI, dated June 3, 1963. Bullet point 12 states:
Claim - *"The post office box in Dallas to which Oswald had the rifle mailed was kept under both his name and that of "A. Hidell."*
Investigation – *"Our investigation has revealed that Oswald **did not** indicate on his application that others, including an "A. Hidell" would receive mail through the box in question, which was Post Office Box 2915 in Dallas. This box was obtained by Oswald on October 9, 1962 and relinquished by him on May 14, 1963."*

DELIVERY OF OSWALD RIFLE TO HIDELL?

When firearms are shipped via the mail the shipper must include with the shipment a form 2162. This form is to be filled out by the receiver of the firearm. U.S Post Office Regulations (846.5.53.A) state:

Per document 38 in Stewart Galanor's Cover-Up, delivery receipts for firearms and statements by shippers of firearms (Forms 2162, 1508) require a retention period of 4 years.

If anyone named Hidell went to retrieve such a package, he or she would have been required, by law, to complete all relevant documentation relating to the sale of the weapon in question. So where is this documentation today? Neither form 2162 nor 1508 exists in the case of "A Hidell."

WAS OSWALD'S MAIL BOX MONITORED?

CE 139 is the rifle found at the scene of the JFK assassination and a key part of the evidence against Lee Oswald, but this weapon has mysteries associated with it.

C.A. Riggs, owner of the apartment duplex on Mercedes where the Oswald family had rented accommodation in 1962, stated as per Commission Exhibit 2189 that he recalled *"The Postal Inspection Service making some inquiries regarding subversive literature while the Oswald's were occupants of 2703 Mercedes."*

But Riggs also told the FBI that there were *"no adverse conditions under which Oswald and his wife moved."* In that time and place, having Postal Inspectors arrive inquiring about a tenant receiving subversive materials would be enough to get said tenant kicked out. We should therefore assume that the inspectors made the inquiries after the Oswald's had vacated.

According to the FBI Hosty Report (CE 829), dated 9/10/63 under the heading Connections with the Communist Party:

"*On September 28th, 1962, Dallas confidential informant T-1 advised that LEE H. OSWALD, who at the time resided at 2703 Mercedes Street, Fort Worth, Texas, was a subscriber to The Worker, an East Coast communist newspaper.*"

How would an FBI informant be privy to the knowledge that Oswald was receiving subversive literature unless his mail was under surveillance?

It would appear that the Inspectors (who may actually have been FBI agents using the title of PO inspectors as cover (because at that time, only PO Inspectors had legal authority to open mail), visited Mercedes Street after September 28, but before Oswald changed his address on October 10 at the Post Office to his newly opened PO Box.

OSWALD LINK TO FAIR PLAY FOR CUBA COMMITTEE

In an undated letter sent to Vincent T. Lee of the Fair Play For Cuba Committee, Oswald asks for money to print pamphlets for the FPCC. He states that he "*Had a placard around his neck handing out Fair Play for Cuba Pamphlets.*" He apparently only had enough money to print some 40 pamphlets.

Oswald also stated that: "*My home-made placard read Hands Off Cuba! Viva Fidel!*" Although the letter bears no date, the words "*Sent 4/19/63*" appears at the bottom of the letter. This is interesting because this information was shared privately in a letter from Oswald to Vincent T. Lee.

However, if we further look at the Hosty Report, we find the following passage:

"On April 21, 1963, Dallas confidential informant T-2 advised that Lee H. Oswald of Dallas, Texas was in contact with the Fair Play For Cuba Committee in New York City at which he advised that he had passed out pamphlets for the Fair Play For Cuba Committee. According to T-2, Oswald had a placard around his neck reading "Hands off Cuba, Viva Fidel."

How was the FBI privy to information shared in a private correspondence between Oswald and Lee? Maybe we can begin to understand why by looking at CE 2718, an FBI document which states:

"Information from our informant, furnished to us on April 21, 1963, was based upon Oswald's own statement contained in an undated letter to the Fair Play For Cuba Committee (FPCC) headquarters in New York City. A copy of this letter is included as Exhibit 61 in our Supplemental Report dated January 13, 1964. Our informant did not know Oswald personally and could furnish no further information. Our Investigation had not disclosed such activity on Oswald's part prior to this type of activity in New Orleans."

According to Vincent T. Lee's testimony before Commission General Counsel J. Lee Rankin, Lee furnished all correspondence relating to Oswald to the FBI only after the assassination of President Kennedy:

Rankin – "Did you have some communications with Lee Harvey Oswald?"
Lee – "*Yes; I did.*"
Rankin – "Have you made a search of your files for all communications that you had with him?"
Lee – "*Upon being communicated with by the Federal agents from the Federal Bureau of Investigation, at their behest, I made an exhausting search throughout the whole Fair Play offices for any and all communications which were there and finding certain communications I turned them over to the Federal agents, particularly Federal Agent Kennedy, in early December 1963.*"
Rankin – "When did you make that search?"
Lee – "*Within a day or two after being contacted by the Federal agents.*"
Rankin – "Can you tell us the approximate date of that contact?"
Lee – "*I believe it was the first week of December.*"
Rankin – "1963?"
Lee – "1963, yes. I am not positive. I am pretty sure it was somewhere around that time."

In chapter 6 of State Secret by Bill Simpich, we find that the FBI had an informant code-named T-3245-S inside the FPCC head office.

Simpich identifies this person as most likely being Victor Vincente who had previously been involved in joint FBI-CIA operations inside Cuba. It is known that T-3245-S passed FPCC information concerning Oswald on to the FBI, including letters he had sent.

While there is no absolute proof that Oswald's mail was under surveillance, it is reasonable to deduce that it was, especially when one takes into consideration all the relevant data pertaining to Oswald's situation at the time. Oswald was no doubt viewed as a communist defector.

The FBI knew that he was receiving subversive mail through his subscription to The Worker. The FBI also knew that Oswald had written to Vincent T. Lee of the FPCC. SA Hosty then quoted information, in his report, which would only have been known to Oswald and Lee at that time. How could the FBI be privy to all this information concerning Oswald but knew nothing of a revolver and rifle ordered to his PO BOX under the name "A. Hidell?"

FBI Special Agent James Hosty kept tabs on Oswald since his return from the Soviet Union yet Oswald was unwatched when the President's motorcade passed in front of the building where Oswald worked on Nov. 22, 1963.

After the assassination, Postal Inspector Harry Holmes could find no one in the postal service who recalled handing a long package over to Oswald as Hidell. This was most likely because it was over 8 months earlier in the year and mail clerks would deal with a lot of mail, packages and customers in that time-period.

A mail-order rifle in those days would not set off alarm bells to ordinary staff. But those who were tasked with surveillance of Oswald's mail had no such excuse. Yet the FBI seemed oblivious when a rifle 'arrived' at Oswald's PO Box addressed to the unauthorized individual "A Hidell."

MAIL ORDER MYSTERY

The mail order for the rifle was purchased at 10:30 a.m. on March 12th, 1963. We know this because of an exhibit contained within the Commission volumes and designated as CE 773. This exhibit depicts the money order and the envelope which the money order was allegedly mailed in. It is clearly timestamped Dallas, Texas, Mar 12. 10:30.

The FBI also checked the "A. Hidell" money order for the latent fingerprints of Lee Harvey Oswald. Had Oswald indeed handled and wrote upon this coupon then any traces of his fingerprints should have been evident. The FBI found no evidence that any of Oswald's prints had resided on the coupon.

Where was Oswald at 10:30 a.m. on March 12th, 1963? Lee Harvey Oswald's time-card, designated as Commission Exhibit 1855, shows that Oswald was present at his place of employment between the hours of 8:00 a.m. and 5:15 p.m.

Oswald took a lunch break from 12:15 to 12:45. Defenders of the Report insist that Oswald must have lied on his time-card because their theory demands that he be present at the post office to complete the purchase of the money order for the Carcano at 10:30 a.m.

Question for the apologists: If Oswald had somehow lied on his time-card and left his place of employment to place the money order for the rifle, then who completed the assigned tasks singed off in his name during the time he was allegedly missing?

Oswald did not own a car, so any venture to the post office would have been completed on foot, thus making the task of ordering the rifle a time consuming venture.

PO BOX SOLELY FOR A. HIDDELL?

A particularly important question seemingly overlooked by the Commission is this:

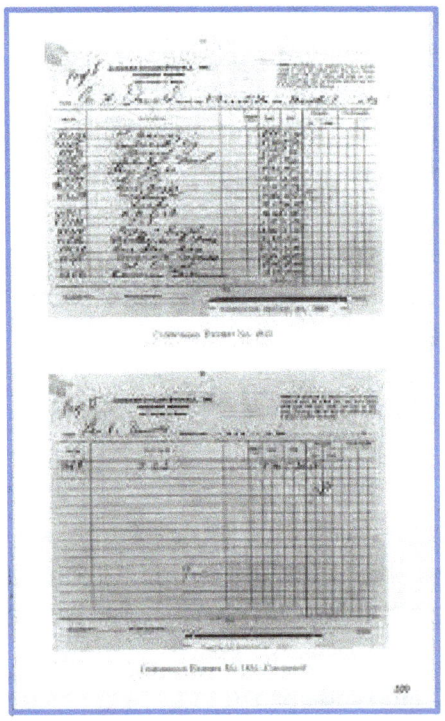

Why would Oswald choose to purchase these weapons through the mail?

Even under the guise of an "A Hidell," these weapons would be traced straight back to PO BOX 2915 in Dallas rented under the name Lee Harvey Oswald.

If we take the official line that Oswald used an alias to hide his connection with these weapons, why would he order them sent to his personal PO BOX?

That action would, without question, lead authorities straight to Oswald. They would then try and use Oswald to find "Hidell." And that is what almost exactly happened in this case.

The evidence the Commission cites against Oswald in this area is a direct result of these weapons being ordered through the mail.

Let us take a look at what options "A. Hidell" had in acquiring a weapon in Dallas in 1963:

Scenario 1

"A. Hidell" could have gone to any store in the Dallas area and purchased a weapon of any kind virtually no questions asked. So why didn't he/she?

Let us assume for argument sake that Oswald and Hidell are one in the same. What then made this scenario so undesirable?

This would have been the most logical route to take. The only thing Oswald would have been gambling on is the clerk in the establishment being able to positively identify him as "A Hidell" nearly nine months after the fact.

The likelihood that a clerk, who would have served hundreds if not thousands of customers between March and November of 1963, could swear under oath that Oswald was "Hidell," would scarcely be believable.

It is the same situation as put forward for the picking up of the weapon at the Post Office. In a court of law, it would simply be Oswald's word against that of the sale's clerk.

If the desire was for these weapons to be untraceable to Oswald, then this is the most viable route to take. This is what makes the mail order scenario very questionable.

Scenario 2

The Warren Commission charged that Oswald ordered weapons delivered to his own PO BOX using the alias "A. Hidell."

The use of an alias in this case is designed to infer that the accused was ready to engage in some kind of criminal act with these weapons. However, by choosing to order these weapons in the manner alleged, Oswald, on the surface, creates a paper trial that strongly links himself to these weapons, the complete opposite of what he would have set out to achieve by using the alias "A. Hidell."

Oswald allegedly uses the rifle to assassinate President Kennedy and proceeds to leave the rifle behind at the crime scene. He would know that the rifle would be found and traced back to PO BOX 2915, rented in his name.

Scenario 3

I pondered a thought for a while: If Oswald was set on mail ordering the rifle and revolver, why didn't he simply rent another PO BOX solely in the name of "A Hidell?"

Why would Oswald concoct an alias to make a purchase only to have the merchandise delivered to a PO Box that is registered in his own name?

Well, maybe Lee could not afford another P.O BOX? I

needed to find out how much money Oswald was making in 1962-63 and how much it cost per month to rent a post office box.

Why would Oswald create the alias A. Hidell and then blatantly link himself to his alias via a shared PO Box in Dallas?

My answer came when I posed this question to lifelong assassination researcher Barry Ernest. I asked him "*This is going to be a longshot, but do you have a rough idea of how much it was to rent a PO Box in 63?*"

Barry replied, "*See WR, Appendix XIV, pp. 741-745, for LHO's expenses, including a PO Box rental.*" I grabbed my copy of the Warren Report and there it was, Appendix XIV titled Analysis of Lee Harvey Oswald's Finances from June 13,1962, Through November 22, 1963. Under the heading 'October 1962' one can read the following:

Receipts:

Net Salary ---------------------------------- $ 228.22
Received from George Bouhe -------- $ 5.00

Expenditures:

Repayment State Department Loan ---- $ 10.00
Rent room, YMCA -------------------------- $ 9.00
Post Office Box Rental -------------------- $ 4.50
Estimated repayment Robert Oswald -- $ 60.00

Estimated cost of food, clothing and
incidental expenses ----------------------------- $ 50.00

Total Receipts ---------------------------------- $ 233.22

Total Expenditures ----------------------------- $ 133.50

Cash on hand, Oct. 31, 1962 ---------------- $ 122.06

This document states that PO BOX 2915 cost Lee Oswald $4.50 per month and that he had an estimated cash surplus of $122.06 that month.

I then flicked through to March 1963, the month the rifle was allegedly ordered. The document stated after all his expenses were taken care of, he had an estimated cash surplus of $184.70.

This document shows that Oswald could have easily afforded another PO Box, one which would serve a short and single purpose. The act of acquiring a "A. Hidell" PO Box would make the venture wholly inexpensive but crucial in his procurement of untraceable weapons.

So, my question now becomes: Why did Oswald not take out a separate PO Box in the sole name of "A. Hidell?"

He could have placed the order for the rifle and revolver to that box, which would have created no paper trail linking him to the transaction or the firearms. Once the weapons were procured, he could have simply ceased the "Hidell" alias and closed the additional PO Box in that name.

These weapons would have been linked to a fictitious

person who had no connection to Oswald, thus making sense of leaving behind the alleged assassination weapon at the crime scene.

The whole process of how the rifle was ordered is nonsensical, especially when it is assumed that Oswald did order these weapons under the guise of "A Hidell."

If one assumes that the Warren Report is accurate, which I do not, then Oswald must have known that when he left the Mannlicher-Carcano behind on the sixth floor of the Texas School Book Depository, in the aftermath of the President's murder then he was leaving behind the most incriminating piece of evidence of all against him.

I charge that this rifle and revolver were never ordered by Lee to his PO Box in Dallas. If Hidell did pick up this Mannlicher at Box 2915, then he/she did so in spite of the previously stated regulations, which strictly prohibit such an action.

The fact that this rifle was not bought over the counter but instead 'purchased' through mail transaction is strong circumstantial evidence that Oswald was indeed being framed for whatever purpose these weapons were to serve.

Since the rifle is the most incriminating physical evidence used by the Warren Commission to name Oswald as the 'lone' assassin of JFK, the discrepancies associated with Oswald and this weapon, as described here, need to be fully investigated by a new formal inquiry.

CONDITION OF THE SIXTH FLOOR RIFLE

The Mannlicher-Carcano, by 1963, was regarded as a cheap, old surplus WW2 rifle, a rifle dubbed by Italian soldiers as "*The Humanitarian Rifle.*" The joke being that the rifle could not hurt anyone on purpose.

Peter Antill is a weapons enthusiast and fellow member of Dealey Plaza UK. Peter is also a long term shooter and highly knowledgeable about classic military small arms who communicated this to me as a response to my query regarding the Mannlicher-Carcano's standing as a rifle:

"As far as accuracy is concerned, if using military surplus ammunition or ammunition that has been reloaded using bullets that are specifically designed for the Carcano (for example, Hornady's 6.5mm Carcano 160 grain round nose bullets), accuracy should be good but it is likely to be better at shorter ranges, due not to any problems with the rifle itself, but with the round nose bullet which is unusually long, and less stable than, for example, the German Mauser 'Spitzer' bullet design.

"Otherwise, reliability and the overall performance of a Carcano will depend firstly, on those variables that can also affect other surplus military rifles, such as how 'eventful' its service life was and how it's been treated in the years since it was sold onto the civilian market i.e. whether it's been rebuilt, how well it's been cared for and how carefully it has been maintained.

"Secondly, is the condition of the ammunition clips. This is critical for those weapons that use the Mannlicher 'en bloc' system, more so than rifles that are fed by 'stripper'

clips where the cartridges are fed into a magazine (such as the German Mauser and British Lee Enfield), as the Carcano feeds the cartridges directly into the chamber from the clip and so any distortion of the clip can lead to problems loading the rifle.

"As far as the M38 Carcano found on the sixth floor of the TSBD goes, the question is not whether a Carcano could do the shooting (magic bullet aside), it's whether <u>that particular</u> Carcano could do the shooting, given the state it was in."

What was the realistic chance of the rifle in evidence, C2766, carrying out the assassination of President Kennedy in its original state?

Had Oswald lived to stand trial, the prosecution would have been required to show that the Mannlicher as of 11/22/63 was in good enough mechanical condition to carry out the assassination.

The answer to that question is displayed in the form of testimony given to Commission Assistant Counsel Melvin Eisenberg by Ronald Simmons of the US Army and FBI Special Agent Robert Frazier. Simmons testified before the commission:

Eisenberg – "Was it reported to you by the persons who ran the machine-rest tests whether they had any difficulties with sighting the weapon?"
Simmons – "*Well, they could not sight the weapon in using the telescope and no attempt was made to sight it in using the iron sight. We did adjust the telescopic sight by the addition of two shims, one which tended to adjust the azimuth and one which adjusted an elevation.*

"The azimuth correction could have been made without the addition of the shim, but it would have meant that we would have used all of the adjustment possible and the shim was a more convenient means - not more convenient, but a more permanent means of correction."

In reference to working the bolt on the weapon, Simmons testified that:

"Yes, there were several comments made particularly with respect to the amount of effort required to open the bolt. As a matter of fact, Mr. Staley had difficulty in opening the bolt in his first firing exercise. He thought it was completely up and it was not, and he had to retrace his steps as he attempted to open the bolt after the first round.

"There was also comment made about the trigger pull which is different as far as these firers are concerned. It is in effect a two-stage operation where the first - in the first stage the trigger is relatively free, and it suddenly required a greater pull to actually fire the weapon." And...

"In our experiments, the pressure to open the bolt was so great that we tended to move the rifle off the target, whereas with greater proficiency this might not have occurred."

Yet more testimony, such as that of FBI Special Agent Robert Frazier, casts more doubt as to the viability of this rifle as the assassination weapon:

Frazier - *"Yes, sir. When we attempted to sight in this rifle at Quantico, we found that the elevation adjustment in the telescopic sight was not sufficient to bring the point of* *impact to the aiming point.*

"In attempting to adjust and sight-in the rifle, every time we changed the adjusting screws to move the crosshairs in the telescopic sight in one direction, it also affected the movement of the impact or the point of impact in the other direction.

When Robert Frazier, the FBI's top firearms and ballistics examiner, testified about the poor operating condition of Oswald's rifle allegedly used to assassinate JFK, the Commission decided to disregard its own expert witness.

"That is, if we moved the crosshairs in the telescope to the left, it would also affect the elevation setting of the telescope. And when we had sighted-in the rifle approximately, we fired several shots and found that the shots were not all landing in the same place but were gradually moving away from the point of impact.

"This was apparently due to the construction of the telescope, which apparently did not stabilize itself -that is, the spring mounting in the crosshair ring did not stabilize until we had fired five or six shots."

Was the accused afforded the necessary luxury of firing *"five or six"* shots to *"stabilize"* the scope before the arrival of the presidential motorcade? No.

An FBI report dated August 20, 1964, from J. Edgar Hoover to General council J. Lee Rankin of the Warren

Commission stated that:

"In connection it should be noted that the firing pin of this rifle has been used extensively as shown by wear on the nose or striking portion of the firing pin, and further, the presence of rust on the firing pin and its spring may be an indication that the firing pin had not been recently changed prior to November 22, 1963."

ASSEMBLING THE RIFLE

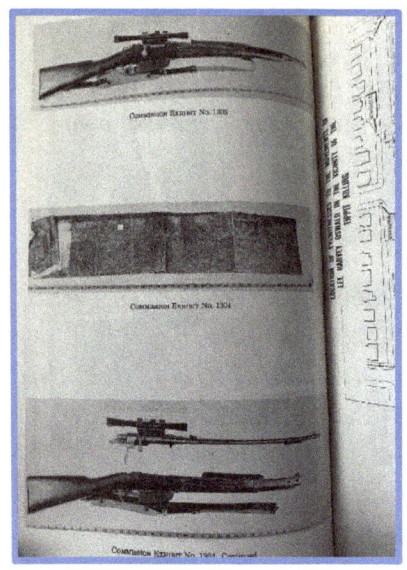

CE 1304 shows the alleged JFK murder weapon fully assembled, the paper bag that was too short and what was said to be the disassembled Mannlicher-Carcano.

One of the most important and overlooked aspects of the case against Oswald is just what it entails to assemble the Mannlicher-Carcano rifle. If we take at face value the information garnered from Commission exhibit 1304 (CE 1304), the dissembled rifle would look like this at left:

The image here is a false indication of what the broken down Carcano would resemble. The Commission, in its quest to bury Oswald as the lone killer, want us to believe that there is minimum effort to assemble the weapon in question.

During his testimony before the Warren Commission,

Special Agent Cortland Cunningham had this exchange with questioning counsel Joseph Ball:

Ball – "Let's take it out of the sack and put it before the Commission. Do you need any special tools to assemble this rifle?"
Cunningham – *"No, sir."*
Ball – "I notice you have a screwdriver there. Can you assemble it without the use of a screwdriver?"
Cunningham – *"Yes, sir."*
Ball – "What can you use?"
Cunningham – *"Any object that would fit the slots on the five screws that retain the stock to the action."*
Ball – "Could you do it with a 10-cent piece?"
Cunningham – *"Yes, sir."*
Ball – "Will you do that - about how long will it take you?"
Cunningham – *"I know I can do it, but I have never been timed as far as using a dime. I have been timed using a screwdriver, which required a little over 2 minutes."*
Ball – "2 minutes with a screwdriver. Try it with the dime and let's see how long it takes. Okay. Start now. Six minutes."
Cunningham – *"I think I can improve on that."*
Ball – "And the only tool you used was a 10-cent piece?"
Cunningham – *"That is correct."*

Why would Ball ask Cunningham if he could have assembled the rifle without the use of a screwdriver? The answer to that question is simple: no screwdriver was found on the sixth floor of the Texas School Book Depository following the assassination.

And why did Ball ask about the use of a 10-cent coin? Because with the absence of a screwdriver or assembling tool, there was a serious flaw in the Commission's theory that Oswald could have assembled the rifle, hence the need for the dime coin speculation.

Regardless of the theory proposed by the Commission, no evidence exists that Oswald ever assembled this rifle, period. If you were planning on breaking this rifle down for transportation purposes and were relying on assembling this weapon in a quick and efficient manner, then without question, you would rely heavily on an assembly tool like a screwdriver.

Anyone who had previously broken down and assembled this rifle would have known the importance of using such a tool. To rely on a dime coin, especially under the intense pressure which Oswald allegedly faced, would have been nothing short of madness.

Without question, the man who had studied this area of research the most was the late, great English researcher Ian Griggs. Ian had conducted various experiments with assembling and disassembling the Mannlicher-Carcano. This is what Griggs has to say on this important matter:

"Well, firstly, it is no simple task to reassemble this rifle. Certainly not as simple as those glib words in the Warren Report or that deliberately misleading CE 1304 photograph would suggest. Secondly, whilst it was reasonably easy to tighten the screws with a screwdriver, it was certainly no simple task using a dime coin. The coin is thin enough to fit the recessed head of the screws but due to its tiny diameter, about two thirds of an inch, there is hardly any leverage and it makes it very difficult to exert sufficient pressure to tighten the screws sufficiently."

Ian also goes on to conclude that:

"Finally, I had practiced many times before undertaking my 'real attempt' at putting the gun together. I knew precisely where each part was and in what order it should be fitted. I knew exactly when I had to change position of the rifle from horizontal (across my lap) to vertical (between my knees).

"There is no evidence that Oswald had either the time or the opportunity to carry out 'dry runs' or rehearsals. How long did it take me to reassemble the Mannlicher-Carcano? Well, my best time was two minutes and four seconds.

"I have to confess that I admitted defeat using a dime coin. Having begun several times and fallen hopelessly behind the clock, I have to look on SA Cunningham's time of six minutes with a certain degree of skepticism. Trying to put that rifle together using just a dime resulted in me sustaining two blood-blisters on my fingers and a small cut on the joint of my right thumb."

The best way to understand the awkwardness of assembling the Mannlicher-Carcano rifle is to watch Ian Grigg's 2004 video, which is listed in this chapter's resources section.

THE BROKEN-DOWN CARCANO

What are the different components that make up the rifle? And what would have been present in the paper bag (CE 142), allegedly carried into the Book Depository by Oswald that morning? They are as follows:

Wooden Stock / Top Stock / Metal Barrel / Firing Mechanism / The Chamber / The Bolt / The Trigger Telescopic Sight / Metal Collar 1 / Metal Collar 2 Five Retaining Screws, Some of which are of different length / Ammunition clip / Four Bullets.

Here is a photograph showing the broken-down rifle in its true form. The rifle has to be fully dissembled to isolate the wooden stock.

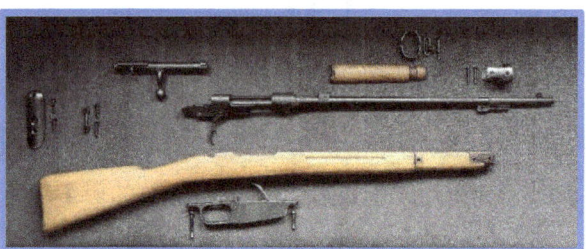

We can clearly see that in its broken-down state, the Mannlicher looks nothing like CE 1304.

Now imagine this: According to the Commission, Oswald is supposed to have carried the paper package (CE 142) containing the broken down Mannlicher on the morning of 11/22/63. There has been no suggestion whatsoever that Oswald put the separate components such as screws, the collars etc. into any sort of envelope to keep all these components neatly together.

We therefore must assume without any evidence to the contrary that Oswald must have thrown every component which makes up the rifle loosely into this paper bag.

With all these different components jangling together, the bag would have been incredibly noisy.

In a communication with me on 4/10/21, Buell Wesley

Frazier responded to my question regarding the noise of the package which allegedly rested on his backseat.

Johnny Cairns – "Did you notice at any time if the package on your back seat was especially noisy? For example could you hear the contents moving around whilst driving? Or if coming to a stop? Do you recall the package being noisy when Lee lifted it from your back seat? I realize I am asking you to recall specific details 57 years after the fact but any recollection would be appreciated."

Buell Wesley Frazier – *"No I do not."*

Why did no other single person see Oswald with this bag or hear him as he walked with it? Surely other co-workers must have seen and heard this?

An employee of the TSBD who witnessed Lee Oswald arrive at the Depository on the morning of 11/22/63 was Jack Dougherty. The Commission stated in its report:

"One employee, Jack Dougherty, believed that he saw Oswald coming to work, but he does not remember that Oswald had anything in his hands as he entered the door." (Warren Commission Report, Page 133) Now compare that statement in the report to Dougherty's actual testimony taken before the Commission:

Ball – "Now, is that a very definite impression that you saw him that morning when he came to work?"
Dougherty – *"Well, oh--it's like this--I'll try to explain it to you this way--- you see, I was sitting on the wrapping table and when he came in the door, I just caught him out of the corner of my eye---that's the reason why I said it*

that way."
Ball – "Did he come in with anybody?"
Dougherty – *"No."*
Ball – "He was alone?"
Dougherty – *"Yes; he was alone."*
Ball – "Do you recall him having anything in his hand?"
Dougherty – *"Well, I didn't see anything, if he did."*
Ball – "Did you pay enough attention to him, you think, that you would remember whether he did or didn't?"
Dougherty – *"Well, I believe I can---yes, sir---I'll put it this way; I didn't see anything in his hands at the time."*
Ball – "In other words, your memory is definite on that is it?"
Dougherty – *"Yes, sir."*

The Commission also never addressed the rationality of why Oswald would transport the weapon in such a way. Picture the scene...Oswald has retrieved his hidden noisy package from somewhere in the building and then proceeds up-to the sixth floor to assemble it.

The area behind the 'shield of boxes' is small, as shown in this picture on the next page that I took in 2018 and affords no space to assemble a rifle.

We must assume if the Commission is correct, that Oswald emptied out all the contents of the bag onto the small floor space available to him and proceeded to sift through the various components to assemble the rifle.

As Ian Griggs points out, two almost identical screws secure the forward collar. These screws are 1/16 of an inch shorter than each other and are not interchangeable.

Can you imagine Oswald up at that window trying to work out which screw goes where, whilst the small space he occupies is drastically reduced by the various other components which surround him?

Then, in spite of all the other hardships he faces, he makes his task of assembling this rifle verging on the impossible by trying to tighten such screws with a dime coin? And on top of that, he must know that at any moment he could be caught in the act of assembly by either his fellow employees, police officers or Secret Service agents. To face that kind of panic and terror would have been unimaginable, no doubt having some effect on his concentration, hand-eye coordination and, by definition, his performance.

Bonnie Ray Williams, a fellow co-worker of Oswald who lunched on the sixth floor until around 10 minutes before the shooting saw or heard no individual up on the sixth floor. How can that be if Oswald was rattling around that south east corner window desperately trying to assemble the rifle?

If I were defense council for Oswald, I would have had a broken down Mannlicher-Carcano in an identical bag as CE 142, thrown in with every single loose component that makes up the rifle. I would have made a replica area of the sixth-floor window, complete with the various boxes that shielded it and what was present in the area itself.

I would have then asked Special Agent Cortland Cunningham to come down off the stand and enter the replica 'Snipers Nest.' I would have asked SA Cunningham to demonstrate the act of assembling this rifle with a dime coin.

I would have relayed to SA Cunningham that as soon as he proceeded to empty the bag of the rifle and its various components, I would begin a stopwatch to establish his time. Whilst crouching in a very confined space, SA Cunningham would have to either match or get close to the "6 minute" time- frame in which he allegedly assembled the rifle with a dime at the Commission hearings. Remember his testimony:

Ball – "Try it with the dime and let's see how long it takes. Okay. Start now. Six minutes."
Cunningham – "*I think I can improve on that.*"
Ball – "And the only tool you used was a 10-cent piece?"
Cunningham – "*That is correct.*"

SA Cunningham apparently found no hardship in this task and thought he could better his time of six minutes. With that in mind, I would then have relayed to SA Cunningham that he would have 10 minutes to assemble the rifle in question.

OSWALD'S PROFICIENCY AS A MARKSMAN

Was Oswald 'proficient' with this weapon and the trigger pull? Proficiency meant two things according to Ms.

Meagher:

1. Familiarity with the action of the bolt itself and the force required to open it.

2. Familiarity with the action trigger, which was a two-stage trigger.

Where is the evidence that Oswald practiced with this weapon? What gun ranges did he frequent in Dallas and New Orleans?

He must have practiced extensively for him to get so proficient with the weapon and the two-stage trigger. Was there any evidence to indicate that he had indeed practiced with this rifle on a range? Were any spent shells linked to C2766 ever recovered on the local ranges? The FBI made extensive searches for any expended shells which could be linked to the Mannlicher. They never found one.

If Oswald practiced much, is there any record of him purchasing a significant amount of ammunition for the Mannlicher? Wouldn't the various establishments who sold the Western Cartridge ammunition in Dallas be familiar with Oswald as an avid shooter?

HISTORICAL BLIND EYE

Warren Commission conclusion: Based on testimony of the experts and their analysis of films of the assassination, the Commission has concluded that a rifleman of Lee Harvey Oswald's capabilities could have fired the shots from the rifle used in the assassination within the elapsed time of the shooting.

The Commission has concluded further that Oswald possessed the capability with a rifle which enabled him to commit the assassination.

But did Oswald have the level of proficiency with a rifle that the Commission attributed to him? We have seen earlier how even master riflemen encountered issues with working the alleged assassination weapon due to its rather poor condition and the two-stage operation needed to work it.

While in the Marines, Lee Oswald proved himself to be a mediocre marksman at best when shooting at a still target. On 11/22/63, his talent was matched by a broken-down mediocre weapon. It just doesn't add up.

During his early days in the Marine Corps, Oswald was given a rifle test. The test was conducted in 1956 with Oswald having registered a score of 212, which was two points over the minimum score for sharpshooter. Sharpshooter classification in the Marine Corp would categorize a Marine as a medium shot. This classification was barely achieved even after a very intensive training period. Also note that during such tests, the Marines would be firing at still targets.

On his last recorded score with a rifle, Oswald registered a score of 191. As a result of this, he dropped into the 'marksman' category, which he made by the skin of his teeth.

If he had dropped a further two points in his rifle scoring, his shooting ability would have dropped out of every known Marine Corp category for a rifleman.

To acquire the feat of Marksman, the tested individual would be ranked at the lowest classification available, indicating a poor shot. How do defenders of the Commission deal with this information?

They speculate that Oswald must have been preoccupied with his subsequent home-coming. This is of course speculation.

Three representatives of the U.S. Marine Corp testified before the Commission regarding Oswald's shooting abilities, Major Eugenie Anderson, Sargent James A. Zahm and Lieutenant-Colonel Allison G. Folsom.

Anderson and Zahm both testified that Oswald's Marine record would indicate Oswald would rank as a *"Good to Excellent shot"* and even an *"excellent shot."*

Major Anderson: *"As compared to a civilian who had not received this intensive training, he (Oswald) would be considered as a good to excellent shot."* WCR—Page 192.

In the words of Mark Lane: *"Compare a nine year old boy who plays sand-lock baseball with my grandmother and he's an excellent baseball player but compare him with anyone in the major leagues and he probably would not do so well."*

Not one fellow Marine who knew Oswald or saw him with rifle in hand would testify that he was a *"Good to*

Excellent shot". On the contrary, such a notion would be scoffed at behind tears of laughter.

When confronted with Oswald's poor score of May 1959, Anderson postulated that the score of 191, and the subsequent marksman classification, could have been down to the weather of the day. Anderson stated: "*It might have been a bad day for firing, windy, rainy, dark.*"

In his book Rush to Judgment, the late Mark Lane helps us to understand how such speculation would be treated in a court of law. Lane states:

"*Whenever weather is a factor in a court case in the United States, the records of the United States Weather Bureau are subpoenaed and presented as a matter of course.*" So, what was the weather like during the test on May 6th, 1959? As pointed out by Lane, *"The Weather Bureau records show that the day was not windy, rainy, dark. It was sunny and bright and no rain fell. There was a slight breeze and the temperature ranged from 72 to 79."*

Why did the Warren Commission rely on the speculation offered by Anderson when they could have easily consulted the report from the Weather Bureau concerning the ideal shooting conditions of that day?

Through his work in this area, Lane has debunked Anderson's speculation and found the basis for its printing in the report to be unfounded.

The Anderson and Zahm conclusions are in stark contrast to the Commission testimony of Lieutenant-Colonel Allison G. Folsom. Folsom testified to counsel

John Ely regarding Oswald's shooting ability:

Ely – "I don't see any point in doing this page by page. I just wonder, after having looked through the whole scorebook, if we could fairly say that all that it proves is that at this stage of his career he was not a particularly outstanding shot."
Col. Folsom – *"No, no, he was not. His scorebook indicates--as a matter of fact--that he did well at one or two ranges in order to achieve the two points over the minimum score for sharpshooter."*

Folsom's interpretation of Oswald's shooting record is of a Marine who was a *"rather poor shot."*

A member of Oswald's Marine unit, Nelson Delgado, testified before the Commission to counsel Wesley Liebeler. Delgado stated with regards to what condition Oswald kept his rifle:

Liebeler – "Do you remember whether or not Oswald kept his rifle in good shape, clean?"
Delgado – *"He kept it mediocre. He always got gigged for his rifle."*
Liebeler – "He did?"
Delgado – *"Yes; very seldom did he pass an inspection without getting gigged for one thing or another."*

Remember the rifle found on the sixth floor of the TSBD was in a clean, well-oiled condition.

Delgado witnessed Oswald's shooting abilities with a rifle first-hand. As he further testified:
Delgado – *"It's broken down into three categories: Sharpshooters--no; pardon me, take that back;*

Marksman is the lowest, Sharpshooters, and Experts. And then Oswald had a Marksman's badge, which was just a plain, little thing here which stated 'Marksman' on it."

Liebeler – "And that was the lowest one?"

Delgado – *"That was the lowest. Well, that was qualifying; then there was nothing, which meant you didn't qualify."*

Liebeler – "Did you fire with Oswald?"

Delgado – *"Right. I was in the same line. By that I mean we were on line together, the same time, but not firing at the same position, but at the same time, and I remember seeing his. It was a pretty big joke, because he got a lot of "Maggie's drawers," you know, a lot of misses, but he didn't give a darn."*

Liebeler – "Missed the target completely?"

Delgado – *"He just qualified, that's it. He wasn't as enthusiastic as the rest of us. We all loved--liked, you know, going to the range."*

Delgado, a first-hand witness to the skill Oswald possessed with a rifle, labeled Oswald's shooting abilities as *"a pretty big joke."*

In an interview with Mark Lane for his film Rush To Judgment, Lane interviewed Nelson Delgado.

In this interview, Delgado mirror's what he told the commission. He states that Oswald was a very poor shot and on the firing range he got a lot of *"Maggie's Drawers,"* which were complete misses of the target.

Delgado also told Lane that he was interviewed by the FBI on numerous occasions. He also stated that he felt the FBI were trying to find holes in his story regarding his recollections that Oswald was a poor shot.

During the show trial of Oswald done for London Weekend Television, Nelson Delgado was called as a witness for the prosecution.

On cross examination, Defense lawyer, Jerry Spence got from Delgado that he felt the FBI were out to harm him because of his Warren Commission testimony, a threat Mr. Delgado took so seriously that he moved he and his family to England.

After hearing this, prosecution council Vincent Bugliosi berated his own witness Delgado by saying:

"If the FBI wanted to get you buddy, don't you think they could do it?"

On recross, Jerry Spence asks Delgado; *"You were actually shot in the shoulder, weren't you?"* To which Delgado replies *"Yes."*

MEDIOCRE BY CONSENSUS

In his book Reasonable Doubt, author Henry Hurt sought out and interviewed over 50 of Oswald's Marine Corp colleagues. These men all had first-hand experience of just how proficient Oswald was with a rifle.

Why weren't any of these men subsequently called to testify before the Commission regarding Oswald's rifling abilities? Men like Sherman Cooley, an expert hunter and fellow Marine colleague of Lee Oswald's shared with Hurt his opinion as to whether Oswald was an excellent, good or poor shot:

"If I had to pick one man in the whole United States to shoot me, I'd pick Oswald. I saw the man shoot. There's no way he could have ever learned to shoot well enough to do what they accused him of. Take me, I'm one of the best shots around, and I couldn't have done it."

James R. Persons, another Marine Corp colleague, stated to Hurt that *"Oswald possessed a lack of coordination that contributed to his being very poor in rifle marksmanship."*

As Hurt points out: *"Many of the Marines mentioned that Oswald had a certain lack of coordination that, they felt, was responsible for the fact he had difficulty learning to shoot."*

On his website, researcher Michael T. Griffith notes that *"Oswald was in the Soviet Union from October 1959 till June 1962. For most of his time in Russia, he lived in the city of Minsk. While there, he belonged to a gun club. The members of his gun club reportedly viewed him as a poor shot."*

In the shooting test's conducted by the Commission, the Commission used riflemen who were rated as 'Master' by the National Rifle Association. How the refurbished Mannlicher, in the hands of these Master Riflemen, could prove that Oswald was capable of the shooting performance attributed to him, was disturbing. As Sylvia Meagher points out:

"In repudiating these tests a priority, it should be pointed out that experiments genuinely comparable to the feat

ascribed to the accused assassin could easily have been conducted. It would be necessary only to rope off the Book Depository area—as was done for the on-site tests—and to tow a car down Elm Street with dummies occupying the positions of the actual victims. Marksmen with the same general level of skill as Oswald's (When he last shot for record) could have been positioned at the sixth floor window, and each one instructed to fire three shots at dummies in the moving car."

Defense council for Oswald would of course have objected to the biased nature of the Commission's tests. The conclusions reached from these tests are wholly irrelevant in determining if Oswald had the skills necessary to carry out this assassination. These tests are also irrelevant in determining if he had the skills to work the assassination weapon in the necessary time available to him.

The fastest the FBI could work the bolt on C2766 was 2.3 seconds. With Oswald's apparent lack of coordination and the intense sense of pressure on him, in all likelihood, it would have taken him considerably longer.

Now, the FBI's time test on C2766's operational ability becomes incredibly important when taken into consideration some of the witness testimony regarding the sequence of the shots. Many witnesses reported the sound of the shots as follows: Bang...Bang,Bang. One witness who stated such was railroad man Lee Bowers who told Mark Lane:

Lane – *"Mr. Bowers, how many shots did you hear?"*
Bowers –*"There were three shots and these were*

*spaced with one shot a pause and two shots in very close order such as perhaps Knock..Knock.Knock (*Bowers taps table to simulate shots*) almost on top of each other while there was some pause between the first and the second shots."*

Many other witnesses to the assassination offer collaboration to Bowers testimony regarding the spacing of the shots. Another such example is Seymour Weitzman who testified:

Ball – "How many shots did you hear?"
Weitzman – *"Three distinct shots."*
Ball – "How were they spaced?"
Weitzman - *First one, then the second two seemed to be simultaneously.*

In his book Kill Shot, Craig Roberts interviewed Carlos Hathcock, one of the most decorated combat snipers in United States military history. Hathcock went on to become the senior instructor for the U.S. Marine Corps, Sniper Instruction School at Quantico.

Hathcock said "*Let me tell you what we did at Quantico. We reconstructed the whole thing, the angle, the range, the moving target, the time limit, the obstacles, everything. I don't know how many times we tried, but we couldn't duplicate what the Warren Commission said Oswald did.*"

An Olympic rifle champion, Hubert Hammerer, said he doubted the assassination could be done with the weapon allegedly used.

The Commission's actual shooting test, from the

perspective of duplicating the conditions of which the assassination took place, was also deeply flawed.

These Master riflemen where located in a tower 30 feet above the targets whereas the alleged 6th floor Book Depository assassin was 60 feet above the street.

The targets were also not spaced out in the correct manner. These targets, which were supposed to simulate the positions of the presidential limousine as it was under fire, did not have the correct distancing.

The master riflemen where instructed to take as much time as they wanted for their first shot. They were also given a rifle rest, a stool and were firing at still targets. These still targets, in opposition to the moving Presidential limousine, were nearly twice as large to which any sixth-floor assassin would have to aim at.

The Commission used selective testimony to determine Oswald's performance with a rifle. This testimony which was in stark contrast to Folsom and Delgado's and of the statements by Cooley and Pearson.

In a letter addressed to Commission counsel J. Lee Rankin from Lieutenant Colonel Folsom, he states the following: Consequently, a low marksmen qualification indicates a rather "*Poor shot.*"

Through the testimony and letter sent by Folsom, we see that Oswald was "*a rather poor shot.*" We also learned from Delgado's testimony that Oswald with a rifle was a "*pretty big joke.*" The Commission must have known that commencing such tests with the use of 'Master' riflemen would be wholly biased against the accused.

Did that stop them from conducting the tests and parading the results as proof that the assassination could be achieved by the accused? No, it did not.

As pointed out in his fantastic book, Reclaiming Parkland, Jim DiEugenio notes what assistant counsel to the Commission Wesley Liebeler stated:

"The fact that most of the experts were much more proficient with a rifle than Oswald could ever be expected to be, and the record indicates that fact... To put it bluntly, that sort of selection from the record could seriously affect the integrity and credibility of the entire report."

None of the Master riflemen were called to testify before the Warren Commission.

OSWALD RIFLE OPERATING CONCERNS

Another alarming aspect of the rifle alleged to have been found on the sixth floor appears in Warren Report Volume XXIV, page 2, CE 1977.

At issue is the condition and reliability of the alleged assassination weapon (serial # C2766). The Commission learned and disregarded evidence that thousands of Mannlicher-Carcano rifles shipped from Italy were of such poor condition, they had to be disassembled to remove defective parts and then reassembled using 'used parts' from other unused rifles.

Contained within CE 1977 is this startling information:

"Concerning the shipment of those rifles to Adam Consolidated Industries, Inc., there is presently a legal proceeding by the Carlo Riva Machine Shop to collect payment for the shipment of the rifles which Adam Consolidated Industries Inc., claims were defective."

William Sucher, who had bought thousands of rifles from the Italian government surplus, told the Commission: *"Many of these rifles were collected from battlefields or places of improper storage and were in very poor condition.*

"These rifles were bought by the pound rather than units. Upon arrival in Canada, defective parts were removed, and salable rifles were sometimes composed of parts of three or more weapons."

Was the rifle allegedly found on the sixth floor of the Texas School Book Depository in usable condition? This evidence suggests that it was not:

Unsightly – The scope on the weapon alleged to have been found on the 6th floor was defective and could not provide an accurate acquiring of the target. The weapon had to be modified by the use of metal shims for test firing purposes.

Bolt Issue – The bolt on the rifle was difficult to operate, a particular problem given the time constraint.

Firing Pin Problem – The master riflemen who test fired the Mannlicher did not want to pull the trigger for fear of breaking the firing pin.

Tricky Trigger – With the trigger pull being a two-stage operation, the marksman's aim when firing this rifle was thrown off considerably.

Now compare that to what the Commission claimed Oswald did with this weapon. He is alleged to have fired this old, rusty, junk rifle at a moving target, scoring two out of three hits in six seconds.

Remember, the FBI test fired how quickly the bolt could be recycled on this particular weapon. It took a minimum of 2.3 seconds to work the bolt and that is without aiming. That left Oswald, on average, a grand total of 1.6 seconds to acquire a target and to fire, and that is assuming he was capable of working the bolt at the minimum time required.

Now with everything which has been stated above, would you, as a rational human being, place your life in the performance of this cheap, old, surplus WW2 rifle with its myriad of problems?

Also, in a legal sense, the rifle poses huge problems for the prosecution in a public trial. When the U.S. Army made modifications to this rifle in the form of repairs to test fire it, the rifle as evidence loses all its credibility.

One could even charge, that in order to test fire the rifle, the U.S. Army had to tamper with one of the most important pieces of evidence in this case.

This rifle, attributed to the accused, could not have been used to assassinate the President within the time constraint of six seconds.

THE PALM PRINT

The next piece of evidence up for discussion is the palm print of Oswald, which was allegedly found on the interior of the Mannlicher- Carcano by Lt. J.C. Day on 11/22/63.

This discovery would lend credence to the charge that Oswald had indeed come into contact with the alleged assassination weapon prior to or on 11/22/63. It needs to be said that it does not prove he ever fired the weapon prior to or on 11/22/63. So, let us take a look at this piece of evidence, study its origin and evaluate how genuine its existence actually is.

Can we establish the authenticity of the evidence in question? The prosecution, in trying to enter this evidence into the record, would fall short in some important aspects.

For starters, NO photograph of the palm print's physical presence on the rifle exists. A photograph of a lift is taken to safeguard against the possibility of losing it. Take for example the statements of FBI Fingerprint Expert Sebastian Letona:

"Primarily, our recommendation in the FBI is simply in every procedure to photograph and then lift."

The absence of any pictorial evidence showing the print on the rifle is very concerning especially when we learn that Lieutenant Day attended an advanced latent print school conducted in Dallas by the Federal Bureau of Investigation.

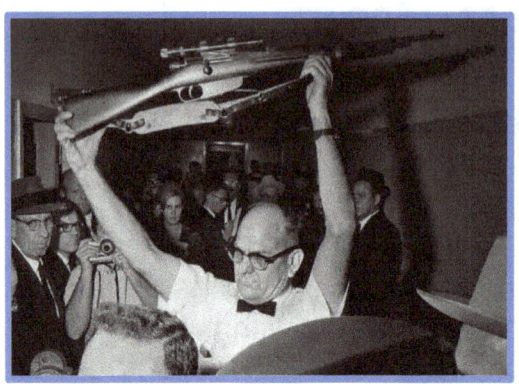

Lt. J.C. Day, a latent print specialist with the Dallas Police Department, carries the alleged 'assassin's weapon' among a crowd of reporters. A public trial of Oswald would have exposed glaring problems with this rifle and how the police handled this weapon in its custody.

There are photographs of partial prints taken by Day which were found on the exterior of the rifle. These prints were found to be valueless by the FBI. (See "A Presumption Of Innocence, Lee Harvey Oswald," Part 3, by Johnny Cairns for more) Day claimed that he had taken these photographs around 8 p.m. on 11/22/63.

Day relayed that he did not take a photograph of the most important latent palm print because he was given orders by Dallas Police Chief Jesse Curry to "*go no further with the processing.*"

However, in an interview conducted by the FBI, Day stated that he received these orders from Curry shortly before midnight. So, by his own admission, Day had almost 4 hours between his photographs of the external prints to the orders from Chief Curry.

Why did Day not photograph the latent print? He must have known that this would be important evidence in any trial of Oswald. Not only is there no evidence that the palm print was ever present on the rifle, when the FBI received the weapon and tested it for prints, they found no evidence of any fingerprint traces or evidence of a lift ever being performed.

Day stated during his testimony that "*The print on the gun...still remained on there...there was traces of ridges still on the gun barrel.*" This is in stark contrast to the findings by the FBI.

Day claimed that he informed FBI agent Vincent T. Drain, who transferred the rifle to Washington DC on 11/23/63, that he had indeed found a print on the rifle. However Agent Drain disputes Day's assertions. This was detailed by author Henry Hurt in his book Reasonable Doubt.

Drain stated to Hurt: Day never showed him any such print or left any indication on the rifle where to look for it. Day even told the Commission during his testimony that he recognized the palm print as belonging to Oswald.

Day also testified that he relayed this information to Curry and Homicide Captain Will Fritz. If he alerted Curry and Fritz about Oswald's suspected palm print on the rifle, why did he not mention it to FBI agent Drain? Day knew the FBI would subject the rifle to fingerprint analysis.

In her book Accessories After The Fact, Sylvia Meagher makes us aware that before the rifle was tested for prints, FBI hair and fiber expert Paul Stombaugh examined the rifle, *stating "I noticed immediately upon receiving the gun that this gun had been dusted for latent fingerprints prior to my receiving it. Latent fingerprints powder was all over the gun.*"

As Meagher points out, "*How could powder survive on the gun from Dallas to Washington, but every single trace of powder and the dry ridges which were present around the palm print on the gun barrel under the stock vanish?"*

It is evident to note that the FBI never did find any of Oswald's prints on C2766. No independent collaboration as to the authenticity of the alleged lift has ever surfaced. Conveniently Day claimed to being alone when he lifted the palm print.

Now when Fritz was asked on Saturday, November 23 if Oswald's prints were found on the rifle, he stated *"No sir."* Curry also made no mention of this important discovery to the media. In fact, the first mention of a palm print discovered on the rifle was announced on 11/24/63 by Dallas DA Henry Wade. This was after the rifle was back in Dallas and after Oswald's murder. Now this part is very hard to swallow:

Day allegedly informed Fritz and Curry on 11/22/63 that he had found a palm print on the rifle which allegedly was used in the killing of President Kennedy and that he had tentatively identified the palm print as coming from the main suspect, Lee Oswald.

With this powerful information in their arsenal, Fritz, Curry nor Wade, who were guilty of making many fraudulent and prejudicial statements of 'fact' against the accused, offered not once to the assembled print media or television reporters on 11/22...23/63 that the existence of Oswald's palm print was indeed found on the suspected murder weapon.

The fraudulent statements of 'fact' emanating from law enforcement officials were so prejudicial against Oswald that it warranted comment from various sources. One of these being Attorney Percy Foreman:

"Authorities are running a serious risk of jeopardizing their case against Oswald by failing to observe his constitutional rights. Officials may have already committed reversible error in the case by permitting the accused to undergo more than 24 hours of detention without benefit of legal counsel."

Citing grounds for reversal, Foreman stated: *"Under recent decision of the United States Supreme Court, Federal procedural guarantees must be observed in state prosecutions. Their abridgment can be grounds for a reversal or even a conviction.*

"This is a new law. They could get a conviction in Texas and get it thrown out on appeal, but it takes a long time for these dim-witted law enforcement officers to realize it."

After Oswald's murder, all the evidence pertaining to the murder of President Kennedy was transferred from Dallas to Washington on Nov 26.

Day's alleged lift of the palm print on the rifle did not reach Washington until Nov. 29. Why did this important piece of evidence not arrive with the others on the 26th? Even the Commission had serious reservations with regards to the late arriving palm print on the rifle. A memo dated 26 August 1964 from the FBI regarding this point reads:

"There was a serious question in the minds of the Commission as to whether or not the palm impression which had been obtained by the Dallas Police

Department is a legitimate latent palm impression removed from the rifle barrel or whether it was obtained from some other source and for this reason this matter needs to be resolved."

For his book Reasonable Doubt, Henry Hurt interviewed Lt. Day and FBI SA Vincent T. Drain. Drain was the agent to whom the rifle was entrusted to escort on its trip from Dallas to Washington DC. Drain relayed the following information to Hurt:

"*I just don't believe there was ever a print.*" He noted that there was increasing pressure on the Dallas police to build evidence in the case. Asked to explain what might have happened, Agent Drain said, "*All I can figure is that it* (Oswald's print) *was some sort of cushion because they were getting a lot of heat by Sunday night. You could take the print off Oswald's card and put it on the rifle. Something like this happened.*"

CONCLUSION

No photographic evidence of the palm print on the rifle exists nor does evidence in the form of powder or dry ridges on the rifle exist, which would indicate that a lift had taken place.

The FBI agent who examined the rifle for prints denies the existence of any traces of the palm print. Day did not relay the information to FBI agent Drain that he found Oswald's print on the rifle. Day also did not provide a note along with the rifle explaining that he had indeed found a print and where.

Although Day testified to it, the lack of any mention of the existence of the palm print by law enforcement authorities prior to 11/24/63 is seriously suspicious when you take into account the morass of fraudulent information which was spewing out of the Dallas Police HQ on 11/22..23/63.

With Day, Fritz, and Curry sure to take the stand at a public trial of Oswald, their stories regarding the existence of the palm print on Friday would be subjected to the art of cross examination.

I am confident that under cross, the fraudulent claim that a palm print had resided on the rifle would have been exposed for what it really was - An attempt to frame the accused defendant, Lee Oswald.

Chapter 5

Debunking the Circumstantial Evidence Used by the Warren Commission to Name Oswald as the 'Lone' Assassin of JFK!

Part 2 – The Problematic Paper Bag

By Johnny Cairns
JFK Assassination Researcher

With regards to the relevance of a hand-crafted paper bag said to have been found near the sixth floor window, it was linked to the alleged murder weapon by this Commission conclusion:

"Oswald carried his rifle into the Depository Building on the morning of November 22, 1963."

The above conclusion was reached by the Commission and was published as fact in the Warren Report. In this section, we will take a look at the available evidence regarding the bag (CE 142).

Is there any physical evidence the Commission presented which would solidify as fact that CE 142 was indeed found around the alleged crime scene on 11/22/63?

The answer to that question is no.

Strange as it may seem, no alleged crime scene photographs exist which show the bag (CE 142) in situ around the southeast corner window.

The Commission had a problem with this.

How can they charge that Oswald brought the Mannlicher to the building if no physical evidence of a paper bag used for transportation purposes exists?

Instead of offering up photographs of the alleged crime scene showing the bag in situ, the Commission instead offered up Commission Exhibit 1302, an alleged crime scene photograph.

CE 1302 is presented under the title "Approximate Location Of Wrapping Paper Bag." The FBI got Robert Studebaker of the Dallas Police Crime Lab to draw a dotted line on a photograph of the alleged crime scene to simulate where, in his opinion, the paper bag was found:

Ball – "Do you recognize the diagram?"
Studebaker – *"Yes, sir."*
Ball– "Did you draw the diagram?"
Studebaker – *"I drew a diagram in there for the FBI, somebody from the FBI called me down - I can't think of his name, and he wanted an approximate location of where the paper was found."*

It gets worse when we find out that that no evidence was removed from the scene until *after "Lieutenant Day and Detective Studebaker came up and took pictures and everything"* (7H 97-98).

Of course, CE 1302 amounts to having an evidentiary value of zero. Furthermore, no prosecution in the land would dare try and admit it into evidence. So why then did the Commission deem it necessary to use 1302 in its exhibits?

The startling absence of any bag housed within the official 'crime scene' photographs presents huge problems for the Commissions case.

Simply stated, without any physical evidence which points to the existence of the paper bag, the Commission's theory that Oswald had indeed carried the rifle into the building is, to be generous, suspect to the most intense scrutiny.

The lower photo (CE 1302) should show the actual paper bag discarded near the sniper's nest, so why did Dallas Police investigators remove the bag from the crime scene and replace it with a dotted outline?

The use of exhibit (1302) by the Commission is heavily prejudicial to the rights of the accused and goes to show the lengths the Commission went to in its quest to bury Oswald as the lone killer of President Kennedy.

What is the physical evidence that CE 142 ever held a broken down Mannlicher-Carcano?

During his testimony before the Commission, FBI Special Agent James Cadigan was asked by assistant counsel Melvin Eisenberg about this point specifically:

Eisenberg – "Mr. Cadigan, did you notice when you looked at the bag whether there were---that is the bag found on the sixth floor, Exhibit 142--whether it had any bulges or unusual creases?"
Cadigan – *"I was also requested at that time to examine the bag to determine if there were any significant markings or scratches or abrasions or anything by which it could be associated with the rifle, Commission Exhibit 139, that is, could I find any markings that I could tie to that rifle?"*
Eisenberg – "Yes."
Cadigan – *"And I couldn't find any such markings."*

So, no such creases or bulges were present on the bag which would indicate that the bag at one time contained the broken down Mannlicher-Carcano rifle.

Remember, when found, the rifle was in a well-oiled condition. Yet no traces of oil were found on CE 142. The lack of markings or oil on the bag in evidence is a serious problem for the Commission's assertions.

HOW WAS THE BAG MADE?

The bag was made from wrapping paper typically used in the Texas School Book Depository building. The man in charge of the wrapping area on 11/22/63 was Troy

West who had worked at the TSBD for a number of years.

He never left his working area. He even preferred to lunch there. For Oswald to have attempted to make a paper bag from the depository stock paper, he would have done so under the watchful gaze of West who testified before Commission counsel David Belin regarding this point:

Belin – "Did Lee Harvey Oswald ever help you wrap mail?"
West – "*No, sir; he never did.*"
Belin – "Do you know whether or not he ever borrowed or used any wrapping paper for himself?"
West – "*No, sir. I don't.*"
Belin – "You don't know?"
West – "*No. I don't.*"
Belin – "Did you ever see him around these wrapper rolls or wrapper roll machines, or not?"
West – "*No, sir; I never noticed him being around.*"
Belin – "Are they paper machines with the rolls of wrapping paper? You have some gum there too, for taping it? When you wrap it, would you tape it with some tape?"
West – "*No, sir. I never seen him.*"

So, West confirmed to Belin that Oswald never approached his station and engaged in the construction of this paper bag. Could Oswald have taken the tape from the machine at the depository and constructed it on the night of 11/21/1963? West again addresses this point in his testimony:

The Commission says Lee Oswald made the paper bag to carry his rifle into work on 11/22/63, but no evidence supports it.

Belin – "If I wanted to use any of that tape, you know the tape you use to seal it, is there a way to make the tape wet so I don't have to lick it myself with my tongue to make it wet and sticky? Or how do you get it to be sticky and stick together?"

West – *"Well, we have those machines with the little round ball that we fill them up with water, and so we set them up. In other words, I got a rack that we set them in, and so we put out tape in a machine, and whenever we pull the tape through, why then the water gets, you know, it gets water on it as we pull it through."*

Belin – "If I wanted to pull the tape, pull off a piece without getting water on it, would I just lift it up without going over the wet roller and get the tape without getting it wet?"

West – *"You would have to take it out. You would have to take it out of the machine. See, it's put on there and then run through a little clamp that holds it down, and you pull it, well, then the water, it gets water on it."*

As West again confirms, to take tape from the machine dry, a person would have to have some knowledge of the machinery to physically open the machine and extract the tape on or prior to 11/22/63.

And as confirmed by Ian Griggs, *"We know from SA*

Cadigan's testimony that the tape on the original paper bag showed unique markings indicating that it had passed through that tape dispenser and no other. It follows, therefore, that the bag was manufactured at West's wrapping table and nowhere else."

TROUBLING TIME OF ASSEMBLY

In his testimony before Commission member Allen Dulles and investigator Eisenberg, James Cadigan of the FBI was asked to identify CE 142 and CE 677:

Dulles (to Eisenberg) – "Could we get - just before you continue there, would you identify what 142 is and 677 is?"
Eisenberg – *"142 is an apparently homemade paper bag which was found in the southeast corner of the sixth floor of the TSBD following the assassination, and which, for the record, is a bag which may have been used to carry this rifle, 139, which was used to commit the assassination. 677 is a sample of paper and tape - and parenthetically, tape was used in the construction of 142. 677 is a sample of paper and tape obtained from the Texas School Book Depository on November 22, 1963, that is, the very day of the assassination."*

Please pay special attention to the fact that CE 677 was taken on 11/22/63. Furthermore, when comparing the paper samples from CE 142 and CE 677, FBI's James Cadigan testified as follows:

Eisenberg – "In all these cases, did you make the examination both of the tape and the paper in each of the bag and the sample?"

Cadigan – *"Oh, yes."*
Eisenberg – *"And they were all identical?"*
Cadigan – *"Yes."*

Now this point is very strange for if Oswald had constructed the paper bag on 11/21/63, then CE 142 and CE 677 could not have been identical matches as Cadigan testified to. On his fantastic website (22november1963.org), Jeremy Bojczuk sums up the problems with this identical match between the bags:

"The TSBD used approximately one roll of paper every three working days (ibid., p.96). For each consignment of 58 rolls of paper, the company ordered a consignment of 500 rolls of tape (Commission Document 897, p.163), the equivalent of using one roll of tape roughly every three working hours.

"The tape on the paper bag supposedly found on the sixth floor seems to have been applied within about three working hours of the samples being taken by the Dallas police. The bag is likely to have been constructed during the period between Oswald's arrival at the TSBD, four and a half hours before the assassination, and the bag's first public appearance in the hands of Detective Montgomery later that afternoon."

So, if the paper sack was made on 11/22/63, how did Oswald use it to transport the Mannlicher-Carcano into his workplace on that morning as claimed in the Warren Report?

CE 142 could not be identified by the only two people who allegedly saw Oswald carry the bag on 11/22/63. These were Buell Frazier and his sister Linnie May.

Both stated Oswald carried a bag roughly 27 inches long that morning. When disassembled, the Mannlicher was 35 inches long. Fully assembled, it was 40 inches long.

Why would Oswald go to the trouble of making a bag 35 inches long to house the broken down Mannlicher, when he could have constructed the bag at 40 inches long to house the fully assembled rifle?

In his 2021 book 'Steering Truth.' Buell Frazier comments upon how much interest the Commission had in his testimony:

"*Unfortunately, several members of the Commission practically slept through my testimony. Honestly, their actions really said they were not interested in finding truth.*"

In a correspondence this researcher had with Buell Wesley Frazier in April of 2021, I asked Mr. Frazier:

Johnny Cairns – "On 11/21/63 prior to, during or after you gave Lee Oswald a ride back to Irving, did you observe at any time Lee with a brown paper bag? Or materials to construct a brown paper bag?"

Buell Wesley Frazier – "*No I did not.*"

PRINTS LINK OSWALD TO BAG?

Two of Oswald's prints were found on the paper bag, a partial print of his right palm and a partial print of his left index finger. This would suggest that Oswald had somehow come into contact with the paper sack at some point.

Lieutenant J.C. Day and Robert Studebaker of the Dallas crime lab examined the bag for prints and both men failed to identify any legible prints on it. The bag was then sent to the FBI, who confirmed through testing that two of Oswald's prints did exist on the bag.

Now I find this rather strange.

Dallas detective Leslie Dell Montgomery exits the book depository with a hand-crafted paper bag claimed to have held Oswald's assassination rifle. In a court of law, this bag would have been problematic for the prosecution.

The accused was supposed to have constructed this bag from scratch. He was also supposed to have placed a rifle inside of it, carried the bag to work, hid the bag, retrieved the bag and emptied the bag of its contents in order to carry out the assassination.

All that handling of this specific item and he only somehow managed to get "*part of a right palm print*" and "*part of a left index print*" on it?

Oswald is credited with its construction and his alleged handling of it on numerous occasions, so how is it conceivable that only two partial prints of his are found on the bag?

If Oswald made and handled CE 142 in the way outlined by the Commission, then undoubtedly his prints would have been all over it.

JFK Case NOT Closed

Of course, even if the partial prints are genuine, the evidence is insufficient to reach the determination that Oswald had constructed the bag or that he carried the bag on 11/22/63.

Also, as I pointed out earlier, firm evidence exists that the bag itself never held a broken down Mannlicher rifle, which then makes the bag wholly irrelevant to the assassination of President John F. Kennedy.

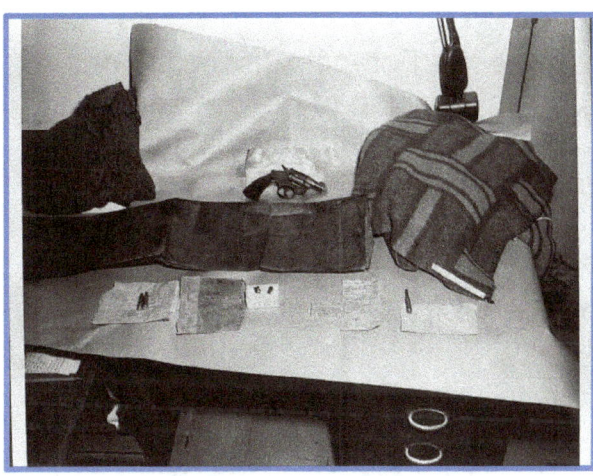

The Dallas police's handling of the physical evidence was abysmal as can be seen in the evidence photograph at left.

Why did the DPD bring together evidence from two separate murder cases and photograph them in this manner?

This cavalier display of physical evidence by the Dallas Police Department shows its reckless handling of the circumstantial evidence against Oswald. Notice how the paper sack and woolen blanket are actually touching each other? We must question all evidence handled by the DPD.

CRUMBLING CIRCUMSTANTIAL CASE

To briefly sum up the evidentiary value of the paper bag as circumstantial evidence:

No Documented Proof – No photographs exist which show the bag in the vicinity of the southeast corner window of the Texas School Book Depository building on 11/22/63. This is odd given that we have photo evidence of the found rifle and the three spent shell casings.

Conflicting Witness Testimony – There are a myriad of problems with regards to the witness testimony about the size of the bag and location of the bag found on the sixth floor.

The Rifle/Bag Disconnect – Forensic inspection of the bag carried out by James Cadigan of the FBI confirmed that the bag had not exhibited any characteristics that it had once held a broken down rifle.

No bulges or creases consistent with the rifle were present and no traces of oil were found on the bag nor were any paper fibers from the bag ever found on the rifle.

Timing Dilemma – The bag under test was found to have the identical characteristics of a paper sample taken from the Depository on 11/22/63 which strongly indicates CE 142 was made on the same day that President Kennedy was assassinated.

Troy West, who was in charge of the wrapping area of the TSBD, testified that he had never seen Oswald engage in constructing the paper bag at the work area he supervised.

Also, West emphatically stated that he never saw Oswald around the work area he supervised on that day or the days prior to Kennedy's visit and that he never left his work station unattended, preferring even to lunch at his work area.

It's pretty conclusive that CE 142 was **not** present on the sixth floor of the Texas School Book Depository on 11/22/63. If it was, where is the evidence for it?

In the words of the late Ian Griggs, who's article The Paper Bag That Never Was is one of the best on the subject..."*If there is no gun sack. There is no gun.*"

Chapter 6

Debunking the Circumstantial Evidence Used by the Warren Commission to Name Oswald as the 'Lone' Assassin of JFK!

Part 3 – The Ammunition Linked to Oswald

By Johnny Cairns
JFK Assassination Researcher

Circumstantial evidence in a murder case such as the assassination of President John F. Kennedy is like methodically assembling a puzzle.

Each piece of evidence should fit perfectly into what eventually becomes a clear picture of what happened on November 22, 1963, how it happened and whether or not the accused was responsible.

This chapter deals with another critical piece of the assassination puzzle, one which the Warren Commission again inadequately covered. Let's start with this question:

Where did Lee Oswald obtain the ammunition he was alleged to have used during the assassination of John F. Kennedy?

It would be necessary for any prosecution of Oswald to ascertain where the accused procured the ammunition allegedly used in the assassination as well as his possession of it prior to 11/22/63.

This evidentiary aspect of the case was investigated by the Dallas police and FBI who's investigation included a canvass of all places of business that sold guns and ammunition in the Dallas and Irving area including hardware stores, pawn shops, department stores, sporting goods stores and Army/Navy surplus stores (CE 2694).

Only two stores where known to have handled the 6.5 mm Western Cartridge Company Mannlicher-Carcano and ammunition. These stores were:

John Thomas Masen, owner of Masen's Gun Shop, 7402 Harry Hines Boulevard in Dallas and John H. Brinegarn, owner of The Gun Shop, 11448 Harry Hines Boulevard in Dallas.

The FBI visited each store and produced a photograph of Lee Harvey Oswald. When shown to Masen, he advised he was *"unable to identify this individual as being a person to whom he had previously sold 6.5 ammunition."*

Masen also stated he bought some ten boxes of the 6.5 mm Mannlicher-Carcano ammunition from the Western

Cartridge Company. He advised that if he had *"sold more than a box or two to any one person he would have remembered the sale."*

Upon further reading of CE 2694, we come across the following in regard to Masen:

Masen claimed, *"He had never seen Lee Harvey Oswald, had no recollection of him ever having come to his place of business, and he had never sold any of this ammunition to Oswald."*

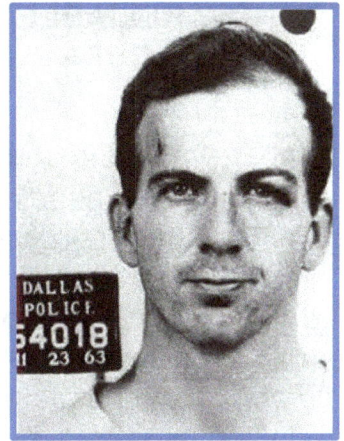

Even though Lee Oswald's face had been splashed all over the news, when the FBI tried to find the store that sold the assassination ammunition to Oswald, no gun store employees could recall seeing the accused assassin in their store.

According to CE 2694, John H. Brinegarn, the owner of the only other store that sold such ammunition, was also shown a photograph of Lee Harvey Oswald. It states:

"A photograph of Lee Harvey Oswald was exhibited to Mr. Brinegarn and he advised he was unable to identify this individual as being a person to whom he had previously sold 6.5 ammunition."

Upon further reading of the documentation, we come across this testimony: *"Mr. Brinegarn stated he did not know Lee Harvey Oswald, had no recollection of ever seeing him and did not believe he had sold him any of this type of ammunition."*

HOW RELIABLE WAS THE AMMUNITION IN CIRCULATION PRIOR TO 11/22/63?

This point was addressed in the Warren Commission Report. Under the heading of 'Speculation and Rumor' on page 646 of the report, we find the following:

Speculation - Ammunition for the rifle found on the sixth floor of the Texas School Book Depository had not been manufactured since the end of World War II. The ammunition used by Oswald must, therefore, have been at least 20 years old, making it extremely unreliable.

Commission's Finding - The ammunition used in the rifle was American ammunition recently made by Western Cartridge Co., which manufactures such ammunition recently. In tests with the same kind of ammunition, experts fired Oswald's Mannlicher-Carcano rifle more than 100 times without any misfires.

This finding by the Commission is in stark contrast to the objections from the critics that the ammunition for the surplus WWII rifle was old and unreliable.

In April of 1965, researcher Sylvia Meagher wrote to Western Cartridge Company about the ammunition for the 6.5 mm Mannlicher-Carcano. A corporate official replied: *"The ammunition had once been produced under a government contract but was no longer available."*

A reply to a second correspondence to Western dated April 20, 1965, prompted this note in Meagher's book Accessories After the Fact – *"The manufacturer stated quite frankly that the reliability of the ammunition still in circulation today is questionable."*

Further, as reported in Mark Lane's Rush to Judgement, in reply to an independent inquiry regarding the ammunition, dated July 14, 1965, the Assistant Sales Manager for the Winchester-Western Division Olin Mathieson wrote:

"Concerning your inquiry on the 6.5mm Mannlicher Carcano cartridge, this is not being produced commercially by our company at this time. Any previous production on this cartridge was made against Government contracts which were completed back in 1944."

The Commission's conclusion regarding the reliability of the 6.5 mm Mannlicher-Carcano ammunition is false. The ammunition was not recently made by Western Cartridge Co. The ammunition was in fact last made by Western in 1944. Thus, the ammunition allegedly used by Oswald would have been over 19 years old come 11/22/63.

WAS ANY AMMUNITION FOUND IN OSWALD'S POSSESSION?

When Oswald was arrested, searches were carried out at two properties with alleged ties to him. One property was located at 1026 North Beckley, Dallas Texas and the other was located at 2515 W. 5th Street, Irving Texas.

During the subsequent searches of these two properties, the police failed to uncover ANY evidence that the accused had, at one time or another, possessed ammunition for any of the weapons attributed to him.

Not one box of ammunition for Oswald's alleged rifle or revolver were ever recovered. Not one stray piece of ammunition for either the rifle or revolver were recovered.

Now ammunition is not sold individually. Bullets are sold by the box load. So, where was the evidence that the accused did indeed possess said ammunition? None existed.

Also, the Police failed to uncover any oil or cleaning solution, which would serve the purpose of maintaining the rifle or revolver. Remember, the rifle allegedly found on the sixth floor was in well-oiled condition.

I shall give the last word on this subject to the late Sylvia Meagher, who brilliantly sums up the state of the Commission's case regarding Oswald ammunition purchase:

"The Commission's rationale seems to be that since Oswald used the bullets to shoot the President, it is entitled to assume that he obtained and possessed them. And since he obtained and possessed them, obviously he used them to shoot the President.

"But this circular reasoning postulates an assassin who:

1. *"Obtained and exhausted a supply of ammunition except for four cartridges which remained in his possession on the morning of the assassination.*

2. *"Covered his tracks so ingeniously that it was beyond the resources of the local and federal investigators to trace the source of the ammunition or to trace expended shells from the largest part of the supply cartridges.*

The Warren Commission could not establish that Oswald purchased or ever had on his possession a six-bullet clip such as this for his alleged assassination rifle.

3. *"Loaded the remaining four cartridges into a clip-fed rifle which can hold seven, firing three times with such phenomenal skill as to make the fourth cartridge superfluous. The alternative is that this singular assassin squandered more than $20 of his meager earnings for a rifle but, unable or unwilling to spend a small additional sum for ammunition, stole, borrowed or found on the street five cartridges that just happened to fit the weapon.*

"Also, those five cartridges sufficed from March through November 1963 for two shooting attempts, an attempted murder of General Edwin Walker and a successful assassination."

No objective person would take any such scenario seriously, yet those who charge Oswald as guilty do just that. It is evident to note here that such an acceptance is not the product of the rational mind but more out of desperation to salvage an irrational theory.

The lack of any evidence which can be attributed to the accused with regards to his possession of the ammunition for the alleged murder weapons leave a gaping hole in the Commission's case.

Simply stated, how could any prosecutor conclude that

the shells discovered in the aftermath of the President's murder be used by Oswald when they can present absolutely no evidence to substantiate its claim that Oswald had in his possession, at any time, ammunition for the Mannlicher-Carcano?

This is an example of the problems a prosecutor would have faced at a public trial of Oswald whereas the Commission could and simply did ignore this inconvenient lack of evidence linking Oswald to the shooting as this section demonstrates.

THE SHELLS

Warren Commission conclusion – *"The three used cartridge cases found near the window on the sixth floor at the southeast corner of the building were fired from the same rifle which fired the above-described bullet and fragments, to the exclusion of all other weapons."*

Now, let's take a look at the shells allegedly found on the sixth floor of the TSBD and the subsequent chain of possession for them (see photo next page). The official theory has three shells found near the southeast corner window after the assassination.

The first man to handle these shells was Captain Will Fritz. These shells were later entered into evidence by Lt J. C. Day. Day testified that he had indeed marked these shells to preserve the chain of custody of the evidence.

The first problem with the shells found near the sixth floor window is that before any official crime scene photographs of the scene were taken, the shells were picked up by Captain Will Fritz, Chief of the Robbery and Homicide Division. According to Tom Alyea, cameraman for local Dallas news WFFA TV:

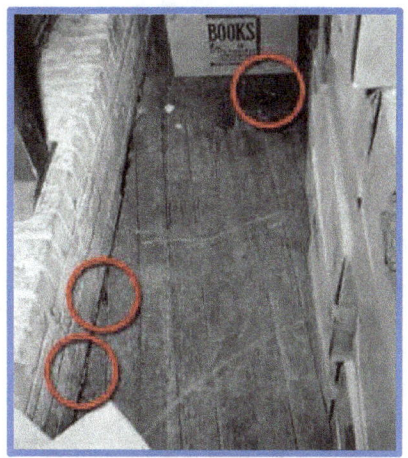

"After filming the casings with my wide angle lens, from a height of 4 and half ft., I asked Captain Fritz, who was standing at my side, if I could go behind the barricade and get a close-up shot of the casings.

Three expended shell casings found near the 6th floor sniper's perch incriminated Oswald in JFK's murder but were never linked to Oswald's possession.

"He told me that it would be better if I got my shots from outside the barricade. He then rounded the pile of boxes and entered the enclosure. This was the first time anybody walked between the barricade and the windows.

"Fritz then walked to the casings, picked them up and held them in his hand over the top of the barricade for me to get a close-up shot of the evidence. I filmed between 3-4 seconds of a close-up shot of the shell casings in Captain Fritz's hand.

"Fritz did not return them to the floor and he did not have them in his hand when he was examining the shooting support boxes.

I stopped filming and thanked him. I have been asked many times if I thought it was peculiar that the Captain of Homicide picked up evidence with his hands.

Capt. Will Fritz improperly handled the three shell casings at the 6th floor window before they were placed into evidence.

"Actually, that was the first thought that came to me when he did it, but I rationalized that he was the homicide expert and no prints could be taken from spent shell casings. Over thirty minutes later, after the rifle was discovered and the crime lab arrived, Capt. Fritz reached into his pocket and handed the casings to Det. Studebaker to include in the photographs he would take of the sniper's nest crime scene.

"We stayed at the rifle site to watch Lt. Day dust the rifle. You have seen my footage of this. Studebaker never saw the original placement of the casings so he tossed them on the floor and photographed them. Therefore, any photograph of shell casings taken after this is staged and not correct."

So, according to witness Tom Alyea, Captain Fritz actually handled the shell casings before any official crime scene photographs were taken. If Captain Fritz' actions do not constitute tampering with a crime scene, I don't know what does.

In a letter to Tom Samoluk of the Assassination Records Review Board (ARRB) on August 18, 1997, Tom Alyea stated that Day and Studebaker's testimony before the Commission was *"Completely false from beginning to end."*

Another serious problem which arises from the shells is this testimony before the Commission by Lt. Day to counselor David Belin as follows:

Belin – "All right. Let me first hand you what has been marked as 'Commission Exhibit,' part of 'Commission Exhibit 543, 544,' and ask you to state if you know what that is."
Day – "*This is the envelope the shells were placed in.*"
Belin – "How many shells were placed in that envelope?"
Day – "*Three.*"
Belin – "It says here that, it is written on here, "Two of the three spent hulls under window on sixth floor."
Day – "*Yes, sir.*"
Belin - "Did you put all three there?"
Day - "*Three were in there when they were turned over to Detective Sims at that time. The only writing on it was "Lieut. J. C. Day." Down here at the bottom.*"
Belin – "I see."
Day - "*Dallas Police Department and the date.*"
Belin – "In other words, you didn't put the writing in that says Two of the three spent hulls."
Day – "*Not then. About 10 o'clock in the evening this envelope came back to me with two hulls in it. I say it came to me, it was in a group of stuff, a group of evidence, we were getting ready to release to the FBI. I don't know who brought them back. Vince Drain, FBI, was present with the stuff, the first I noticed it. At that time there were two hulls inside. I was advised the homicide division was retaining the third for their use. At that time, I marked the two hulls inside of this, still inside this envelope.*"
Belin – "That envelope, which is a part of Commission Exhibits 543 and 544?"

Day – "*Yes, sir; I put the additional marking on at that time.*"
Belin – "I see."
Day – "*You will notice there is a little difference in the ink writing.*"
Belin – "But all of the writing there is yours?"
Day – "*Yes, sir.*"
Belin – "Now, at what time did you put any initials, if you did put any such initials, on the hull itself?"
Day – "*At about 10 o'clock when I noticed it back in the identification bureau in this envelope.*"
Belin – "Had the envelope been opened yet or not?"
Day – "*Yes, sir; it had been opened.*"
Belin – "Had the shells been out of your possession then?"
Day – "*Mr. Sims had the shells from the time they were moved from the building or he took them from me at that time, and the shells I did not see again until around 10 o'clock.*"
Belin – "Who gave them to you at 10 o'clock?"
Day – "*They were in this group of evidence being collected to turn over to the FBI. I don't know who brought them back.*"
Belin – "Was the envelope sealed?"
Day – "*No, sir.*"
Belin – "Had it been sealed when you gave it to Mr. Sims?"
Day – "*No, sir; no.*"

Belin, seeing the problem the Commission had with trying to establish the chain of possession, continues:

Belin – "Your testimony now is that you did not mark any of the hulls at the scene?"
Day – "*Those three; no, sir.*"

Further, in his testimony, Day states he recognizes CE 543 because it has the initials GD on it.

Belin – "Now, I am going to ask you to state if you know what Commission Exhibit 543 is?"

Day – *"That is a hull that does not have my marking on it."*

Belin – "Do you know whether or not this was one of the hulls that was found at the School Book Depository Building?"

Day – *"I think it is."*

Belin – "What makes you think it is?"

Day – *"It has the initials 'G.D.' on it, which is George Doughty, the captain that I worked under."*

Belin – "Was he there at the scene?"

Day – *"No, sir; this hull came up, this hull that is not marked came up, later. I didn't send that."*

So, we have Day testifying that his identification of CE 543 is based solely on the fact that GD is on the bullet. How George Doughty's markings could be on the bullet when he wasn't even at the crime scene didn't seem to bother Belin.

In a letter to the Commission dated April 23, 1964, Day then throws his identification of CE 543 and the chain of custody question of the hull's into even more doubt:

Sir:

In regard to the third hull which I stated has GD for George Doughty scratched on it, Captain Doughty does not remember handling this.

Please check again to see if possibly it can be VD or VED for Vince Drain.

Very truly yours,
J. C. Day

This really is extraordinary. By reading Day's testimony we illicit that he DID NOT mark the shells at the scene of the crime even though they were in his possession. Furthermore, he placed these unmarked shells into an open envelope.

By Day's own admission, he has brought the authenticity of the shells into serious disrepute. Day testified that Dallas detective Richard Sims took possession of the shells. Below are excerpts from Sims' Commission testimony to assistant counsel Joseph Ball:

Ball – "Who picked up the hulls?"
Sims – *"Well, I assisted Lieutenant Day in picking the hulls up."*
Ball – "There were three hulls?"
Sims – *"Yes, sir."*
Ball – "Now, what kind of a receptacle did you put them in?"
Sims – *"He had an envelope."*
Ball – "Did he take charge of the hulls there?"
Sims – *"I don't know."*
Ball – "Did he take them in his possession, I mean?"
Sims – *"I don't remember if he took them in his possession then or not."*
Ball – "But you helped him pick them up?"
Sims – *"I picked them up from the floor and he had an envelope there and he held the envelope open."*
Ball – "You didn't take them in your possession, did you?"
Sims – *"No, sir; I don't believe I did."*

Further in his testimony to Commission assistant counsel Joseph Ball, Sims reverses himself and states that he did take possession of the shells:

Ball – "What is the fact as to whether or not you now independently remember putting that envelope in your pocket?"
Sims – "*I do, yes, sir.*"
Ball – "Did Captain Fritz tell you that he saw you put them in your pocket?"
Sims – "No; he didn't say anything about the envelope or pocket. I remember he told me to be sure and get the hulls."

Ball also asked Sims if he had marked the shells:

Ball – "Where were these hulls when you last saw them, or saw the envelope in which they were?"
Sims – "*In Captain Fritz' office, I believe.*"
Ball – "Were they just laying on his desk, or in his physical possession?"
Sims – "*In this envelope.*"
Ball – "Was the envelope on his desk?"
Sims – "*I don't remember if I actually gave them to him or put them there on the desk in front of him.*"
Ball – "But he was there when you left there?"
Sims – "*Yes.*"
Ball – "And that is the last time you saw them?"
Sims – "*Yes.*"
Ball – "Do you remember whether or not you ever initialed the hulls?"
Sims – "*I don't know if I initialed the hulls or not.*"

These three shells, which were allegedly used during the assassination of President John F. Kennedy, were for a time in the sole custody of detective Sims and he cannot remember if he marked these shells or not?

Did Sim's ever work on a more important homicide case in his life? These actions reek of incompetency. But as we have seen, incompetency from the Dallas Police is nothing new in relation to the murder of President Kennedy.

This is what should have happened; According to Tom Alyea, Fritz was the first detective on the scene to come into contact with the shells. So, if that is the case, Fritz should have marked these shells at the scene. Fritz then gave the shells to Det. Studebaker.

Studebaker should have then proceeded to mark these shells at the scene. Studebaker then threw the shells down on the floor of the so called 'Snipers Nest' and proceeded to capture the *"undisturbed crime scene"*

Lt. Day then retrieved the shells from the floor with help from Det. Sims. Day should have marked these shells at the scene. Instead, Day gave up possession of the shells without adding his markings, which in turn lay in an unmarked, unsealed envelope.

The envelope remained unsealed when Day took back possession of these hulls at 10 p.m. on 11/22/63. Sims should have marked the shells at the crime scene while in his possession. But according to his testimony, he did not remember if he marked them or not.

There are established rules in the judicial system that every police department must follow with regards to the preservation of evidence. By no stretch of the imagination did the Dallas Police comply with any of them.

Instead, they treated key evidence, to put in kindly, in a cavalier fashion. And in doing so they left the veracity of the evidence to be challenged at every turn. The preservation of evidence is so important in protecting the rights of the accused against the real possibility of evidence tampering, which no doubt happened in this case.

Now can you imagine what this would have meant in a court of law for the state's case against Oswald?

For the prosecution to enter CE 543, CE 544 and CE 545 (shell casings) into evidence, they would have had to be able to document every step of the custody process in order to vouch for their veracity.

This would include hearing testimony of the witnesses in the chain and establishing their markings on the exhibit. Markings which, in some cases, do not exist.

This again is paramount to the state's case in proving Oswald's guilt. There is a very real possibility that the defense council for Oswald would have brought a motion to the judge to rule CE 543, CE 544 and CE 545 as inadmissible on the basis of their non-existent chain of custody.

Alternatively, the defense could have allowed the shells into evidence, thus exposing their flaws through the art of cross examination.

Either way, the shells would raise serious doubt with the jury regarding the authenticity of the state's other circumstantial evidence against Oswald.

Barry Krusch, researcher and author of Impossible: The Case Against Lee Harvey Oswald, is offering $5000 to anyone that can authentic the shells via chain of custody. (see link in resources section).

For a more in-depth look at the shells please see part 3 of my article "A Presumption Of Innocence, Lee Harvey Oswald" on KennedysandKing.com.

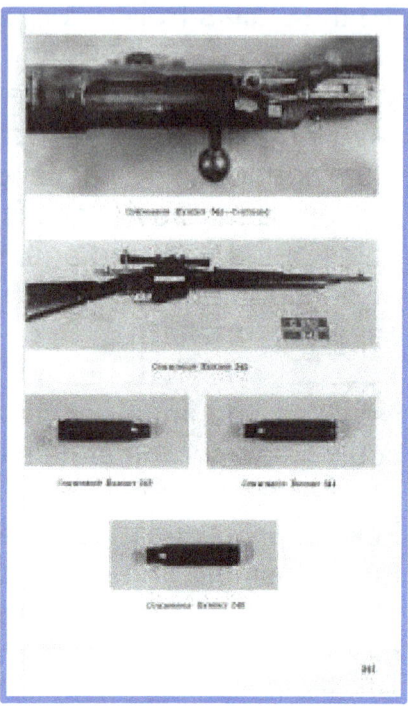

The Warren Commission claimed the three spent shell casings at the bottom of the exhibit were ejected by Oswald's rifle at the time of the assassination, but would a court of law have heard differently?

COULD THE SHELLS HAVE BEEN USED IN THE ASSASSINATION?

Of the three spent shells found on the sixth floor after the assassination, CE 543 presents a real problem for the commission and their thesis that three shots were fired from a lone gunman at President Kennedy.

In his excellent article The Dented Bullet Shell: Hard

Evidence Of Conspiracy In The JFK Assassination, Michael T. Griffith expertly shows how CE 543 could not have been used on 11/22/63.

Griffith quotes fellow researcher Dr. Michael Kurtz as saying: "*There is no doubt that CE 543, i.e., the dented shell, could not have fired a bullet on the day of the assassination, and, moreover, that it could not have been fired from the rifle that Oswald allegedly used.*"

In 2020, I contacted Peter Antill. I asked Peter if he would be so kind to explain the various problems which surround CE 543:

"*CE 543 is one of three cartridge cases found on the Sixth Floor of the Texas School Book Depository (TSBD) following the assassination of JFK on 22 November 1963, the others being CE 544 and CE 545. In addition, a 6.5mm Carcano (CE 139, sometimes referred to as a Mannlicher-Carcano) Model 91/38 rifle was found with a live round (CE 141) in the chamber.*

"*Controversy has surrounded CE 543 for many years as to whether the case actually took any part in the events of that day, the basic problem being that if it didn't, then the Carcano could only have fired two rounds and therefore there must have been at least one other gunman. Any arguments one way or another have to take into account the following factors*:

The Dented Lip

"*One of the more striking characteristics of CE 543 is a significant inward-facing dent in the case lip. This raises the question of how and when this damage could have* occurred.

JFK assassination researcher Peter Antill's study of the shell casings found near the sniper's nest window provides an example of how key physical evidence would have been problematic at a public trial of Oswald.

"Researchers have experimented in throwing an empty Carcano case against a wall or standing on it but failed to do any damage. However, one researcher inflicted exactly the same damage seen on CE 543 on an empty cartridge case while he was loading it into his own rifle.

"Firing a round results in both the case and its lip expanding slightly and hence there is an increased chance of the case catching on a lip below where the barrel meets the breach if someone tries to subsequently chamber it.

"If CE 543 had been a live round, such damage would not have been possible as the bullet would have helped to guide the round smoothly into the chamber. This means that either the damage was done before the assassination (and therefore the case could not have been used that day) or if it occurred during it, it raises the question as to why the shooter would waste time trying to manually chamber an empty case.

Signs of Being Dry Fired

"According to CE 2968 (a letter from FBI Director J. Edgar Hoover to Commission Counsel J. Lee Rankin, dated 2 June 1964) CE 543 was found with three sets of marks on the base which were not found on the other cases fired through the Carcano, as well as other marks which indicated it had been loaded into, and extracted from a weapon, at least three times. In addition, CE 543 had a deeper, more concave dent in its primer (where it had been struck by the firing pin), a characteristic found with dry fired cartridge cases. The FBI actually reproduced this effect on CE 557, an empty case dry fired in the Carcano for comparison purposes.

Marks from the Magazine Follower

"The only marks that link CE 543 to the Carcano were produced by the magazine follower. These marks are caused by the pressure of the magazine follower on the last round in the clip, which pushes the remaining rounds in the clip upwards as their predecessors are chambered and then ejected from the rifle.

"When the final round is chambered, the clip falls past the magazine follower and drops out of the bottom of the magazine well. While other cases had similar marks, the point is that these marks could not have been caused by the Carcano's magazine follower on the day of the assassination as the last round in the clip (CE 141) was unfired and still chambered in the rifle when it was found.

The Chamber Impression

"CE 543 lacks a characteristic displayed by all the other cartridge cases (CE 544, CE 545 and CE 577) that have been chambered in the Carcano - a distinct impression along one side. Even CE 141 (the live round), showed a similar, if less pronounced, impression.

"This was probably because it wasn't fired - firing (where the case expands slightly) would accentuate any marks or impressions caused by the chamber. If CE 543 is supposed to have been fired in the Carcano, how could it be missing this distinct impression?"

This detailed information by Peter would have caused serious problems for any prosecutor trying Oswald. For in the state's quest to have the shells admitted into evidence, not only could they not prove that Oswald purchased and owned any ammunition, they also cannot document through legal means the veracity of the evidence.

Furthermore, the independent study carried out on CE 543 by various researchers and experts compound the fact that CE 543 could not have been used during the assassination of John F. Kennedy.

Defense council also could have pointed to the fact that one of the shells allegedly found on the sixth floor of the TSBD, charged as being used to hold a bullet which killed John Kennedy, actually could not have participated in the assassination.

And if that's not enough, not one of Oswald's fingerprints were found on the hulls allegedly found on the sixth floor.

All this leads to the only logical conclusion available - the shells found near the southeast corner window of the TSBD had been planted, along with the rifle, to incriminate the defendant Lee Harvey Oswald.

Chapter 7

Debunking the Circumstantial Evidence Used by the Warren Commission to Name Oswald as the 'Lone' Assassin of JFK!

Part 4 – CE 399: The 'Magic' Bullet

By Johnny Cairns
JFK Assassination Researcher

CE 399 is the near pristine bullet found on a stretcher at Parkland Hospital where President John F. Kennedy and Governor John B. Connally were taken after the shots rang out in Dealey Plaza.

This piece of evidence is so vital to the prosecution that without it, the crime being committed by a lone individual cannot even be considered by a jury. This bullet is said to have caused all seven non-fatal wounds inflicted upon both Kennedy and Connally as follows:

* The bullet passed through Kennedy's upper back and lower neck.
* The bullet exited Kennedy's throat just below the Adam's apple.

CE 399

* The bullet entered Governor Connally's back close to his right armpit and passed through his body, smashing several inches of his fifth right rib, exiting the right side of his chest.
* CE 399 allegedly then passed through his right wrist, breaking the distal radius bone, before embedding itself in his left thigh.

Once at Parkland Hospital, the Commission stated that whilst Connally occupied his stretcher, the bullet wriggled its way out of his thigh. It then fell between the gurney's black vinyl pad and its metal edge where it was discovered by hospital employee Darrell C. Tomlinson.

CE 399 CHAIN OF POSSESSION

The Commission concluded that the bullet designated as CE 399 was indeed the bullet which was found on 'Connally's' stretcher at Parkland Hospital in the aftermath of the Presidents murder. Tomlinson testified with regards to his discovery of a bullet:

Tomlinson – "*I pushed it (the stretcher) back up against the wall.*"
Specter – "*What, if anything happened then?*"
Tomlinson – "*I bumped the wall and a spent cartridge or bullet rolled out that apparently had been lodged under the edge of the mat.*"

Tomlinson then proceeded to retrieve the bullet from the edge of the gurney and upon inspection of it, gave it to his boss, O.P. Wright, Parkland's personnel director. Wright was a retired Dallas deputy chief of police, in charge of patrol division in the 1950's.

Once Wright had studied this bullet, he sought out a Secret Service Agent and handed it over to him. This agent happened to be Richard E. Johnsen. The Parkland bullet for a time was in the sole possession of Agent Johnsen who retained it until he got back to Washington DC with the martyred Presidents body. He then gave this bullet that he acquired from Wright to Chief Rowley, head of the Secret Service.

Chief Rowley then gave the bullet to Special Agent Elmer Lee Todd of the FBI Washington office. Todd allegedly marked this bullet and then handed it over to Robert Frazier of the FBI crime lab. This chain of possession is officially recognized as how the bullet found on a stretcher at Parkland ended up in the FBI crime lab in Washington DC later that night.

IDENTIFYING CE 399

In a court of law, the witnesses who took possession of CE 399 would have been called to testify at the trial of Lee Harvey Oswald. Each witness in the custody chain would have been asked by council to identify the bullet in evidence (399) as the bullet they took possession of that fateful day in Dallas.

Let's start with Darrell Tomlinson.

Tomlinson appeared before the Warren Commission on March 20th, 1964. Oddly enough, Tomlinson was not shown CE 399 during his hearing and consequentially was not asked to ID it as the bullet that he had discovered at Parkland on 11/22/63.

This is strange behavior from the Commission as Tomlinson was an important witness in the custody chain to this vital piece of evidence.

According to this FBI document housed within the Warren Commission Hearings, vol. 24, page 412 (CE 2011), Darrell C. Tomlinson was shown Exhibit C1 (CE 399), a rifle slug, by Special Agent Bardwell D. Odum, Federal Bureau of Investigation.

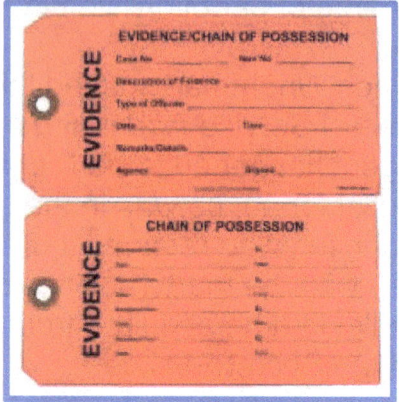

A lack of formal Chain of Possession record-keeping of CE 399 resulted in the Warren Commission not hearing from key people about the custody of this vital piece of evidence. Such would not have happened at a public trial.

Tomlinson stated it appears to be the same one he found on a hospital carriage at Parkland Hospital on November 22, 1963, but he cannot positively identify the bullet as the one he found and showed to O.P. Wright.
Did Tomlinson concede that CE 399 strongly resembled the bullet he held in his possession that day?

O.P. WRIGHT

Wright was not called to testify before the Commission. His absence was a notable one for he too was an important witness in the custody chain to the identification of CE 399.

According to an FBI document housed within the Warren Commission Hearings, O.P. Wright, advised Special Agent Bardwell D. Odum that Exhibit (CE 399), a rifle slug, shown to him at the time of the interview, looks like the slug found at Parkland Hospital on November 22, 1963.

Wright advised he could not positively identify (CE 399) as being the same bullet which was found on November 22, 1963. Again, like Tomlinson, did Wright concede that CE 399 resembled the bullet he held in his possession that day?

In November of 1966, researcher and author of Six Seconds in Dallas, Josiah Thompson, visited Tomlinson and Wright at Parkland Hospital in Dallas.

Thompson, accompanied by the two men, had set off to reenact Tomlinson's discovery of the stretcher bullet. For reenactment purposes, Wright had given Thompson a .30 Caliber projectile to use.

Thompson later asked Wright to describe the bullet he got from Tomlinson on 11/22/63. Wright described the bullet he obtained as having a *"pointed tip."*

In reference to the earlier reenactment done with Tomlinson, Wright stated to Thompson that the stretcher bullet looked *"like the one you got there in your hand,"* referencing the .30 caliber projectile.

This description from Wright was in stark contrast to CE 399. When Thompson showed Wright a picture of CE 399, (CE 572) similar bullets from Oswald's alleged rifle

Pioneering researchers like Josiah Thompson (Six Seconds in Dallas) have done what the Warren Commission wouldn't to solve the JFK assassination.

and CE 606, similar bullets from Oswald's alleged revolver, Wright had **rejected** all of these as resembling the bullet Tomlinson found on 11/22/63 on the stretcher at Parkland.

Thompson stated that while he was getting ready to leave Parkland, Wright approached him and said *"Say, that single bullet photo you kept showing me... was that the one that was supposed to have been found here?"* Thompson replied *"Yes."*

Thompson states that Wright *"Looked right at me, his face expressionless"* and Wright said, *"Uh...huh"* Then Wright turned and went back to his office."

To Thompson, Wright had rejected CE 399 as the bullet Tomlinson handed over to him that day. Tomlinson also could not Identify CE 399 as the bullet he found on the stretcher on 11/22/63.

In a declassified document dated 6/20/64 from Gordon Shankland, SAC Dallas, to FBI Director J Edgar Hoover, Shankland states: *"Neither Parkland's DARRELL C. TOMLINSON nor O. P. WRIGHT, can identify this bullet."*

It is a fact that as of June 20th, 1964, the FBI knew that neither Darrell C Tomlinson nor O. P. Wright could identify CE 399 as being the bullet which came from a stretcher at Parkland Hospital on 11/22/63.

TROUBLING SECRET SERVICE TESTIMONY

When the Parkland bullet was turned over to the Secret Service, the chain of possession continued to be problematic.

Page 412 of Warren Report volume XXIV features the testimony of Secret Service agent Richard E. Johnsen and Secret Service Chief James Rowley.

When agent Johnsen was shown CE 399 by FBI Special Agent Elmer Lee Todd, Johnsen advised that he could not identify this bullet as the bullet he obtained from O.P. Wright and subsequently turned over to Chief Rowley on November 22, 1963.

Additionally, when FBI Special Agent Todd asked Secret Service Chief James Rowley if CE 399 was the bullet turned over to him on the evening of the assassination, Chief Rowley stated that he could not identify CE 399 as being that bullet.

IS ELMER TODD'S MARKINGS ON CE 399?

According to the FBI document CE 2011, in 1964, Special Agent Elmer Lee Todd, Washington D.C... Identified C1 (CE 399), a rifle bullet, as being the same one he had received from James Rowley, Chief, United States Secret Service, Washington, D.C... on November 22, 1963.

This identification was made from initials marked Theron by Special Agent Todd at the Federal Bureau of Investigation Laboratory upon receipt.

So according to CE 2011, SA Elmer Todd, was able to ID the bullet, CE 399, because of the initials Todd had placed upon the bullet in keeping with the chain of custody.

Well respected Kennedy researcher John Hunt wanted to establish if the bullet which sits in the National Archives today in fact bares the marking of Special Agent Elmer Lee Todd.

Hunt 'managed to put together an illustration using photographs of CE 399.' He was then 'able to track the entire surface of the bullet using four of NARA's preservation photos.'

Three markings are present on the bullet in evidence today, these markings consist of RF, CK, JH. RF is Robert Frazier, CK is Charles Killion and JH is Cortland Cunningham.

JH was used by Cunningham to save any confusion over the markings of CC, which can be interpreted as 'Carbon Copy'. JH was also confirmed to be Cunningham's markings by Robert Frazier. These markings are of the three FBI examiners who examined the bullet in Washington DC.

Hunt has proven that the initials of Special Agent Elmer Lee Todd do not appear on the historical CE 399. As Hunt states in his fine essay on this subject:

"There is no question but that only three sets of initials appear on CE-399. There is likewise no question that they have all been positively identified: RF was Robert

Frazier, CK was Charles Killion, and JH was Cortland Cunningham." And "It can be stated as a fact that SA Elmer Lee Todd's mark is not on the historical CE-399 bullet."

We also find further collaboration for Hunt's work from Dr. David Mantik. At NARA in June 1994, Dr Mantik and astronomer Steve Majewski confirmed that Todd's initials are not on the historical CE 399. In an email communication with the author, Dr. Mantik stated: *"The other initials are precisely as described by John Hunt."*

FBI SPECIAL AGENT BARDWELL ODUM

When researchers Gary Aguilar and Josiah Thompson tracked down retired FBI Special Agent Bardwell Odum in 2002, Odum agreed to review some documents for them. One of these documents was CE 2011. Remember this document pertained to Odium himself and the subsequent chain of possession for CE 399.

CE 2011

This FBI memorandum states that Special Agent Odum had showed CE 399 to both Tomlinson and Wright at Parkland prompting Odum to reply to Aguilar as follows:

"Oh, I never went to Parkland Hospital at all. I don't know where you got that!"

When Aguilar brought up CE 399, the bullet allegedly found on a stretcher at Parkland soon after the assassination, Odum offered this:

"I didn't show it to anybody at Parkland. I didn't even have any bullet. I don't know where you got that from but it is wrong."

Odum insisted to Aguilar that he never saw CE 399 let alone have it in his possession. Now Odum knew O. P. Wright. If Odum had a bullet in his possession said to have been used in the assassination of President Kennedy and showed it to Wright, wouldn't he have remembered it?

WHAT STRETCHER?

The Commission concluded, out of necessity, that Tomlinson found the bullet (CE 399) on the stretcher which once occupied Governor Connelly. Whilst at Parkland, Thompson asked Tomlinson about this point. Thompson concluded once all the facts had been ascertained that the bullet Tomlinson found at Parkland on 11/22/63 was in fact found on the stretcher of a little boy named Ronald Fuller.

Fuller was present at Parkland's Emergency department on 11/22/63 because of an injury the boy had sustained to his cheek.

Time Discrepancies

In John Hunt's fine essay "The mystery of the 7:30 Bullet," we come upon some information which further brings the Commission's evidence into serious question. Upon examination of Robert Frazier's detailed notes, we come across the following information: "Reed Elmer Todd, 11/22/63 – 7:30 p.m." So according to this detailed account penned by Frazier, Frazier took custody of the bullet from Todd as of 7:30 p.m. on 11/22/63.

Upon examination of the envelope filled out by SA Elmer Lee Todd upon receipt of the bullet from Chief Rowley, we come across more important information - Received from Chief Rowley, USSS, 8:50 p.m. 11/22/63 E.L. Todd.

How could Todd have given Frazier the stretcher bullet at 7:30 p.m. when he didn't receive that bullet from Rowley until 8:50 p.m.?

This documentation proves that a serious discrepancy exists regarding the time some witnesses took custody of the alleged stretcher bullet. It is a discrepancy that any defense council for Oswald would have no doubt paraded at his trial.

Through Hunts fine work on this aspect of the case, we ascertain that Frazier had a bullet as of 7:30 p.m. on 11/22/63. But this bullet could not have been the bullet recovered on a stretcher at Parkland Hospital because Todd did not take custody of that bullet until 8:50 p.m. This discrepancy raises further serious doubt about the veracity of the Commission's evidence.

NEUTRON ACTIVATION ANALYSIS ON CE 399

Defenders of the Commission claim that the bullet found on a stretcher at Parkland Hospital on 11/22/63 is unquestionably the same bullet that transited both President John F. Kennedy and Governor John Connally whilst riding in the open motorcade through Dallas.

This bullet, labelled CE 399, was allegedly the very same one which was shown to Tomlinson, Wright, Johnson and Rowley. Although none of those men could positively identify it as the same one they handled on 11/22/63, the argument that it was the same bullet persists.

Unfortunately for those making the argument that CE 399 is scientifically linked to the Mannlicher in evidence this presumption is based on a debunked scientific process known as Neutron Activation Analysis (NAA). Tests conducted by chemist Dr. Vincent Guinn have proven, they say, that the fragments taken from Connally's wrist matched CE 399.

In 1977, Guinn was tasked by the HSCA to compare the fragments taken from the presidential limousine and the fragments taken from Governor Connally's wrist, CE 842 to CE 399.

Dr Guinn concluded via Neutron Activation Analysis that the fragments taken from John

TABLE 12.3 Neutron Activation Analysis Results for the Bullet Fragments

Sample	Description	Silver ppm	Antimony ppm	Conclusion
Q1	Bullet from Governor Connally's stretcher	8.8 ± 0.5	833 ± 9	Bullet No. 1
Q9	Governor Connally's wrist	9.8 ± 0.5	797 ± 7	
Q2	Large fragment recovered from car	8.1 ± 0.6	602 ± 4	
Q4	Fragment from JFK's skull	7.9 ± 0.3	621 ± 4	Bullet No. 2
Q14	Small fragment recovered from car	8.2 ± 0.4	642 ± 6	

from Vincent P. "JFK Assassination: Bullet Analyses," Analytical Chemistry, vol. 51, pp. 484A–493A, 1979.

Neutron Activation Analysis led the Commission to conclude that fragments taken from Connally matched CE 399 but the science has been so discredited, it is no longer used by the FBI for matching purposes.

Connally's wrist did indeed match CE 399. Dr Guinn also concluded that fragments found within the car matched a fragment allegedly removed from the Presidents head during his autopsy. The HSCA, a body who heavily relied on Dr Guinn's work in this area, concluded the following:

"The single bullet theory was substantiated by the findings of a neutron activation analysis performed for the committee...It was highly likely that the injuries to Governor Connally's wrist were caused by the bullet found on the stretcher in Parkland Hospital."

The neutron activation analysis further supported the single bullet theory by indicating that there was evidence of only two bullets among the fragments recovered from the limousine and its occupants.

The consultant who conducted the analysis concluded that it was *"highly likely"* that CE 399 and the fragments removed from Governor Connally's wrist were from one bullet; [and] that one of the two fragments recovered from the floor of the limousine and the fragment removed from the President's brain during the autopsy were from a second bullet. Neutron Activation Analysis showed no evidence of a third bullet among those fragments large enough to be tested.

This new development seemed damning to the charge that others besides (or instead of) the main suspect were involved in committing this crime.

This led to the most famous Warren Commission apologist of all, Vincent Bugliosi, to proclaim as *"fact"* that it was scientifically proven that the rifle allegedly attributed to Oswald was solely responsible in carrying out the assassination of President John F. Kennedy. Bugliosi and many others have used the conclusion reached by the HSCA through Guinn to prop up the claim that Oswald bore sole guilt in this affair.

To quote the late prosecutor during his show trial cross examination of Dr. Guinn: *"If fifty people had fired at Kennedy that day, your science indicates they all missed except Oswald?"* Guinn agreed.

NEUTRON ACTIVATION ANALYSIS DEBUNKED?

In 2006, Erik Randich (PhD) and Patrick M. Grant (PhD), metallurgists and statisticians, put Guinn's conclusions to the test and released an article pointing out the damming flaws in his conclusions.

A second experiment to either confirm or refute the findings of Dr Guinn was conducted in 2007 by Cliff Spiegelman, William A. Tobin, William D. James, Simon J. Sheather, Stuart Wexler and D. Max Roundhill titled Chemical and Forensic Analysis of JFK Assassination Bullet Lots: Is a Second Shooter Possible?

This equally damning article on NAA as a science applied to CE 399 can also be found in the resources section. The following is a quote from the introduction in this paper:

"The assassination of President John Fitzgerald Kennedy traumatized the nation. In this paper, we show that evidence used to rule out a second assassin is fundamentally flawed."

Did Bugliosi ever contact Randich and Grant after their essay dealing with the major flaws in NAA were published

Famed Charles Manson prosecutor Vincent Bugliosi believed he would have convicted Oswald at trial based on circumstantial evidence but that evidence no longer holds up to scrutiny.

in 2006? A full year before his book Reclaiming History was published? The unsurprising answer is no.

The article by Spigelmen and co along with the earlier work by Randich and Grant, debunk the work and conclusions carried out and reached by Vincent Guinn.

These later evaluations show that Neutron Activation Analysis cannot be used to determine the origin of bullet fragments. As a result, the most we can say is that the source of Connally's fragments remains unknown.

The notion that NAA is valid for testing the origin of bullet fragments has been officially debunked as evidenced by the FBI's decision to no longer use it for such purposes.

CE 399 CONCLUSIONS

As previously indicated, CE 399 cannot be scientifically linked to the fragments taken from the Governor during surgery (CE 842). As for the chain of possession and witness identification question, CE 399 would have proven to have been an evidentiary debacle for the state's case.

In order for evidence to be ruled as admissible in a court of law the item must have an intact chain of possession. If a certain piece of evidence does not have an intact chain, then this evidence is wide open to serious scrutiny by a defense attorney. The defense can also bring a motion to the judge that such evidence be ruled as inadmissible.

Why would the prosecution want Tomlinson, Wright, Johnson, and Rowley testifying in a court of law that CE 399 was not the bullet each of them took possession of that day?

Why would the prosecution want Todd testifying that he marked the bullet in evidence when in fact the bullet in evidence does not bare his marked initials?

Why would the prosecution want Frazier to take the stand and testify under oath that he had received the Parkland bullet from Todd at 7:30pm when the bullet from Dallas wouldn't be received by Todd until 8:50pm?

Hypothetically, why would the prosecution want Randich or Grant or Spiegelman or the many others who have written articles pointing out the serious flaws in Guinn's work to take the stand and testify under oath that CE 399 cannot be scientifically matched to the fragments taken out of Connally that day?

Each man who took possession of the Parkland bullet was a vital link in the custody chain and without positive identification and subsequent witness markings, the defense would most likely petition for CE 399 to be thrown out of court. Without CE 399 being proven beyond a reasonable doubt that it had indeed been found at Parkland and had caused all the non-lethal wounds sustained by President Kennedy and Governor Connally, there cannot be a 'lone' gunman.

It is also interesting to note that the Warren Commission omitted to hear testimony from O.P Wright, SS Agent Richard Johnson and SA Elmer Lee Todd.

Mark Lane, quoting Mark Twain, summed it up best when he said..."Who so clinging from a rope by his hands severith it above his hands must fall. It being no defense to claim that the rest of the rope is sound."

SUMMATION OF CHAPTERS 4, 5, 6 & 7

"Ladies and Gentlemen of the jury, for you are the only jury, the American people, the only jury that Lee Harvey Oswald, shot to death in the basement of an American court house in Dallas, whilst handcuffed to law enforcement officials, the only jury that he will ever have."

- Mark Lane, first generation researcher

In the 48 hours following his arrest as an accused murderer, Lee Oswald's constitutional and human rights were grossly violated by the Dallas Police and Prosecution officials.

During his all but brief detention at the hands of the Dallas Police, Oswald vehemently protested his innocence at every turn. I started my four chapters for JFK Case NOT Closed with one of his statements of innocence.

With his shocking murder, Oswald has been left in a kind of legal limbo. Although legally innocent of the murders wrongfully attributed to him, that has not stopped official investigations and the news media from branding him as guilty of the murders of President Kennedy and patrolmen Tippit.

With his murder, the American people were deprived of the right to evaluate Oswald's innocence or guilt in an open legal proceeding. Through my work documented in this book, I have presented the case for Oswald's innocence. That innocence, in my opinion, has been well established through evaluating the key evidence of the case.

I have tried to show what a competent legal defense of Oswald might have looked like, a defense the accused was not permitted in life or in death before any of the official investigations into the murder of John Fitzgerald Kennedy. The evidence in this case is far from conclusive as to who shot President Kennedy.

Its veracity with respect to Oswald being the lone person responsible can and is challenged at every turn. This case in a legal sense is a non-starter. The prosecution, which for all intent and purposes the Commission served as, presented a weak circumstantial evidence case against Oswald.

They also relied on the testimony of Oswald's wife in certain aspects, something the prosecution in a court of law certainly could not do due to the Marital Privilege Law. There is also a moral question to be asked: How credible is the word of Marina Oswald in this case? The

Commission had serious reservations about using her testimony but did so out of necessity.

The HSCA (House Select Committee On Assassinations) were equally as skeptical regarding Marina's credibility. So much so that they compiled a report titled: Marina Oswald Porter, Statements Of A Contradictory Nature. The report is 29 pages long and can be found in the Resources section for Chapter 7. Read the report and make up your own mind regarding her credibility in this case.

A CASE FOR OSWALD'S INNOCENCE

To me, Oswald's innocence has been established beyond all doubt. There is no evidence in this case which you could base a verdict of guilty on. The rifle? There is zero evidence to indicate that he had the weapon in his possession prior to 11/22/63.

There is also no evidence that he became proficient with this weapon, an absolute must in the opinion of Simmons if one wants to equate themselves to the weapon's two stage trigger operation.

There is also Oswald's poor shooting ability to take into account. This ability could be put down to his very poor hand-eye coordination.

There is also no evidence the accused purchased or had in his possession, at one time or another, the ammunition for the Mannlicher-Carcano. The crime being committed by Oswald cannot be considered without relevant proof of his ownership of the ammunition.

The weapon itself was in poor operational condition on 11/22/63. It was in such poor condition, the U.S. Army had to refurbish it prior to its participation in rifle tests, which in turn invalidates the rifle as evidence in this case.

No one in Dealey Plaza could testify reliably that they witnessed the accused commit the crime. The best eyewitness the Commission could find was Howard Brennan.

There are a myriad of problems with Brennan's testimony such as not being able to pick Oswald out of a police lineup on 11/22/63 despite seeing him on TV and the numerous other pictures of the accused prior to the lineup is just one of them.

Oswald also gave his real name and place of work at these lineups, information which was highly disseminated through the news media to the world. The lineups conducted by the Dallas police were completely fraudulent and geared solely for witnesses to pick out Oswald as the accused.

For example, Ted Calloway, alleged witness to someone fleeing from the scene of patrolman Tippit's murder, was told by Captain Will Fritz prior to viewing the lineup that:

"We want to be sure. We want to try and wrap him up real tight on killing this officer. We think he is the same one that shot the President and if we can wrap him up tight, on killing this officer then we have got him."

Researcher Larry Harris asked Dr. Robert Buckout in 1979 to evaluate the Dallas Police lineups. Dr. Buckout, who was a leading U.S. expert on eyewitness testimony and identification procedures concluded:

"By any stretch of the imagination, virtually every rule in the book was violated in the conduct of these lineups. The results of any of the line-ups conducted as poorly and under hysterical circumstances, as they were, should be regarded as utterly worthless."

FINGERPRINT PROBLEMS

There were also no fingerprints found around the trigger guard or anywhere else on the rifle which would link the shooting to Oswald. As discussed in chapter 6, the late arriving palm print is, to put it kindly, of a severely dubious nature.

The shells found around the sixth floor window also presents problems. One of them, CE 543, could not have been fired during the assassination. Also, none of Oswald prints were found on them.

The clip also bore no fingerprints which could be attributed to the accused. The rifle was never tested to see if it had been fired recently on 11/22/63.

The chain of custody for the shells designated CE 543, CE 544 and CE 545 is completely and utterly broken, thus rendering the shells useless as evidence in any criminal case brought against the accused.

Another myth was that Oswald had constructed the alleged shield of boxes that congregated around the sixth floor southeast corner window. The claim was that he had done so to remain hidden during the assassination and since his prints were found on some of the boxes, this speculation is heralded as fact by those who charge Oswald as guilty.

Well, an innocent explanation for Oswald's prints being on some of the boxes is this - The man worked in the building! He had done so for or over a month. Some of his duties whilst employed at The Texas School Book Depository involved handling boxes for order processing.

He had a right of access to these boxes, so this charge has no evidentiary value.

Oswald's fellow co-worker Bonnie Ray Williams was part of the floor laying crew on the sixth floor. At the time of the assassination, the sixth floor was being refurbished. Bonnie Ray testified regarding the arrangement of boxes around the sixth floor window:

"We had to move these books to the east side of the building, over here, and those books - I would say this would be the window Oswald shot the President from. We moved these books kind of like in a row like that, kind of winding them around."

Another myth promulgated by those who charge Oswald as guilty is easily debunked. Joe Tonahill, council for Jack Ruby, stated in an interview whether or not Oswald would have been found guilty in a court of law:

Interviewer – "Mr. Tonahill, what, in your opinion, would have been the outcome of a trial, had Oswald gone to trial?"

Tonahill – "*In my opinion…. Under Texas Law… a trial judge, trying him… the judge would have had a weak circumstantial evidence charge to go to the jury. In my opinion he wouldn't have had that. He would have been forced to instruct the jury to return a verdict of Not Guilty, on the grounds of insufficient evidence.*"

In Mark Lane's 'A Brief For The Defense,' he outlines the myriad of problems in the case against Oswald in a section titled The People vs Oswald as stated by the American Civil Liberties Union:

"*It is our opinion Lee Harvey Oswald, had he lived, would have been deprived of all opportunity to receive a fair trial by the conduct of the police and the prosecution officials in Dallas, under pressure from the public and the news media.*

"*From the moment of his arrest until his murder two days later, Oswald was tried and convicted many times in the Newspapers, on the radio, and over television by the statement of the Dallas law enforcement officials. Time and again high ranking police and prosecution officials state their complete satisfaction that Oswald was the assassin. As their investigation uncovered one piece of evidence after another, their results were broadcast to the public. Oswald's trial would, have been nothing but a hollow formality.*"

The ACLU also weighed in as follows:

"*The concessions to the media resulted in Oswald not only being deprived of his day in court, but of his life as well.*"

J. Edgar Hoover, FBI director, told President Lyndon Johnson on 11/23/63 that:

"This man in Dallas, we of course have charged him with the murder of the President. The evidence that they have at the present time is not very, very strong. The case as it stands now is not strong enough to get conviction."

The case, approaching 58 years after the fact, is still not very strong and certainly would not result in a conviction of Oswald.

There are other areas I have not touched upon. For example, the chain of possession of the Presidential limousine in which President Kennedy was shot. The chain of possession of the fragments taken from the car. Also, the chain of possession for the body of President John F. Kennedy. These are also major problems for the state's case.

Time and again, the Commission failed to call important witnesses to testify. Witnesses like the President's own personal physician, Dr. George Burkley. Admiral Burkley, who witnessed the President wounds first hand, stated in an interview:

Interviewer – "Do you agree with the Warren Report on the number of bullets which entered the Presidents body?"
Burkley – *"I would not care to be quoted on that."*

In 1969, Dallas Chief Of Police Jesse Curry stated in an interview with the Dallas Morning News: *"We don't have any proof that Oswald fired the rifle, and never did. Nobody's yet been able to put him in that building with a gun in his hand."*

After viewing the Zapruder film, Chief Curry also stated his belief that Kennedy and Connally were hit by separate bullets.

AND THE VERDICT IS...

Under Texas Law, an autopsy must be performed by the medical examiner in the jurisdiction where the homicide occurred in order to have a homicide complaint issued or subsequent indictment occur.

The 'military' autopsy of President Kennedy was performed in Bethesda Maryland, not by forensic pathologist Earl Rose in Dallas County.

Therefore, even if Oswald had lived, according to Texas law, no trial could have been heard regarding the murder of President Kennedy. If Oswald had lived and had he faced trial, the facts of the assassination would have been brought to light.

Instead, his murder has allowed these facts to be locked away in archives and buried under the pretense of national security.

Kennedy researcher and author of The Assassination Tapes, George O'Toole, ran his Psychological Stress Evaluator (PSA) results by former army intelligence agent L.H. "Rusty" Hitchcock. Hitchcock was one of the most experienced polygraph examiners in the United States. Below is the outcome of Hitchcock's own conclusions with regards to Lee Oswald's pronouncements of innocence whilst detained by the DPD:

Dear Mr. O'Toole:

As you requested, I have analyzed with the Psychological Stress Evaluator the tape recordings you provided of the voice of Lee Harvey Oswald's comments regarding the circumstances of his arrest and his statements that he had been denied legal representation show considerable situation stress.

When he is asked, "*Did you kill the President*," his reply, "*No, I have not been charged with that*," shows no harder stress than that found in his earlier comments. In replying to the question, "*Did you shoot the President*," his reply, "*No, I didn't shoot anybody, no sir*" contains much less stress than I found in his earlier statement regarding legal representation, made only moments before this.

My PSE analysis of these recordings indicates very clearly that Oswald believed he was telling the truth when he denied killing the President. Assuming that he was not suffering from a psycho-pathological condition that made him ignorant of his own actions, I can state, beyond a reasonable doubt, that Lee Harvey Oswald did not kill President Kennedy and did not shoot anybody else. /s/ Lloyd H. Hitchcock.

I rest my case.

Note: For more information on the physical evidence in this case by researcher Johnny Cairns, visit the following links on the KennedysandKing.com website:

- **https://www.kennedysandking.com/john-f-kennedy-articles/a-presumption-of-innocence-lee-harvey-oswald-part-1**

- **https://www.kennedysandking.com/john-f-kennedy-articles/a-presumption-of-innocence-lee-harvey-oswald-part-2**

- **https://www.kennedysandking.com/john-f-kennedy-articles/a-presumption-of-innocence-lee-harvey-oswald-part-3**

Chapter 8

Seeing ISN'T Believing? Putting the JFK Film and Photo Myths to Rest Once and For All

The Zapruder film recording of the death of President Kennedy would have been a pivotal piece of evidence at a public trial of Lee Harvey Oswald.

Perhaps to a lesser extent, the same can be said for the Orville Nix film which also captured the fatal head shot from a different angle.

Lesser still are several other short films that shed little or no light on those tragic few seconds in Dallas but still make a contribution.

And let's not forget the hundreds of still photographs taken in Dealey Plaza by pros and amateurs alike that have also stirred unending controversy (see chapter 11 for the most disturbing example).

All these years later, we can say for certain that at least snippets of the Zapruder or Nix films would have been entered at trial as evidence of guilt by State prosecutors or evidence of innocence by Oswald's defense counsel.

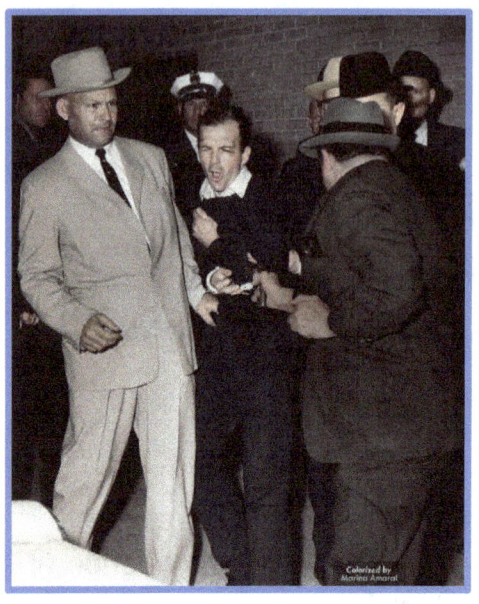

Tragically for history, the Zapruder and Nix films never became evidence at a public trial. Jack Ruby saw to that when he gunned down prisoner Oswald before he got his day in court (left). For this purpose, let's focus on the 26.6-second film by Abraham Zapruder.

Had a trial occurred, a first generation copy of Zapruder's film would have been shown to a jury of 12 people, no doubt broken down frame-by-frame as argued evidence of guilt or innocence.

Instead, without having been seen by hardly anyone outside of government, an expansive Warren Report was issued a year later with the Zapruder film cited as key evidence of Oswald being guilty as the '**lone**' assassin of JFK. Is that a verdict a jury would have rendered upon seeing it several times? Consider this:

For the next 11 years following the Warren Report, with only frame-by-frame still photographs up to the lethal head shot (frame 313) published in Life Magazine, which had bought the film from Zapruder, the American public had no cause to disbelieve the apparent exhaustive work of the Warren Commission thanks to a compliant mainstream media that lazily seconded the findings of Oswald's guilt.

A VISUAL RECKONING!

Despite a 12-year head start in publicly propagandizing Oswald as the *'lone nut'* assassin of the nation's 35th President, which began within hours of Oswald being arrested and charged, it took only 26.6 seconds of what our eyes were seeing to cause us to question what we had been told about the historic event.

On March 6, 1975, Geraldo Rivera, Robert Groden and Dick Gregory showed the entire silent 8 mm color Zapruder film for the first time to a national TV audience on ABC's Good Night America.

Once the Zapruder film was finally seen by the public 12 years after the JFK murder, controversies started to emerge such as the relevance of a man unfurling an umbrella for only the duration of the shots.

For millions of people coast-to-coast, a mere 26.6 seconds of stunning horror on their TV screens unraveled 12 years of presumed fact about their President's murder and the man named as his killer.

How was it possible, millions of viewers pondered at the same time, that Oswald shot JFK from above and behind, yet the President's head and upper body were slammed violently backward as a result?

In just 1/2 second of elapsed time, JFK went from slumping forward to almost bump heads with wife Jackie (312) to being slammed back against the back rest of his car seat (323). The bullet that caused this reaction came from behind? The Commission says yes.

As explained in detail in chapter 3, per Newton's Second Law of Motion, why wasn't Kennedy's head propelled violently forward from the fatal head shot that came from '*behind*?'

If you haven't already done the demonstration in chapter 3, do it now. Gently tap the back of your own head with an open hand and observe the result. As you can see, your head moves forward in the same direction as the incoming force (your hand).

So, why wouldn't a high velocity, high energy bullet impact to the back of JFK's head not cause his head to move forward more than the gentle tap of your own hand?

After those history-challenging 26.6 seconds on TV, the Zapruder film, after this initial public viewing, would become the most analyzed film ever.

Thanks to the work of film expert Robert Groden, not only would the fatal head shot come to be used to question

Oswald's guilt as a lone assassin, the film also caused us to doubt the Commission's imperative 'Single Bullet Theory' (see chapter 10).

These two critical aspects of the Commission's case against Oswald as the President's 'lone' assassin have been hotly debated ever since the TV showing.

GIVING BIRTH TO CONSPIRACY

Because the film was kept from the public until 1975, growing skepticism opened the door to the ultimate JFK conspiracy theory, namely:

The Zapruder Film was Tampered With!

Absurd you say?

While such a claim comes mostly from extreme conspiracy theorists that long pre-date the emergence of QAnon, can we emphatically deny such a possibility when we learn in chapter 16 that Kennedy's autopsy photos and X-rays were altered to remove evidence of any shots from a second location?

Douglas Horne, former chief analyst of military records for the Assassination Records Review Board, claims that the CIA's National Photographic Interpretation Center (NPIC) got access to the Zapruder film two days after the assassination and has quoted NPIC photo interpreter Dino Brugioni as saying: "*The film in the National Archives today is not the film I saw the day after the assassination.*"

The allegation is that any alteration of Zapruder's film took place in a narrow 12-hour window on Sunday, November 24 at a film lab called Hawkeye Works with the same intent being to remove evidence of shots that didn't come from the 'Oswald' window in the Book Depository.

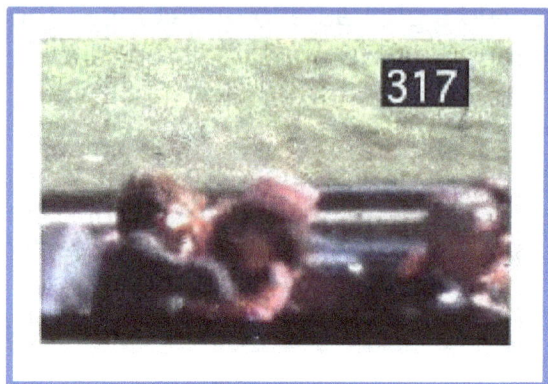

Was Zapruder frame 317, just 1/5th of a second after the fatal head shot, altered in any way to hide evidence of a shot from the front?

Given the time constraints with the film and lack of technology available, it is alleged JFK's dramatic 'backward' head snap could not be adequately sanitized from the film.

Instead, approximately five frames immediately after the head shot (frame 313) were either removed or altered to get rid of images that show "*exit debris*" coming from the back of Kennedy's head that flew out to the rear of the limousine, which would indicate the fatal head shot came from the front.

At best, they may have been able to marginally diminish the violent rearward snap of JFK's head and at least cause confusion by removing frames that showed the direction of the exit debris.

Could this be what forced the Warren Commission to

come up with the 'neuromuscular reaction theory' to explain how Kennedy's head could have snapped back toward the origin of the shot?

The neuromuscular reaction explanation worked because it has prompted decades of debate about the fatal head shot whereas an unaltered Zapruder film may have proven a conspiracy at a public trial of Lee Oswald as early as 1964.

Let's not forget the jury's reaction in 1969 when New Orleans District Attorney Jim Garrison failed to convict Clay Shaw for conspiracy to murder John Kennedy.

Those 12 jurors were the first general public to see the full Zapruder film. Many of the jurors later stated that while Garrison failed to prove Shaw's guilt beyond a reasonable doubt, the film established in their mind the probability of more than one gunman, hence a conspiracy.

Priority One of any new investigation needs to be the application of modern film imaging technology to a first generation copy of the Zapruder film in the National Archives.

It is hard to believe that any film alterations done in 1963 could still go undetected in 2022. Secondly, if alterations are found, an investigation into the chain of possession of the Zapruder film in the hours and days following 11/22/63 could lead us directly to those responsible for the assassination and corresponding cover-up!

SEPARATING FACT FROM FICTION

While the integrity of the Zapruder and Nix films must be verified for a new official inquiry to be viable, we can't expect every claim of dismissed, ignored, altered or suppressed evidence to be investigated.

Some claims are too absurd to mention, but some allegations warrant probing because they potentially speak to a second conspiracy in this case – the conspiracy to cover it up.

For instance, although effectively dismissed as hogwash, the claim persists that Secret Service agent William Greer, driver of the JFK limousine that day, did two things that implicate him and/or the Secret Service in this case.

1. Shooter? – The Zapruder film shows Greer turns in his car seat, looks back toward JFK and points what appears to be a handgun at him. This is one theory that modern film analysis techniques should be able to dispel forever.

Some conspiracy theorists also claim that both the Zapruder and Nix films show that Greer stopped the limousine on Elm Street as the shots were being fired, making JFK an easier target for the assassin(s). A reality check indicates that Greer may have slowed the car down for only a moment during the shooting before accelerating the limousine to get JFK to escape Dealey Plaza.

JFK Case NOT Closed

All these years later, can new technology prove or disprove that this image shows a man in a police uniform taking aim at JFK with a rifle?

2. **The Badge Man** – In a still photograph taken by Mary Moorman, some believe that it shows a sniper firing at JFK from under trees lining a picket fence along the grassy knoll.

The man appears to be wearing a police uniform that shows his police badge and a flash of light from a shot being fired.

Of all the mysterious images of the shooting, the Badge Man persists and should be examined when advancements in photo analysis permits.

ALSO WORTH INVESTIGATING

1. **Missing Nix Camera and Film** – The family of Orville Nix claim that the second most famous film footage of the JFK assassination has gone missing after heirs to Nix turned it over to the House Select Committee on Assassinations for its investigation in 1975. How could this happen and why? This directly implicates the government in a potential cover-up and needs to be investigated.

2. **Missing Oliver Film** – Beverly Oliver, also known as the 'Babushka Lady for a red scarf she wore that day, claims she filmed the assassination at close range on Elm Street opposite to where Zapruder was filming.

Very soon after the shooting, Oliver turned her film over

to FBI agent Regis Kennedy and it has not been seen since. A new inquiry needs to hold the FBI accountable for this missing vital piece of evidence.

3. **More Evidence Missing or Destroyed** – In addition to the Stemmons Freeway sign that was removed, as well as smaller street signage and allegations of a street lamp disappearing that may have been damaged by a bullet or fragment, we know that damage occurred to the limousine front windshield and/or windshield frame that was not accounted for by the Commission.

If these pieces of physical evidence supported the Commission's 'lone' gunman conclusion, you would think they would have been presented as evidence of such.

Instead, having gone missing, speculation has been allowed to flourish about what happened to this physical evidence and what they reveal about the shooting in Dealey Plaza.

There are dozens of theories about evidence and witnesses that could be listed here, most of them to be stuck in the Twilight Zone forever.

However, an attempt to resolve a few of these mysteries need to be part of a new official investigation.

It's why a new inquiry should include representatives of both the 'lone gunman' and 'conspiracy theory' communities.

Chapter 9

The Natural, Instinctive Physical Reactions of Three Key People in Dealey Plaza that Prove a Second Gunman!

Of the more than 600 people who had a rendezvous with history at 12:30 p.m. in Dealey Plaza on November 22, 1963, just three of them share a gruesome telling moment that could finally bare truth to the biggest lie of the 20th century, namely that:

> *President John F. Kennedy was fatally shot by a 'lone' assassin positioned above and behind him.*

In naming Lee Harvey Oswald as the '**lone**' assassin perched at the 6th floor southeast corner window of the Texas School Book Depository building, the Warren Commission concluded that the third and last shot he fired entered the rear crown area of JFK's head and explosively exited just above his right ear, causing non-survivable damage.

Is this really how John F. Kennedy died?

Despite the many ignored eyewitness and earwitness claims of at least one shot coming from the right-front of

Zapruder frame 313 shows the horrific impact of the fatal bullet. Do the immediate reactions of JFK and two others point to a second gunman in Dallas?

the President's limousine (see chapter 15), what happened to these three key individuals distinguishes them from everyone else in Dealey Plaza.

Apart from the clearly visible physical reaction of President Kennedy as a direct result of a gunshot to his head, it must be asked why two other people experienced identical instinctive physical reactions to JFK's fatal head shot at the exact same time.

The first of these two unique witnesses was the First Lady of the United States, Jackie Kennedy, seated at left of her husband in the open limousine.

It's not her riveting testimony as to what happened that compels us to this day. Due to the shock of the moment, she had no conscious recollection of what occurred during those critical moments.

The other unique witness, on the other hand, offered problematic testimony as to what he heard and subsequently happened to him as a direct result of the JFK lethal head shot.

Accordingly, his testimony was omitted from the summary edition of the Warren Report and was buried in the 26 supplemental volumes that few people ever read.

That witness, Dallas police motorcycle officer Bobby Hargis, riding along the left rear bumper of the President's limousine at the time of the shots, is forever linked to Jackie and Jack Kennedy by these points of commonality:

Motorcycle cop Bobby Hargis, seen over Jackie's left shoulder, testified with good reason that the JFK kill shot came from the right-front of the car. His account was not included in the widely-read summary edition of the Warren Report.

As a result of the fatal head shot, all three experienced identical instinctive, natural physical reactions beyond their control

and

*The shot that killed JFK and caused the corresponding instinctive, natural physical reactions of Hargis and Mrs. Kennedy could **NOT** have come from above and behind the limousine!*

BUILDING BLOCKS OF EVIDENCE

What's fascinating about the two survivors is that they are witnesses who tell us what happened to President Kennedy not so much by what they saw or heard but how they subconsciously reacted immediately after the lethal head shot.

It is important to reiterate that Jackie Kennedy and Bobby Hargis experienced immediate '*natural, instinctive physical*' reactions to the President's headshot that mirrored each other's subconscious reaction to what just happened. This makes them unique to everyone else at the crime scene.

The sudden and unscripted reactions of Jackie and Bobby Hargis, though not known to each other at that moment, confirm each other's actions as evidence of how JFK died – which is at odds with how the Commission says Kennedy died.

As the Abraham Zapruder and Orville Nix films show JFK's head snapping violently backward as an immediate result of a bullet impact to his head, there are only two ways to explain his uncontrollable reaction:

1. **Commission Says** – Kennedy's head snapped back toward the origin of the shot because he experienced a 'neuromuscular reaction' instantly after the head shot.

2. **Science Says** – Per Newton's Second Law of Motion, Kennedy's head slammed back against the backrest of his car seat because a headshot came from the right-front of the car and exited the rear of his skull.

To be discussed momentarily, a third option has emerged as the more likely truth about how JFK died thanks to the independent research of four respected medical scientists

– Dr. Cyril Wecht, Dr. David Mantik, Dr. Michael Chesser and Dr. Gary Aguilar.

But first, let's look at how the instinctive, natural, physical reactions of Jackie Kennedy and officer Hargis immediately as a result of the fatal JFK head shot disproves the Commission's lone gunman conclusion:

JACKIE'S INSTINCTIVE REACTION

Jackie Kennedy didn't remember jumping out onto the trunk of the limousine but why she 'instinctively' did so would pose a big problem for a 'lone' assassin firing from behind.

To everyone's horror when watching the Zapruder film, we are stunned to see Jackie reacting to her husband being fatally shot by jumping out <u>onto the trunk</u> of the limousine.

Why did she leave her car seat and mortally wounded husband to crawl out onto the trunk?

It was a completely subconscious reaction to the trauma of the moment. Apart from knowing that her husband had been shot, she did not recollect her reaction.

Only when shown the Zapruder film did she know that she had instinctively and physically acted out in this manner and why she did it.

Mrs. Kennedy saw a piece of her husband's skull fly out of the car and land on the trunk. Out of pure instinct, she went after the skull bone, retrieved it and clasped it in her hand until a nurse at Parkland Hospital got her to give it up.

From an evidence standpoint, Mrs. Kennedy's 'instinctive' physical reaction is quite telling. The key point is that she jumped out over the '**back**' of the car seat and onto the trunk because that's where the skull bone went as a result of a bullet striking her husband's head.

This strongly indicates that the bullet that caused the President's head to be thrown violently back and to the left, instantly followed in the same direction by a sizeable piece of his skull bone, came from the right-front of the limousine.

Had the head shot come from the so-called 'Oswald' window above and behind as concluded by the Commission, why wouldn't we have seen JFK's head be thrust violently *'forward'* upon impact followed by brain and skull debris being propelled into the jump seats ahead occupied by Nellie and John Connally?

In reaction to a shot from the rear, we might expect to see Jackie chasing a piece of skull into the jump seats ahead of her. This didn't happen.

As both Mr. and Mrs. Connally testified before the Warren Commission, only a fine reddish mist of the President's blood and brain matter reached them in the limousine.

Had Oswald lived to stand trial, the instinctive physical reaction of Jackie and the corroborating testimony of Nellie and John Connally would have been used by Oswald's defense team to show that he could not have fired the shot that killed President Kennedy.

SIMILAR REACTION, SAME CONCLUSION

Dallas motorcycle police officer Bobby Hargis had quite a different experience that day but it affirms what happened to Jackie and Jack Kennedy as a result of the deadly head shot.

Hargis did not see the bullet impact to JFK's head but like the skull bone that flew back and to the left onto the trunk as a result of the head shot, his immediate reaction helps us understand why Jackie did what she did.

Officer Hargis was riding along the left rear bumper of the President's limousine on Elm Street, placing him just over Jackie's left shoulder as the shots rang out.

Hargis told the Commission that as the motorcade was proceeding along Elm Street, from his position at the left rear bumper, he heard what he took to be a gunshot.

Very soon after the sound of the shot, Hargis says the protective shields on his motorcycle and helmet were spattered by a spray of misty blood and brain tissue that startled him enough to momentarily disorient him and cause him to slightly lose balance on his bike.

At this moment, Hargis' experience with firearms kicked in as he recognized the sound as a gunshot versus, for instance, a motorcycle backfire, both of which he was quite familiar with.

Hargis also testified, despite being told by Commission counsel that all the shots came from above and behind the limousine, that the direction of the flow of blood and brain matter that hit him had to be the result of a gunshot coming from his right-front.

Having to make an instant decision to either help escort the President's car to a nearby hospital or stay at the crime scene, Hargis chose to park his motorcycle at the scene.

Based on his position in relation to Kennedy at those critical moments, Hargis followed his instincts and ran to the west end of the grassy knoll at his right-front. He raced to the picket fence where he thought the shot came from but did not see anything suspicious.

TWO GUNMEN TRIFECTA

Here we have three key people who had similar instinctive physical reactions apparently caused by the origin of the fatal head shot being the grassy knoll to the right-front of the car.

These telling reactions are supported by dozens of witnesses in Dealey Plaza who report a gunshot as coming from the grassy knoll that Hargis also suspected.

Obviously, the victim never got to testify but his uncontrolled physical reaction as graphically seen on the Zapruder and Nix films substantiate what Hargis experienced.

Survivor Jackie Kennedy got to testify but her recollection was impaired by the personal trauma of the moment. Again, her instinctive physical reaction to the head shot is consistent with her husband's involuntary reaction and that of officer Hargis.

Witness Bobby Hargis got to testify to an unreceptive Warren Commission. Although what happened to Hargis and how he reacted to it totally aligns with what happened to the President and Mrs. Kennedy in the car very near him, the Commission made sure that Hargis' testimony would be known to as few people as possible.

NEW TECHNOLOGIES, NEW FINDINGS

Since the deadly shot to President Kennedy's head has become so vital to the lone gunman versus multiple gunmen debate, the instinctive physical reactions of these three individuals needs to be examined by any new official inquiry.

Simply stated, if any new technology can be applied to the mysteries surrounding the JFK head shot, in addition to proving or disproving the 'Single Bullet Theory,' there still exists a chance to solve this case.

A collaboration between science and Hollywood special effects may be our best bet. It would be imperative to replicate the crime scene precisely in every detail, especially the mass and bone structure of JFK's head, not to mention the position of these three key people in relation to each other.

Or as chapter 17 details, it may no longer be necessary to reconstruct the crime scene or the shooting sequence thanks to the modern wonders of imaging.

And as demonstrated in chapter 16, modern technologies applied to existing physical evidence by qualified medical experts is changing the official historical record of the events of 11/22/63.

One example pertaining to JFK's death by gunshot damage to the head is the research by these four doctors, all of whom have independently examined the medical evidence in the National Archives.

After what is clearly a lethal shot impact to Kennedy's head, the Zapruder film shows a very brief forward movement of JFK's head, which is quickly and abruptly halted and followed by a much more violent and rapid snap of Kennedy's head back and to the left.

The Warren Commission explained the double head movement as follows:

Frontal Movement – Was caused by a bullet fired from the 6th floor Book Depository window that struck JFK in the rear crown area of his head.

Backward Movement – Within a nano-second of the bullet impact to the rear of JFK's skull, driving his head forward, the President experienced a 'neuromuscular reaction' that suddenly reversed the direction of his head and upper body, slamming him to the back of the car seat.

A neuromuscular reaction occurs when muscle

contractions take over the body's movement as a result of a sudden trauma.

The Commission used this explanation to claim that the fatal head shot came from Oswald's rifle above and to the rear of the target.

Would a neuromuscular reaction hold up to modern day testing? It would have to establish beyond reasonable doubt that it's possible that Kennedy's barely noticeable frontal movement as a result of a bullet impact to the head was abruptly halted by a neuromuscular reaction with a force able to reverse his upper body movement many times greater than the initial force of the bullet's impact.

Dr. Michael Chesser, a neurological scientist whose research is featured in chapter 13, doesn't believe the Commission's neuromuscular reaction narrative to be valid.

"I think that the violent head movement backwards was caused by the mechanical force of a shot from the front," he states.

"I don't know of any type of neuromuscular reaction which would cause a movement of the head which would be this rapid.

"The most common reaction to a massive traumatic brain injury of this type would be a sudden loss of muscle tone, termed flaccid paralysis.

"A seizure could be triggered by brain trauma, but there wasn't any movement of President Kennedy which would suggest a seizure, and again, the backwards head movement was too violent and rapid," Dr. Chesser offers.

But what about the brief frontal movement of JFK's head cited by advocates of the Commission's 'Oswald acted alone' conclusion?

*"I think that the short forward movement of the head was caused by **the first head shot** entering low in the right occipital region, the WC entry site,"* reasons Dr. Chesser in support of the original autopsy finding of a bullet entry at the back of the skull.

As chapter 13 details, Dr. Chesser's study of the autopsy photos and x-rays in the National Archives confirmed a trail of bullet fragments in the upper skull that could only have come from a bullet entering near the hairline of the forehead.

Additionally, Dr. Chesser notes that the 'snowstorm' of bullet fragments he tracked from the front of the skull to near the back of the skull could not have been deposited by a 6.5 mm copper jacketed bullet fired by Oswald's Mannlicher-Carcano rifle.

Lastly, Dr. Chesser's expert eyes detected what appears to be a medical incision on the right side of the forehead obscured by JFK's hair. The size of the incision appears to be designed to conceal a small wound at that location, such as a bullet entry wound.

THE INSTINCTIVE PHYSICAL REACTIONS EXPLAINED

Thanks to the research by Drs. Wecht, Mantik, Chesser and Aguilar, we can now explain the identical physical reactions of President Kennedy, Mrs. Kennedy and officer Hargis as follows:

The initial gunshot that struck Kennedy in the back of the head, causing his head to move forward, was instantly followed by a gunshot that entered the front of the skull, driving his head and upper body violently back and to the left against the car seat!

A different caliber weapon and bullet fired from the front scientifically explains Kennedy's considerably more violent rearward head movement than the Commission's neuromuscular reaction theory.

Dr. David Mantik cites evidence of a second shot to the head by a forward sniper but as Dr. Chesser points out, *"Whether there was one or two shots from the front, the Warren Commission's lone gunman position becomes a moot point."*

In addition to explaining the double movement of JFK's head after Zapruder frame 313, a lethal shot from the front also explains the instinctive, physical reactions of Mrs. Kennedy and officer Hargis.

"The bloody fluid which hit officer Hargis in the face hit him with such force that it could only have been caused by an exit wound at the back of the head," offers Dr. Chesser.

And clearly the bone fragment that Mrs. Kennedy chased onto the trunk of the car was also the result of an exit wound at the rear of JFK's head.

Sorting fact from fiction may be sooner than you think despite the passage of time.

Toward that end, any new investigative body would be wise to recruit the imaging and 3D realism talents of the group featured in chapter 17.

Without applying all new technologies to the next official inquiry, any such effort runs the risk of becoming just the latest whacky conspiracy theory.

Chapter 10

The 'Magic' Bullet May be Less Magical than We Thought but Still NOT Possible!

Any new formal investigation into the assassination of President John F. Kennedy could very well change the history books by focusing specifically on one pivotal controversy –

The flightpath of the 'Magic' Bullet!

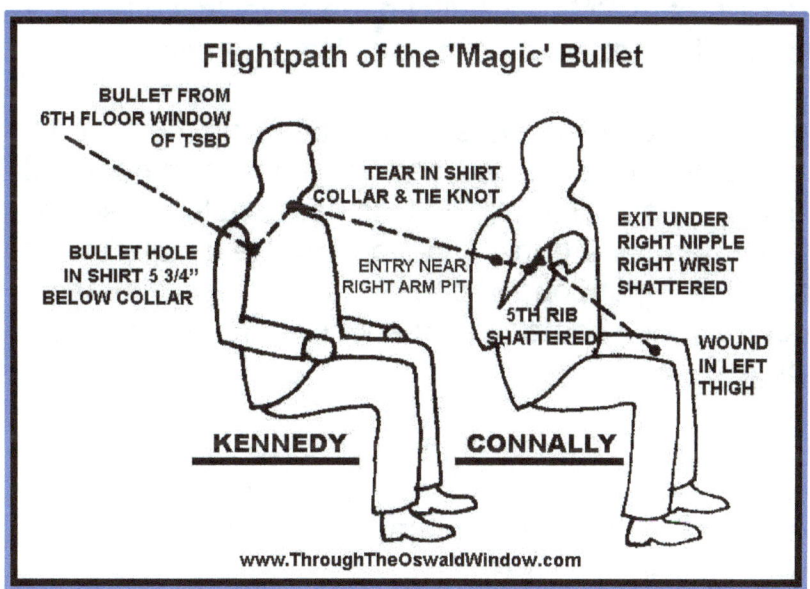

The Warren Report states that one bullet fired by Oswald from the 6th floor Book Depository window caused all seven non-fatal wounds suffered by Kennedy and Texas Governor John Connally.

If the Warren Commission's stated flightpath of the 'Magic' bullet (at left) is not correct, its most essential conclusion that Lee Harvey Oswald was the '**lone**' assassin of President Kennedy is completely destroyed.

Conversely, if the Commission's stated flightpath of the 'Magic' bullet is accurate, even the most ardent conspiracy theorists have to concede that a single assassin is possible.

If we took no other evidence into regard, solving the flightpath of the 'Magic' bullet debate would settle once and for all the question of one or more gunmen.

The gravest consequence of Oswald being murdered by Jack Ruby before the accused 'lone' assassin got his day in court is that it allowed the Commission, the designated replacement for a public trial, to fabricate a bullet's magical flightpath based on no evidence and cite it as proof that one shooter was responsible for the history-changing event.

It is disturbing to realize that had Oswald lived to stand trial, the state prosecutor would not have presented a 'magic' bullet scenario to a jury because of the obvious absurdity of it.

However, with the accused "*lone nut*" out of the way and

the Warren Commission operating with the understanding that key evidence exculpatory to Oswald would be suppressed from the public until 2038, the Commission denied Oswald any posthumous legal representation during its hearings.

ANATOMY OF ALTERED EVIDENCE

This allowed it to treat evidence as it pleased and even shape evidence to fit its case against Oswald.

For instance, we know that what appeared to be a bullet 'entry' wound was documented in the autopsy report face sheet shown here as being located 5 ¾ inches below Kennedy's collar line and no more than one inch to the right side of the spinal column.

We also know that when Dr. James Humes probed this wound with his pinky finger, he could feel the end of the opening and could not penetrate past the second knuckle.

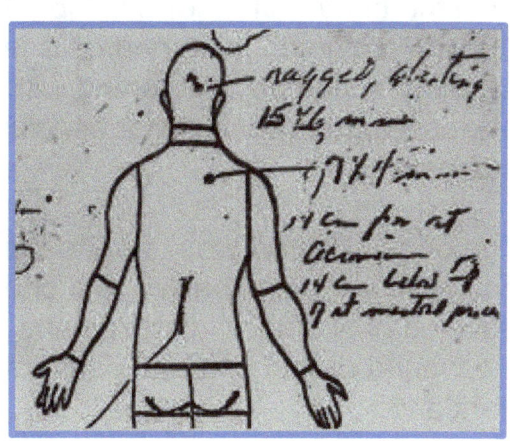

Further to this point, when Dr. Pierre Finck attempted to dissect the back wound to search for a lodged bullet or determine the missile's pathway inside the body, military superiors present at the autopsy ordered him to abandon this routine procedure (see chapter 12).

Denying this customary post-mortem process would prove consequential the next day when the autopsy surgeons learned that they had not accounted for a small circular wound on the President's throat located just below the Adam's apple.

They didn't know such a wound existed because when JFK arrived at Parkland Hospital after the shooting, Dr. Malcolm Perry obliterated the tiny wound to perform an emergency tracheal incision to insert a breathing tube.

This is what the autopsy surgeons believed they were viewing once JFK's body reached the autopsy table (see next page).

With the body no longer available for examination, Dr. Humes, acting on military orders or on his own, burned his original autopsy notes and without citing any evidence, changed a major conclusion in his official autopsy report.

The original report was to state that the bullet that entered Kennedy's back 5 ¾ inches below the collar line traveled only a short distance and most likely fell out of the wound during external cardiac message performed at Parkland.

A bullet found at Parkland Hospital in virtually pristine condition, Commission Exhibit 399 above, was labelled the bullet that caused this wound, and six others on two men, having lost only 2.4 grains of metallic substance at the nose.

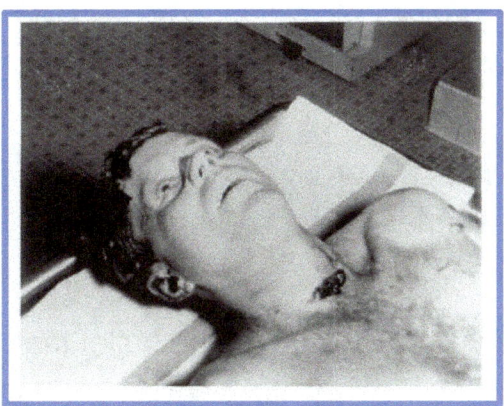

JFK autopsy surgeons recognized this throat wound as a tracheal incision. What they didn't know is that the incision obliterated a small circular wound at the same location.

This account of the back wound was verified by an FBI autopsy report submitted by two agents present at the autopsy to record the findings and retrieve any bullets or fragments as evidence.

Yet, because of the late discovery of JFK's throat wound, this important finding would change dramatically by the time the Warren Report was released.

A THEORY WITHOUT EVIDENCE

The throat wound on JFK had to be accounted for. Again, with no evidence cited, the Commission declared that the bullet entering Kennedy's back, in fact, **DID** transit his chest and exited at his throat.

What are the odds that this sudden change in flightpath not only turned CE 399 into the 'Magic' bullet, it also enabled the Commission to put forth its 'Single Bullet Theory' necessary to name Oswald as the '**lone**' assassin?

In saying that CE 399 did transit JFK and exited at his

throat, the Commission was now able to conclude that this bullet also went on to strike Governor John Connally and cause all five of his wounds (insert huge sigh of relief here).

This became necessary because the Zapruder film shows Connally reacting to his wounds so soon after Kennedy, only two possibilities exist:

1. **Same Shot** – Connally was hit by the same bullet that first struck Kennedy…

or

2. **Separate Shot** – Connally was hit by a separate shot fired almost simultaneously by a second sniper.

This is how important the Magic' bullet and its corresponding 'Single Bullet Theory' is to historical truth.

CE 399 LESS MAGICAL?

In recent years, conspiracy theorists have had to endure a setback when it was learned that CE 399 wasn't as magical in its flightpath as once thought.

A long held argument was that CE 399, upon leaving JFK's throat, had to make a left-to-right turn in mid-air in order to strike Connally in the back near his right armpit.

However, it has been established that such a turn in mid-air was not necessary because Connally was not seated directly in front of JFK.

Connally, in fact, was seated in his jump seat in front of

Kennedy slightly left of JFK, thus possibly aligning the two wounds without necessitating a left-to-right turn of the bullet in mid-air.

Problem solved, right?

Not exactly! Less magical than what conspiracy theorists claimed? Yes, but not enough to validate the Single Bullet Theory as fact.

Yet, with the 'Single Bullet Theory' presented as fact, the 'Magic' bullet could not be declared ordinary in its flightpath despite deceiving efforts by the Commission when confronted with another trajectory dilemma.

STILL DOESN'T LINE UP

With the official autopsy report now having CE 399 piercing JFK's upper body and exiting at his throat, the Commission could claim that this bullet went on to strike Connally and cause all of his wounds.

As it turns out, the 'Magic' bullet wasn't magical at all, so problem solved?

Not quite yet.

The Commission discovered that eliminating the left-to-right turn in mid-air by CE 399 upon leaving JFK's throat only solved half of the problem.

The panel found itself unable to explain another trajectory problem for CE 399. How could this bullet exit Kennedy's throat at what must have been an 'upward' angle but still manage to travel 'downward' to hit Connally near his right armpit?

Two things proved problematic for the Commission:

1. Back 'Entry' Wound – As measured by autopsy surgeon J. Thornton Boswell, the 'entry' wound on JFK's back was 5 ¾ inches below the collar line and slightly to the right of the spinal column.

2. Throat 'Exit' Wound – According to the only man who saw the tiny wound at Kennedy's throat before he destroyed it via an incision, the hole was center on the throat, just below the Adam's apple.

Military autopsy surgeons completed the autopsy on JFK not knowing a small circular wound as shown here was obliterated by a tracheal incision. Upon learning of the oversight, key findings by the Warren Commission would change to incriminate Oswald – courtesy Robert Groden's The Killing of a President.

As you recall, the Commission was quick to accept the throat wound as the point of 'exit' because it needed to explain how all the non-lethal wounds on the two men were caused by the same bullet, CE 399.

The Commission reached this conclusion even though Dr. Perry told the panel that he could not offer an opinion of the wound being entrance or exit.

In a handwritten letter to this 16-year-old researcher in

1968 (see Appendices section), Dr. Perry states:

"As I noted in my testimony (and verified by the transcript of the press conference), I did not know how many bullets struck him and could not state that the neck wound was either entrance or exit. I, unfortunately, in response to questions speculated about possible trajectory, and this was subsequently reported out of context as my opinion."

Without any evidence to verify the nature of the throat wound, the Commission deemed it to be the point of exit for the bullet that also struck Connally despite this glaring obstacle - The point of entry on Kennedy's back is almost six inches lower than the point of exit at his throat.

Yet we are asked to believe that the bullet entering JFK's back (CE 399) penetrated at a 'downward' angle having come from a window 60 feet above the ground aback of him.

Despite evidence to indicate the projectile penetrated only a short distance **downward**, the Commission disregarded this autopsy finding to declare that the bullet did tear through Kennedy's chest to exit at his throat.

However, in doing so without any supporting evidence, CE 399 is required to deflect **upward** in Kennedy's chest despite not hitting any hard substance such as bone so that it can travel 'up' to the throat.

And even if the bullet somehow did manage an 'upward' trajectory to reach the soft tissue in the neck, how could it exit and suddenly make an abrupt 'downward' turn in mid-air to find Connally's back?

The Warren Commission came up with a solution that would not have satisfied a jury had Oswald lived to defend himself at a public trial.

GLARING WOUND ALTERATION

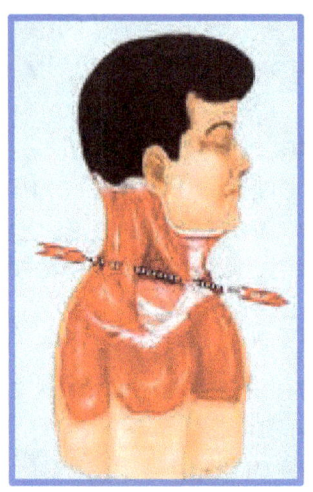

Notice how this drawing used by the Commission shows a bullet entry wound almost six inches higher than the autopsy face sheet shown earlier.

Believe it or not, rather than admit that Kennedy and Connally were hit by separate bullets fired from behind by separate snipers, the Commission simply moved the entry wound on JFK's back up nearly six inches so that it was now slightly higher than the exit wound at his throat!

To get away with it, the Commission suppressed the original autopsy photos and duped medical illustrator Harold Rydberg into drawing the sketch on this page to show an entry wound at the base of the neck rather than the upper back (see Chapter 14).

Upon presenting the Rydberg drawing (CE 385) in its report as a factually correct representation of the President's two non-lethal wounds, the Commission was able to then introduce the 'Single Bullet Theory' to explain how one bullet, fired by Oswald, also caused all the wounds sustained by Connally.

The Warren Commission also applied one of its favorite techniques by ignoring other evidence of the back wound location, such as the testimony of Secret Service agent Clint Hill, who helped to disrobe the President at Parkland to ready him for medical care.

Agent Hill had this exchange with Commission member Hale Boggs:

Boggs – "Did you see any other wound other than the head wound?"
Hill – "*Yes, sir; I saw an opening in the back about six inches below the neckline to the right-hand side of the spinal column.*"

Hill's testimony would become significant because there is no record of the doctors at Parkland examining or treating JFK's back wound. They were more concerned about the obvious head wound and the President's labored breathing.

Even more alarming, the Commission also ignored physical evidence it found contrary to its '**lone**' assassin assertion.

Commission Exhibit 59 is the suit jacket worn by President Kennedy on 11/22/63. Without explanation, both the shirt and suit jacket were not taken into regard as evidence of bullet trajectory.

Both garments clearly show, per the photo here, that a bullet struck the President precisely where the autopsy face sheet and the testimony of Clint Hill places it – 5 ¾ inches below the collar line and slightly to the right of the spinal column.

There is only one explanation as to why the Commission chose to ignore both eyewitness testimony and physical evidence of a shot entering Kennedy's upper back – it was not congruent with its position that only one man was responsible for all the shots!

At least some 'lone nut' believers tried to explain how CE 59 was not representative of the shot Kennedy received from behind. They argue that JFK's shirt and suit jacket were bunched up because of a back brace he wore that day thus producing a bullet hole lower than what it actually was.

CE 59 is the suit jacket worn by JFK on 11/22/63. It shows a bullet entry wound in the upper back, not the neck as depicted in the medical drawing above. Why this discrepancy?

However, this theory simply does not hold up when you examine the Zapruder film. It shows Kennedy to be upright with his clothing in perfect order as he brings his hands to his neck in reaction to this shot.

This pattern of dismissing, ignoring, altering or suppressing evidence exculpatory to Oswald was rampant throughout the Warren Report.

The next official investigation into the JFK assassination must start with one simple operating premise – it must examine and evaluate any and all evidence in this case – especially any and all evidence dismissed, ignored, altered or suppressed by the Warren Commission.

Only then do we have a chance to definitively reconstruct the shooting sequence and the wounds attributable to each shot.

Chapter 11

Altering Vital Photographic Evidence to Declare Oswald as the 'Lone' Assassin of JFK!

They say a picture is worth a thousand words.

As it relates to one iconic photo of the JFK assassination, four of those words are deceive, alter, frame and suppress!

This famous James Altgen's photo would be severely cropped before appearing in the Warren Report. Why?

One famous example of history captured in a photograph

is the Altgens 6 black and white still photo that shows the moment President Kennedy reacts to the first shot fired that day, a bullet that inflicts a non-fatal wound to his upper back.

This wound is documented in the official JFK autopsy report, the eyewitness testimony of Secret Service agent Clint Hill, the FBI autopsy report and the shirt and suit jacket worn by President Kennedy that day (see previous chapter).

Like a fist to the back between the shoulder blades, the bullet impact causes him to be winded. As the photo here shows, JFK's hands instinctively rise to his neck.

Compare this James Altgen's photo published in the Warren Report to the full photo above. Was this photo cropped for sinister reasons?

Had this been the only shot that horrible day, the 46-year-old President would have survived and history as we know it would be dramatically different, many argue for the better.

Tragically for historical truth, the actual photo you see below never appeared in the Warren Report. Only a cropped version of it did, exactly as presented on the previous page.

Was this nothing more than innocent editing with no ill intent? At first glance, it appears the two vertical and horizontal sections of the photograph were cut out merely to accentuate Altgens capturing the moment history changed.

However, the cropping of this photo of JFK being shot, if the omitted sections of the image possibly include evidence that the shot could NOT have come from the 6th floor southeast corner window of the Book Depository, suggest dubious intent to cover-up a second assassin to the rear of the limousine.

Based on two visits to Dealey Plaza, stunning observations from the so-called 'Oswald' window and overcoming the Commission's blatant attempt to conceal the limousine's position on Elm Street at the precise moment of this shot, this researcher believes the Altgens photo was purposely altered for sinister reasons.

POSITION ON ELM STREET

The one thing the Commission could not suppress was that JFK is seen reacting to the first shot that struck him.

As we isolate JFK in the limousine as seen here in the circle, he is partially obscured by the rear-view mirror attached to the windshield. However, inside the yellow circle, we see his hands at his neck, the left white cuff of his shirt and the bent left elbow of his suit jacket. This is the first moment we see him under attack.

The Warren Commission could not hide this fact, but it soon realized that it had to make it impossible to tell where the limousine was on Elm Street at this very moment in order to declare Oswald as the 'lone' assassin in Dealey Plaza. How did it go about suppressing this vital information?

First, it cropped the top of the picture to remove any sign of the oak tree in front of the Book Depository building. This is germane to at least the first of three shots put forth by the Commission, all of which it said came from the

Tragically for historical truth, the actual photo you see below never appeared in the Warren Report. Only a cropped version of it did, exactly as presented on the previous page.

Was this nothing more than innocent editing with no ill intent? At first glance, it appears the two vertical and horizontal sections of the photograph were cut out merely to accentuate Altgens capturing the moment history changed.

However, the cropping of this photo of JFK being shot, if the omitted sections of the image possibly include evidence that the shot could NOT have come from the 6th floor southeast corner window of the Book Depository, suggest dubious intent to cover-up a second assassin to the rear of the limousine.

Based on two visits to Dealey Plaza, stunning observations from the so-called 'Oswald' window and overcoming the Commission's blatant attempt to conceal the limousine's position on Elm Street at the precise moment of this shot, this researcher believes the Altgens photo was purposely altered for sinister reasons.

POSITION ON ELM STREET

The one thing the Commission could not suppress was that JFK is seen reacting to the first shot that struck him.

As we isolate JFK in the limousine as seen here in the circle, he is partially obscured by the rear-view mirror attached to the windshield. However, inside the yellow circle, we see his hands at his neck, the left white cuff of his shirt and the bent left elbow of his suit jacket. This is the first moment we see him under attack.

The Warren Commission could not hide this fact, but it soon realized that it had to make it impossible to tell where the limousine was on Elm Street at this very moment in order to declare Oswald as the 'lone' assassin in Dealey Plaza. How did it go about suppressing this vital information?

First, it cropped the top of the picture to remove any sign of the oak tree in front of the Book Depository building. This is germane to at least the first of three shots put forth by the Commission, all of which it said came from the southeast corner window 60 feet above street level.

Second, they edited out the two police motorcycle cops on the right side of the picture. The inside cop is Bobby Hargis, a key witness downplayed by the Commission.

The critically important testimony of officer Hargis, as discussed in chapter 9, suggested the fatal head shot came from the grassy knoll, not the 6th floor Book Depository window.

The Commission not only dismissed Hargis' testimony, it excluded it from its 888-page summary edition, which was mass printed and released to the public.

Instead, what Hargis heard, saw and personally experienced was buried in the 26 supplemental volumes of evidence of which very few copies were printed and made available.

The Commission did not want the public to know about officer Hargis, what happened to him and especially his position on Elm Street at the time of the shots, so he was conveniently cut out of the Altgens photo published in the Warren Report as part of this cover-up.

In altering this photographic evidence, the most important omission of all is the left-front tire of the limousine touching the white road marker on Elm Street as seen above in the complete Altgens photo indicated by the red arrow.

The cropped version of the Altgens 6 photo omits the tire's contact with this white road marker to ensure that the car's position on Elm Street at the time of this particular shot cannot be established. The reason for this deception will become alarmingly apparent.

A DIFFERENT PERSPECTIVE

The Altgens photograph sync's up with Zapruder frames 225-230 when we compare the position of JFK's left hand, arm and elbow in each image.

The Umbrella Man stands immediately to JFK's right when the first shot rings out.

Not visible in the full Altgens photo are two markers of sorts on the passenger side of the limousine that enable us to identify the exact location of the white road marker on Elm Street being touched by the left-front tire.

Why is this important? It allows us to discover what the Commission didn't want us to know – the exact location of the car on Elm Street at the precise moment the first shot sounded, striking President Kennedy in the upper back.

These two markers, as captured on the Zapruder film, are the large Stemmons Freeway sign at left on frame 225 above and the infamous 'Umbrella Man' standing at the right edge of the sign where you can see ½ of his unfurled black umbrella.

Using the Altgens 6 still photograph and the Zapruder film at the moment the limousine is parallel to the highway sign and the Umbrella Man, when I returned to Dealey Plaza in 1983, I was able to position myself at the sign exactly where the Umbrella Man was standing.

From that vantage point, as Zapruder frame 225 above shows, by looking slightly to my right, I could see the white road marker on Elm Street appearing in the Altgens photo that was touched by the left-front tire as shown by the red line and pointing arrow.

A SHOCKING DISCOVERY

Knowing precisely where the car was positioned on Elm Street at the very moment the first shot was fired, imagine my surprise when I walked directly out onto the road to the white marker from the position of the Umbrella Man and looked up at the Book Depository building. Guess what I couldn't see?

I couldn't see the sixth floor southeast corner window sniper's nest because the oak tree blocked my view from where Kennedy was hit!

This discovery affirmed a visit to Dealey Plaza four years earlier when I became one of the few researchers ever granted access to the Book Depository when it was locked and sealed to the public.

From the so-called 'Oswald' window, soon after the House Select Committee on Assassinations was there to re-enact the assassination, I was able to take this photo of the kill site below, clearly showing the oak tree as an obstacle to an assassin firing from that window.

What I didn't know then was the exact location of the limousine on Elm Street at the moment the first shot is said to have been shot from this window by Oswald.

With the two visual perspectives now available to me, I was able to discern that an assassin at this position could NOT have fired the first shot that struck Mr. Kennedy because the oak tree blocked the view of his target on Elm Street at this moment!

Instead, the first shot fired that afternoon had to have come from a second location to the rear of the President's car, likely the Dal-Tex Records building on the corner of Houston and Elm Streets.

THE OAK TREE

Like you, I had to wonder if the photo I took looking down on Elm Street was close to what the assassin would have seen on 11/22/63.

My Dallas County host during that visit, William Smith, informed me that at the time of the assassination, the oak tree was already mature and fully grown.

Notwithstanding the freak winter storm of mid-February 2021, winters in Dallas tend to be mild. Unlike the northern states, leaves on old, rugged oak trees during the change of seasons in Dallas don't tend to fall off the limbs. They merely change from green to yellow as seen in the above picture.

Accordingly, the foliage of a fully grown oak tree in Dallas tends to remain in full bloom. When the House Select Committee did its re-enactment shortly before my visit, efforts to trim the foliage to make the tree as identical to 1963 as possible proved to be unnecessary.

THE UMBRELLA MAN: FROM MYSTERY TO MYSTERY SOLVER?

The HSCA discovered the identity of the Umbrella Man to be Louie Steven Witt and bought his story of being in Dealey Plaza to protest Joseph Kennedy's appeasing of Adolf Hitler.

By unfurling his umbrella, Witt argued, he was merely trying to be noticed by Kennedy as he passed by. However, with no signage to reflect his protest, it is a mystery how the President, if he even noticed Witt, could have understood what Witt was trying to convey in protest.

Mystery continues to surround the Umbrella Man. Was his unfurling of his umbrella on a bright sunny day for only the duration of the shooting a signal to the assassins in Dealey Plaza that the target was in position for all to participate?

Or was he what he claimed to be – a protester without a sign.

It is disturbing to realize that the FBI and Warren Commission failed to identify this odd character at JFK's assassination or locate him or if they even tried.

What's even more alarming is that Witt is hardly alone as a witness who never got to tell his or her story to the Warren Commission.

As detailed in Chapter 15, of the more than 600 witnesses in Dealey Plaza that day, only a handful testified before the Commission hearings!

What's presented in this chapter doesn't have to remain subject to speculation. The good folks profiled in Chapter 17 are applying their imaging techniques to not only this shot, but all possible shots fired that day.

The group's finished work needs to be presented to any new official inquiry into JFK's death to help answer the many unanswered questions left to history by the Warren Commission.

Solving this one bullet trajectory alone could tell us if a shooter in the 6th floor southeast corner window of the Texas School Book Depository building could have changed history all on his own.

Chapter 12

Why the 'Military' Autopsy Alone Would Have Acquitted Lee Harvey Oswald at Trial

By the time the post mortem examination on the body of President John F. Kennedy got underway on the evening of his assassination, the accused murderer in police custody was *"emphatically"* denying he killed anybody.

A defiant Lee Oswald would not confess to killing JFK and didn't live to see his day in court.

Nonetheless, before sunrise the next morning, Lee Harvey Oswald was formally charged with assassinating both the President and Dallas police officer J.D. Tippit.

And by the time the late night autopsy on the young President was completed, Dallas Police Chief Jesse Curry had publicly proclaimed that they had their man and that no other suspect was being pursued.

Once Oswald was murdered in police custody almost 48 hours after he allegedly assassinated Kennedy, nullifying a public trial, FBI Director J. Edgar Hoover was circulating a memorandum stressing that the public needed to be convinced as soon as possible that Oswald was the 'lone' assassin. This was to quell suspicions of conspiracy such as the Soviets being behind it.

Did any of this help to shape the autopsy report that would conclude all wounds on JFK were caused by shots fired from above and behind the limousine where the accused was said to have been positioned?

Connecting these dots may be a stretch but how else are we to explain the autopsy calamity of errors, omissions of procedure and blatant incompetence?

For goodness sake, this was a post mortem on the **President of the United States**!

If you or I were killed by violent means, a qualified forensic pathologist from the local Medical Examiner's office would be called upon to ascertain the exact cause of death.

On November 22, 1963, the 35th President of the United States was not afforded that customary right. Instead of Dallas Medical Examiner Earl Rose being summoned to perform Mr. Kennedy's autopsy, the body was illegally whisked out of Dallas and turned over to military custody.

Rather than calling upon qualified forensic pathologists in Maryland or the District of Columbia to perform this historic post mortem, three unqualified 'military' pathologists were ordered to conduct an autopsy well beyond their expertise.

For my first book Through The 'Oswald' Window, Dr. Cyril Wecht, one of America's most acclaimed forensic pathologists who has examined the autopsy materials in the National Archives, noted that the three military pathologists assigned to the President's autopsy were 'general hospital' pathologists. *"The autopsy report is salacious,"* fumes Wecht and explains why:

Noted forensic pathologist Dr. Cyril Wecht believes Oswald defense council would have exposed the JFK autopsy as a fraud at a public trial.

"A hospital pathologist deals primarily with patients who have died from natural causes. His job usually is to confirm a diagnosis already arrived at, or for research purposes.

"A forensic pathologist, often associated with the medical examiner's office (like Wecht and Rose), *must frequently determine the exact cause and manner of death caused by violence,"* says Wecht.

As Dr. Wecht claims, Commander James J. Humes, Colonel Pierre Finck and Colonel J. Thornton Boswell were unqualified pathologists ordered to conduct President Kennedy's autopsy because they all had one thing in common:

Not one of them had ever before conducted an autopsy involving death by gunshot!

Colonel Pierre Finck had some forensic pathology training purely at the academic level but had not conducted an actual autopsy involving death by violent means. Further, at the Kennedy autopsy, whatever expertise he could bring to the table was thwarted by military superiors in attendance.

At the time of JFK's autopsy, Oswald was alive and in police custody. It boggles the mind to contemplate why unqualified autopsy surgeons would be tasked to undertake an historically significant procedure beyond their ability when it must have been known that a post mortem examination would be essential evidence in the pending public trial of the accused!

Or at the risk of sounding like a QAnon conspiracy theorist, did the autopsy on President Kennedy take place under military command knowing that the procedures and findings would not be analyzed and debated in a court of law?

VITAL PART OF A COVER-UP?

The many consequences of the military autopsy conducted by three unqualified 'hospital' pathologists instead of a local 'forensic' pathologist like Earl Rose doesn't end with the surgeons involved.

In addition to the history-challenging conclusions reached by Dr. David Mantik's examination of the autopsy x-rays addressed in chapter 16, you will read in chapter 13 the eye-opening revelations by Dr. Michael Chesser and Dr. Gary Aguilar that point to much more than a clumsily botched autopsy.

The three scientists, upon reviewing the medical evidence in the National Archives on several occasions, provide expertise analysis of sinister attempts to not only incriminate Oswald as the 'lone' assassin, but also cover-up any evidence of multiple gunmen.

While the investigation of the Assassination Records Review Board in the mid 90's began to tangibly unravel JFK's fraudulent autopsy, further study of the medical evidence by Drs. Cyril Wecht, Mantik, Chesser and Aguilar establish that the Warren Report's lone assassin conclusion would not have stood up at a public trial of the accused Oswald.

As you will read, even without the newer examinations of the medical evidence, forced and unforced errors during the JFK autopsy, as well as the buffoonish incompleteness of the official autopsy report, resulted in a post-mortem that would have provided all the reasonable doubt needed in a court of law to find defendant Oswald 'not guilty' of murdering the President.

And that's a tragedy. This researcher agrees that Oswald did not fire a shot that day and therefore did not murder Kennedy.

However, as I detailed in Through The 'Oswald' Window, it is highly improbable that people completely unknown to Oswald could have set him up to take the fall as the '**lone**' assassin.

It is far more reasonable to conclude that Oswald's role in the assassination was to use his access to the 6th floor as an employee in the building to ready the sniper's window for one of the actual assassins.

This would reasonably explain how Oswald was framed by his fellow conspirators, how they could have taken his rifle from his home and stashed it near the sniper's lair and planted three matching shell casings near the sniper's window as well as a pre-fired bullet at Parkland Hospital to set him up as the assassin. At best, Oswald should have faced a charge of conspiracy to murder the President.

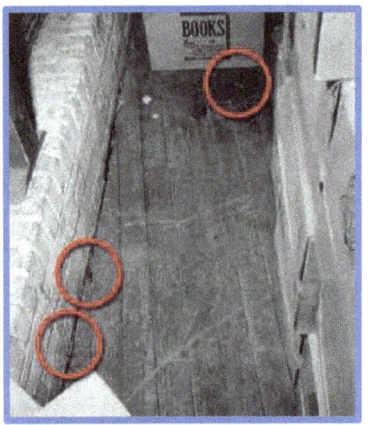

In Chapter 6, researcher Johnny Cairns argues that the three shell casings were planted at the scene because one of them was damaged and could not have been fired that day.

Even if the framing of Oswald is pure poppycock, the analysis of the JFK autopsy X-rays by the above noted experts scientifically establish that even if Oswald was the shooter at the 6th floor Book Depository window, he was **NOT** the only assassin in Dealey Plaza!

So, the question becomes; Why and how was the autopsy conducted with deliberate intent to suppress historical truth?

The 'why' is that the government, for its own clandestine reasons, had to attribute President Kennedy's assassination to a 'lone nut' nobody.

The reasons for that are anybody's guess as presented in hundreds of books that promote conspiracies that could electrify a QAnon convention.

BUNGLING AN AUTOPSY

The 'how' behind this bungled autopsy is so mind-boggling, it would have become the most ridiculed post mortem examination ever presented as evidence in a courtroom.

One consequence of the military takeover of Kennedy's body for autopsy was to ensure that a proper 'forensic' post mortem would never happen.

In a typical pre-trial stipulation, the court would usually allow the defense to undertake its own post mortem examination by a forensic pathologist of its choosing, but with the accused also dead and the President buried just two days later, Oswald was denied this vital right to his defense.

But would a second autopsy have mattered in a court proceeding? Imagine a competent defense attorney like Mark Lane, with the help of qualified expert witnesses, arguing these points before a jury:

Body Chain of Possession

Evidence suggests that President Kennedy's body left Parkland Hospital in an elegant bronze ceremonial casket but arrived at the Bethesda Naval Hospital in a standard military aluminum shipping casket.

This has been verified by several people at the Bethesda morgue who say JFK's body was removed from this ordinary casket and placed on the autopsy table.

However, some 20 minutes later, a bronze ceremonial casket arrived at Bethesda accompanied by Jackie Kennedy and the President's brother Robert, said to be the same casket that left Parkland with the deceased President's body.

And rumors persist that a third stylish mahogany casket arrived with the President's body, prompting conspiracy theorists to have a field day.

A possible change of caskets also opens the door to the President's body being removed for nefarious reasons.

JFK's casket boards Air Force One. Evidence suggests this was not the casket that arrived at Bethesda Naval Hospital for autopsy several hours later.

Testimony by Bethesda personnel, Parkland personnel and Secret Service agents at a public trial would have set the gossip tabloids ablaze if the precise chain of possession of JFK's body and caskets could not be adequately explained.

The chain of possession problems, as well as evidence that Kennedy's body was diverted for surgery to alter his head wounds before arriving at Bethesda is brilliantly outlined by researcher and Assassination Records Review Board staffer Douglas Horne in his 2021 National-Security State and the Kennedy Assassination series webinar for the Future of Freedom Foundation (see resources section).

In the chapters contributed by fellow researcher Johnny Cairns, he does an excellent job exposing the chain of possession problems associated with other key physical evidence in this case.

Can a chain of possession for Kennedy's body and other physical evidence be resolved today by a new inquiry with subpoena power to unseal the remaining government records? It needs to be explored.

Body Alterations?

The allegation that President Kennedy's body was moved coffin to coffin raises the question of why?

Was it to take possession of the body to perform surgical procedures to conceal evidence of any shots from the front of the President?

Before you dismiss this allegation as absurd, noted radiation oncologist Dr. David Mantik reveals in Chapter 16 that an Optical Densitometry technique he applied to the JFK autopsy X-rays in the National Archives in 1993 reveals that some of the X-rays have been *"altered to incriminate Oswald!"*

The next chapter gives credibility to clandestine efforts made by both the Warren Commission and House Select Committee on Assassinations (HSCA) to suppress the autopsy X-rays and photos and replace them in the public record with completely inaccurate depictions of the wounds sustained by Kennedy, which also just happen to incriminate Oswald.

And in chapter 13, Dr. Michael Chesser exposes direct evidence of at least one surgical procedure performed on JFK's head to conceal a bullet entry wound from the front!

The Shocking Phone Call

There can only be three reasons for the very first mistake made by the autopsy doctors on the night of the assassination:

1. Inexperience in performing a 'forensic' post mortem examination.
2. Gross incompetence.
3. Following orders by military superiors.

As laymen, even you and I would have had the common sense to call the doctors at Parkland Hospital to gather their observations and nature of treatments performed on President Kennedy **BEFORE** proceeding with the autopsy!

This did not happen and the consequences of this one mistake would no less than falsify the historical record of the death of a President.

For some inexplicable reason, lead JFK autopsist Commander James Humes did not call Parkland on the night of the assassination to speak to the attending physicians or request copies of any reports they may have compiled. Instead, Dr. Humes proceeded with the autopsy as if he were the first medical professional to see the body.

JFK Case NOT Closed

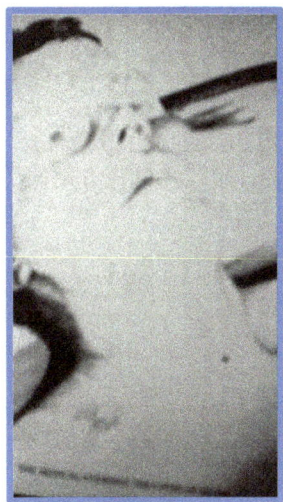

Dr. Malcolm Perry observed a small wound like this under JFK's Adam's apple but obliterated it with a tracheal incision to insert a breathing tube. The autopsy doctors saw the incision but didn't know this wound existed - courtesy Robert Groden's The Killing of a President.

The consequences of this oversight would become shockingly apparent the next morning when Dr. Humes placed a phone call to Parkland's Dr. Malcolm Perry.

What Dr. Perry told Dr. Humes was so flabbergasting, Dr. Humes felt compelled to burn his own autopsy notes in his home fireplace and change his official autopsy report.

Imagine how Dr. Humes felt when he hung up the phone with Dr. Perry who informed him that the obvious tracheotomy incision on Kennedy's throat he saw on the autopsy table in fact obliterated a small pencil-sized wound just below the Adam's apple!

It would have bluntly occurred to Dr. Humes that only hours earlier, he had just committed one of the most dreaded sins of a post mortem examination:

He had just completed an autopsy on the President of the United States that failed to account for all the wounds on the body!

Without ever seeing this wound, Dr. Humes declared it to be a bullet 'exit' wound, thus enabling the Warren Commission to concoct the 'Single Bullet Theory' that would have us believe the 'magical' flightpath reported in chapter 10.

A simple pre-autopsy phone call by Dr. Humes to Parkland Hospital may have also prevented a deliberate medical cover-up of the fatal wound on JFK.

Autopsy Versus Parkland Doctors

It is astounding to realize that had Dr. Humes spoken to ANY of the doctors at Parkland Hospital who treated the President or even just saw the body prior to conducting the autopsy, he would have had to deliberately lie about how JFK died.

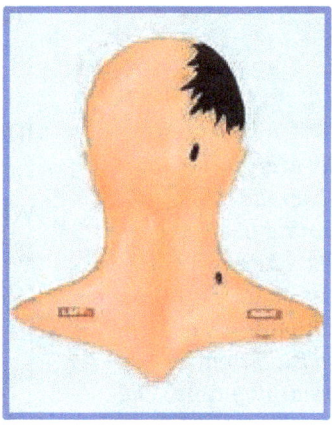

CE 386

Based on a verbal description by Dr. Humes months later, medical illustrator Harold Rydberg, a Naval corpsman, drew what would become CE 386 which depicts all the wounds inflicted upon JFK as accepted by the Warren Commission.

This diagram shows a small bullet entry hole in the rear of the head with a corresponding large gaping exit wound above the right ear.

As detailed in the following chapter, there's only one problem – if the head wounds depicted in CE 386 are what Dr. Humes saw at autopsy, they do not reflect what the Parkland doctors saw before the body left their care.

Dr. Robert McClelland points to where he saw a fist-sized exit wound on JFK's head. What he and all other doctors at Parkland saw was ignored.

More than a dozen Parkland doctors, nurses and trauma room attendants ALL described the fatal exit wound they saw on President Kennedy, as demonstrated here by Dr. Robert McClelland, as being at the right rear occipital region of the head!

How can this possibly be? Something is wrong here. For his entire life, Rydberg said he was duped into drawing erroneous depictions of Kennedy's wounds and was never allowed to see the original autopsy photos – but he wasn't the only professional artist caught up in the deception.

Fifteen years later, as described in the next chapter, the HSCA also ignored the Parkland doctors and had medical illustrator Ida Dox draw a black and white schematic showing a small entry wound in the center rear of the skull and the right rear of JFK's head to be fully intact.

Compare the black and white Dox illustration on the next page to the color drawing beside it that reflects what several medical professionals at Parkland observed.

In my previous book, forensic pathologist Dr. Cyril Wecht is on record as saying the JFK autopsy photos are fake.

This is echoed by radiation oncologist Dr. David Mantik in chapter 16, who further states that at least one head

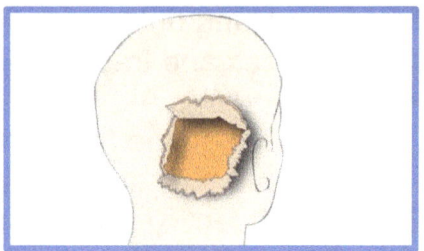

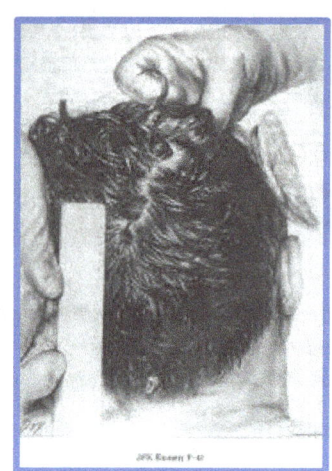

X-ray was altered *"to incriminate Oswald"* as the only shooter.

Thankfully, this physical evidence still exists and needs to be a priority target of a new investigation to explain why the official autopsy report on President Kennedy does not match the medical evidence uncovered by researchers in the National Archives.

TWO CONFLICTING AUTOPSY REPORTS

Not only did Dr. Humes modify his own autopsy report to account for a wound on JFK that he never saw, a second autopsy report by two FBI agents present at the procedure demonstrates yet another critical change in findings made after the fact.

FBI agents James Sibert and Francis O'Neill were assigned to the autopsy proceeding to:

A) Retrieve bullets, fragments or other physical evidence during the post mortem examination.

B) Record the findings of the autopsy surgeons with the body present.

At issue here is the back wound on the President, which was measured at time of autopsy as being located 5 ¾ inches below the collar line and slightly to the right side of the spinal column (see diagram at right).

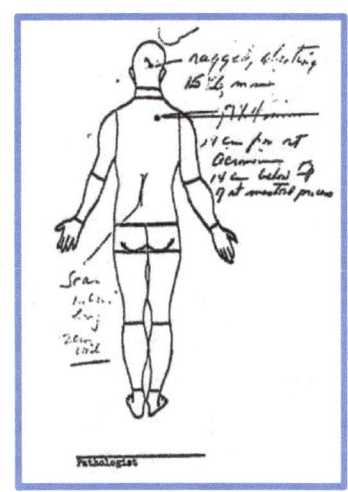

Autopsy face sheet by Dr. Boswell showing bullet hole in the upper back.

The Sibert-O'Neill FBI autopsy reports states: *"During the later stages of this autopsy, Dr. Humes located an opening which appeared to be a bullet hole which was below his shoulders and two inches to right of the middle line of the spinal column."*

While this description matches the autopsy face sheet shown above, it was not convenient to the Commission's Single Bullet Theory, so it was ignored.

Even more shocking is what the FBI autopsy report says happened once this back wound was discovered:

"Dr Humes probed this opening with a finger at which time it was determined that the distance travelled by this missile was a short distance inasmuch as the end of the opening could be felt with the finger."

To account for the short distance travelled by this projectile, the FBI report adds: *"Dr. Humes stated that the pattern was clear. The bullet that had entered at this point…fell out of the point of entry during external cardiac massage at Parkland Hospital."*

Wait just a minute here. To create the 'Single Bullet Theory' and blame Oswald as the '**lone**' assassin, the Commission not only ignored the autopsy face sheet, the FBI autopsy report and JFK's clothing by moving the back wound up to the base of the neck, it also ignored the finding of Dr. Humes as recorded by the FBI report that the bullet only penetrated a short distance!

The Commission not only ignored all that evidence, it cited no evidence in concluding that the bullet that entered at JFK's back did transit his body, exit his throat and strike John Connally, causing all of his wounds.

Even if the body were to be exhumed, Dr. Cyril Wecht believes that the normal decomposition of muscle and soft tissue would make it highly unlikely that this bullet trajectory in the body could still be ascertained.

As for agents Sibert and O'Neill? After affirming their FBI autopsy report in an interview with Commission chief investigator Arlen Specter, who created the 'Single Bullet Theory,' Sibert and O'Neill were never called before the Warren Commission hearings.

NEWS FLASH CHANGES EVERYTHING

When Dr. Finck was ordered by military superiors to not dissect the President's back wound, the consequence of this decision became more alarming when an announcement was made in the autopsy room.

The autopsy doctors were informed that this nearly pristine bullet below was found at Parkland Hospital. Accept for a miniscule 2.4 grains of metal missing at the

 nose of the bullet, it looked as if it hadn't even been fired.

Without any confirming evidence, the bullet was immediately associated with the entry wound in JFK's upper back.

And despite this bullet's condition being consistent with the 'shallow' wound in Kennedy's back, it was decided this bullet transited JFK's chest after all, exited his throat and went on to strike Connally, causing a total of seven wounds on two men, including two broken bones in the Governor.

Believe it or not, that's how the historic 'Single Bullet Theory' and '**lone**' gunman conclusion came to be!

The Missing Brain!

One of the great mysteries of the JFK assassination is that his badly damaged brain, removed at autopsy, suddenly went missing. It has never been located.

Normally, in a case involving death by gunshot to the head, the brain would be removed at autopsy and be placed in a stainless steel container of formalin solution for at least a couple of weeks.

Once the brain is hardened in the solution, it is incised into very thin slices to reveal evidence of a bullet, fragments or bullet pathway inside the brain as a means of establishing where the related shot or shots came from.

Tragically, this was never done. As a result, many questions remain unanswered even though the Zapruder film clearly shows JFK's head struck by a fatal bullet.

Fortunately, the expert eyes of neurologist Michael Chesser, as detailed in the next chapter, has found stunning evidence of a bullet pathway in JFK's head that is most problematic for lone gunmen advocates.

Speculation endures that the brain was taken by Robert Kennedy and buried with the body in Arlington National Cemetery. Even if the brain was found, it is debatable whether it would still be viable for forensic examination.

However, when it comes to the many controversies surrounding the JFK autopsy, not all is lost. As discussed in Chapter 16, modern advancements are starting to reveal the secrets within the archived X-rays in the National Archives that are proving contrary to the findings of the Warren Report.

Although not even the government can force the exhumation of President Kennedy's body for a proper post mortem procedure, the autopsy on JFK needs to be a focal point of any new official inquiry into the events of 11/22/63.

Chapter 13

Shocking Discoveries by Two Experts Who Reviewed the JFK Medical Evidence and Found Conspiracy and Cover-Up!

When independent medical experts get the rare opportunity to examine the original JFK autopsy/medical evidence under lock and key in the National Archives, two trends emerge:

1. The Original Sin – The seriously bungled JFK autopsy may have been due, in part, to incompetence by unqualified pathologists but there was a 'deliberate' altering of wounds, x-rays and photographs separate from the autopsy to purposely conceal evidence of more than one gunman.
2. Ongoing Cover-Up – No less than three other government investigations not only affirmed the medical findings of one gunman, they ignored and altered evidence of multiple gunmen and even suppressed such evidence from their own investigators.

Dr. Michael Chesser, Board certified in adult neurology and clinical neuro physiology, found such evidence when he studied the original JFK autopsy x-rays and photos in 2015.

Neurologist Michael Chesser saw clear evidence of a frontal shot to JFK's head when he studied autopsy x-rays in the National Archives.

More specifically, Dr. Chesser found evidence in the x-rays that challenges the official autopsy report on JFK on the night of his violent death on November 22 of 1963.

One issue is a "snowstorm" of bullet fragments Dr. Chesser noted in a lateral (sideview) x-ray at the top of JFK's skull.

Dr. Chesser, in an April 14, 2021, presentation for the Future of Freedom Foundation's National-Security State and the Kennedy Assassination webinar series, noted that the pattern of deposited metallic debris extended from the front of the skull to very near the rear of the skull.

He opined that the characteristics of the debris field appear consistent with a bullet entering the '**front**' of the head and travelling toward the back with no signs of the projectile exiting at rear.

Further, Dr. Chesser stated in the webinar that the trail of metallic fragments is highly inconsistent with a metal-jacketed bullet fired from a Mannlicher-Carcano rifle. This is the weaponry attributed by the Commission to 'lone' assassin Lee Oswald positioned above and behind the limousine.

"Instead, an M-16 bullet could cause a 'snowstorm' of fragments located at the frontal skull," **states Dr. Chesser.**

JFK Case NOT Closed

DISTORTING THE EVIDENCE

As Dr. Chesser points out, the autopsy surgeons did not ignore the trail of bullet fragments at the top of JFK's skull. After all, they had to be accounted for.

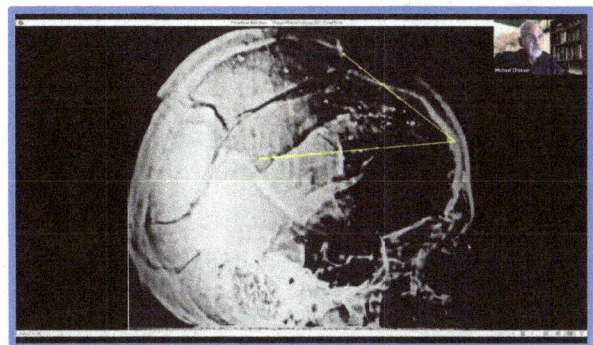

The yellow triangle captures a 'snowstorm' of bullet fragments (white specs) left by a bullet entering the right forehead of JFK and ending near the back of the skull – courtesy Dr. Michael Chesser

In an interview with this researcher, Dr. Chesser notes: "*The Warren Commission autopsy report falsely stated that the trail of metallic fragments extended from their designated entrance at the lower occipital region* (lower right rear of skull) *to the proposed exit in the frontal-parietal region* (above the right ear).

"*Dr.* (David) *Mantik and I agree that the smallest fragments are seen in the right frontal region, and I saw a cluster of tiny fragments just inside a gap in the right side of the frontal bone, which I believe is evidence that there was an entry in this region.*" states Dr. Chesser.

As the x-ray image from Dr. Chesser's power point presentation above illustrates, the trail of metallic fragments at the top of the skull cannot possibly be associated with a bullet entry wound in the lower right

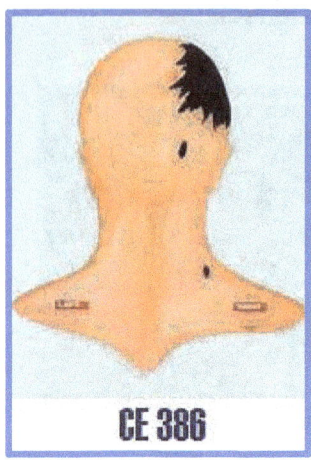

This diagram released by the Commission depicts a bullet entry at the right rear occipital area of the skull. This wound does not explain a trail of metallic fragments found near the top of Kennedy's head.

occiput area as per the diagram below, which is where the Commission places the fatal head shot bullet entry.

Instead, the trail of metallic fragments along the top one-third of the skull can be associated with a frontal entry wound at the right forehead area at the hairline, per Dr. Chesser's quote above.

And Dr. Chesser says the authentic autopsy photographs bear evidence of wound alteration to hide a bullet entry from the front, thus establishing the deliberate cover-up of a second gunman.

In the original autopsy photo (next page), an incision on Kennedy's forehead is visible to the expert eye of Dr. Michael Chesser and his colleagues (see red rectangular box).

This was confirmed by autopsy surgeon J. Thornton Boswell when he testified before the ARRB probe on 2-26-96.

"There was an incised wound up there that extended into the right eye socket and then back across his temporal and frontal bone," **stated Boswell.**

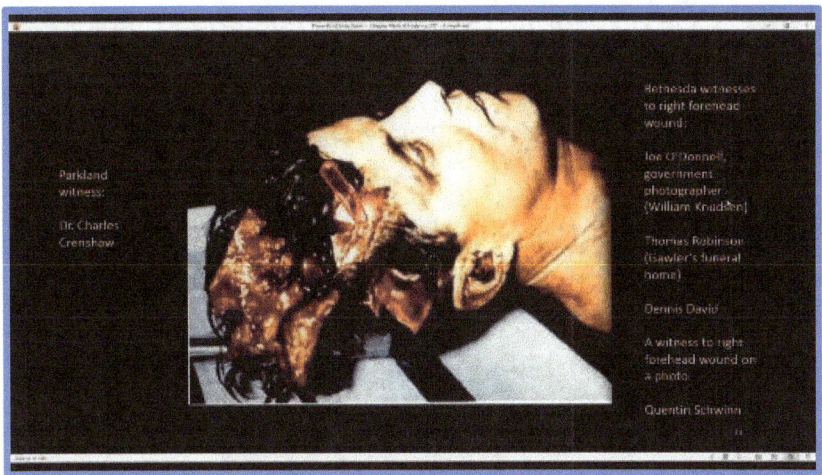

According to the expert eye of Dr. Chesser, this autopsy photo shows an incision (red box) at the right forehead that had to have occurred between the body leaving Parkland Hospital and arriving at Bethesda Naval Hospital for autopsy - courtesy Dr. Michael Chesser

"*We* (Mantik and Chesser) *think that the incision in the right forehead* (*which was not seen in Dallas but was present when the official autopsy began*) *was part of a pre-autopsy manipulation of the wounds to remove evidence,*" continues Dr. Chesser.

"*This incision could not have been part of a legitimate autopsy procedure because it extends well into the forehead,*" adds Dr. Chesser, who dismisses any claims of the incision being associated with the procedure to remove JFK's brain.

"*All incisions which are made to remove the brain at autopsy must be within the hairline, so that the incisions can be covered by the hair and not visible to family,*" asserts Dr. Chesser, who worked as a morgue attendant in medical school and assisted med-school pathologists during autopsies.

And as Dr. David Mantik quips, "*Scalpels cause incisions. Bullets cause wounds.*"

A MORE SINISTER APPROACH

While the Warren Commission, perhaps believing the JFK autopsy photos and x-rays would not be seen by anybody until their scheduled release in 2038, associated the trail of metallic fragments to a bullet entry wound in the lower-right occipital region of the skull without any supporting evidence, future government inquiries were even more brazen in dealing with the inconvenient debris of fragments.

"*The government appointed medical panels that followed the Warren Commission stated the autopsy pathologists were wrong about the entry location* (in the lower right occipital region) *and moved it up about four inches.*

"*It is mind-boggling to think that they would overrule the pathologists who participated in the autopsy,*" exclaims Dr. Chesser.

Despite moving the back-of-the-skull entry wound up four inches to make it easier to associate it with the troublesome trail of metallic fragments, experts who have since examined the autopsy x-rays are not fooled. This includes two of the original autopsy pathologists, Dr. Finck and Commander Boswell, both of whom insisted before the Assassinations Record Review Board in 1995 that the bullet entry wound at the rear of the head was in the lower occipital region.

If there is to ever be another formal investigation into the murder of President Kennedy, it is clear that it cannot be left to the government without oversight by independent researchers as well as experts in medicine and ballistics.

Whereas every government body since the Warren Commission has altered evidence to support a one shooter scenario, Dr. Chesser notes the existing x-ray evidence establishes multiple gunmen in Dealey Plaza.

"Whether there was two or three shots to the skull is a moot point," contends Dr. Chesser. *"In both scenarios, the official version(s) fall apart."*

The collective observations of Drs. Mantik and Chesser rule out the damage to JFK's skull being caused by a single shot entering the lower right rear of the skull.

A scenario of three separate shots to Kennedy's head is far more likely based on the following:

Shot #1 – The autopsy evidence supports a shot from behind, entering the lower right occipital region of the head.

This shot is the only explanation for JFK's apparent slight 'forward' head movement following the initial impact (see chapter 3). This was followed by one or possibly two nearly instantaneous frontal shots that slammed his head and upper body 'rearward' against the backrest of his seat.

Shot #2 – The discovery of the 'snowstorm' debris of bullet fragments strongly indicates entry of a bullet at the right forehead that travels nearly to the rear of the skull without exiting.

The incision noted by Dr. Chesser is evidence that a pre-autopsy surgery was performed to obscure a bullet entry at the front of the skull.

Dr. Michael Chesser agrees with this researcher's discussion in chapter 9 that a spray of JFK's blood and brain matter that flew back and hit officer Bobby Hargis (behind Jackie's left shoulder) is consistent with a shot from the right-front.

Shot #3 – The fist-sized blow-out wound at the right rear of Kennedy's skull denotes a shot from the right-front of the limousine that entered the temporal region above the right ear.

The sizeable exit wound at the back of Kennedy's head cannot be associated with either the bullet that left a 'snowstorm' of fragments at the top of the skull or a bullet entering the back of the skull at the location of the fist-sized blow-out wound.

As Dr. Chesser points out, while he cannot state for certain, head shot #3 would account for what happened to Dallas motorcycle cop Bobby Hargis as detailed in chapter 9.

For those of you disbelieving of deliberate action to frame Oswald by tampering with the official medical records, then why, as you are about to read, would subsequent government investigations also falsify autopsy findings and key testimony by medical professionals?

Years of Ongoing Government Cover-Up Revealed by Medical Sleuth!

While Dr. David Mantik and Dr. Michael Chesser were discovering evidence of altered JFK wounds and x-rays to purposely incriminate Lee Oswald as a 'lone' assassin, Dr. Gary Aguilar found disturbing proof of a systematic government cover-up of other autopsy evidence that would have placed multiple gunmen in Dealey Plaza.

Dr. Gary Aguilar's study of the JFK autopsy photos didn't jive with other evidence about the fatal head wound. Then he discovered that all follow-up medical inquiries based their findings on erroneous medical records put forth by the Warren Commission.

Like Drs. Mantik and Chesser, the practicing Ophthalmologist and Clinical Professor of Ophthalmology at the University of California, San Francisco, has examined the JFK autopsy x-rays and photographs in the National Archives in Maryland.

However, when Dr. Aguilar examined the JFK autopsy photographs on record and found them to be at odds with other known medical evidence, it sent him on a research journey that resulted in him writing the groundbreaking report: How Five Investigations into JFK's Medical/Autopsy Evidence Got it Wrong.

It turns out that that not only did all the follow-up government investigations get it wrong, they got it purposely wrong!

What jumped out at Dr. Aguilar was that the purported authentic autopsy photographs in the Archives showed no visible wound at the rear of the President's head that matched the descriptions given by the Parkland medical professionals.

The scalp and hair at the lower right of the skull appeared undisturbed as shown in the photo below left. Yet Dr. Aguilar was aware of the consistent eyewitness accounts of at least 20 Parkland Hospital nurses, physicians and trauma room attendants who all reported observing a fist-sized blow-out type wound at the lower right occipital region of Kennedy's skull, as shown in the diagram below right.

Not only did the Warren Commission accept the falsified autopsy photo (below left) as proof that Lee Oswald fired the kill shot from above and behind Kennedy, it never called any of the hospital witnesses to testify as to the fatal head wound they observed on the President before the body left Parkland!

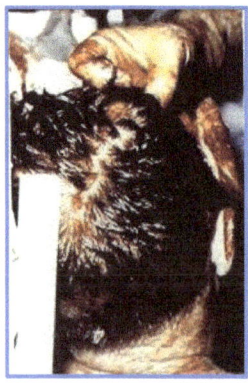 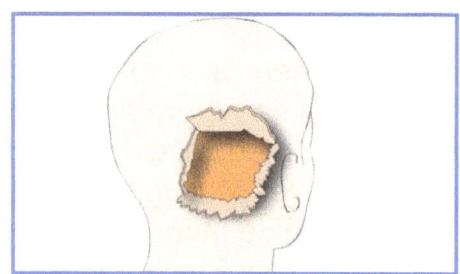

Equally shocking is that any and all testimony and evidence published in the Warren Report places the small rear entry wound at the lower right occipital region of the skull where you instead see the massive exit wound in the diagram on the previous page.

Evidence of photographic forgery appears in the autopsy photo at left on page 252. It shows an entry wound at the center of the skull in the crown area near the top of the ruler. Yet, no medical testimony or evidence supports this location as a bullet's impact to JFK's head.

What is the reason for this deliberate deceit? The Warren Commission could not acknowledge a sizeable exit wound at the right rear of Kennedy's head without admitting to more than one gunman.

THE ULTIMATE SUPPRESSION

Even more disturbing, Dr. Aguilar discovered that this gaping head exit wound versus small bullet entry wound discrepancy was not corrected by three successive government panels tasked to analyze the medical evidence.

This included the Clark panel (1968), the Rockefeller Commission (1975) and the House Select Committee on Assassinations (1976-79).

In fact, the HSCA not only failed to correct this history-changing piece of evidence, it took steps to ensure that its own forensics advisory panel:

1. Did not know that this autopsy photo was a forgery, allowing the panel to accept the photo, as well as other altered photos and x-rays as factually correct.

2. Withheld the observations of the Parkland medical specialists and other evidence that challenged the accuracy of the photo of the back of JFK's head.

Another stunning finding to come out of Dr. Aguilar's research of the original autopsy report and all other government examinations of the medical evidence is that _none_ of the inquiries accepted the small entry wound location at the rear crown area as depicted in the photo (page 252) as factually correct.

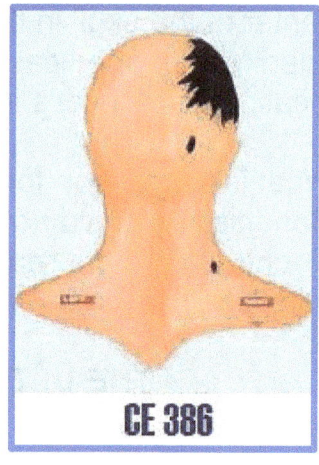

This Rydberg drawing was presented as accurate by the Commission, but the entry wound at the back of the head does not match the forged photo above that shows the entry wound center skull in the crown area. How could this happen?

Instead, starting with the original autopsy report, the bullet entry point on JFK's head is described as being at the lower occipital region above the cerebellum on the right side of the skull.

This location is falsely documented on Harold Rydberg's medical illustration where the Parkland staff and other evidence instead place the explosive exit wound.

While the Commission ignored this key conflicting evidence, subsequent panels recognized that a bullet entering at the lower right quadrant of the head could not be associated with the 'snowstorm' of metal fragments at the top of the skull as noted earlier by Dr. Chesser. How was this dealt with?

Dr. Aguilar discovered ARRB documents that reveal the bullet entry point was moved up four inches on the back of the skull to better connect it to the trail of fragments. In doing so, they attempted to attribute the metallic debris to a bullet fired by a 'lone' shooter at the 6th floor Book Depository window.

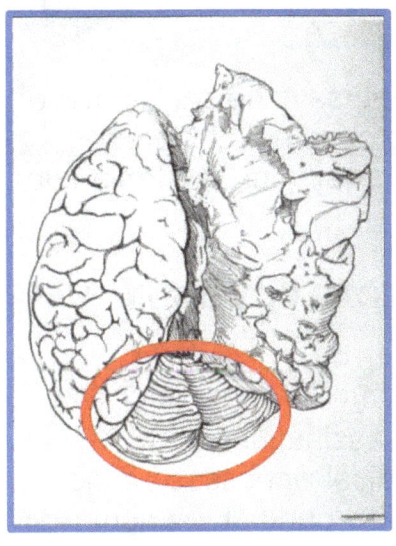

Doctors at Parkland Hospital observed severe damage to the cerebellum at the bottom rear of JFK's head (circled). Yet, 'official' autopsy photos do not show this explosive exit wound. Why?

Dr. Aguilar contends that the original JFK autopsy was seriously flawed and that all subsequent 'official' government investigations operated under the premise that the autopsy report accepted by the Warren Commission was factually correct.

They did so despite key autopsy x-rays and photos appeared in conflict with other related documented aspects of the Humes autopsy report.

Dr. Aguilar's investigation raised two critical examples of ongoing governmental cover-up in support of the Warren Commission's lone assassin conclusion.

First, the original autopsy report makes no mention of a massive blow-out wound at the lower right occipital region of the skull despite the consistent observations of more than a dozen Parkland medical professionals.

These expert witnesses not only saw a fist-sized hole at the lower right rear of Kennedy's head, Dr. Robert McClelland at right, stationed directly over the  President's head during treatment, says he saw damaged cerebellum that caused tissue to ooze out of the exit wound and fall on the autopsy gurney (see illustration on previous page).

EXPANDING THE MEDICAL COVER-UP

Like the Warren Commission some 15 years later, the House Select Committee on Assassinations (HSCA) decided to ignore the expert medical witnesses on the Parkland staff about a gaping exit wound at the right rear of Kennedy's head. Only, it took the medical cover-up a couple of steps further.

According to documents within the Assassination Records Review Board (ARRB) uncovered by Dr. Aguilar, the HSCA also suppressed the testimonies of 26 additional expert medical witnesses who observed the autopsy procedure at the Bethesda Naval Hospital on the night of the assassination.

Aguilar discovered that every one of these medical professionals had submitted testimony that placed a sizeable blow-out wound at the lower right occipital region at the back of the President's skull at the precise location reported by as many as 20 Parkland doctors, nurses and emergency staff.

Several of these medical experts present at the autopsy also submitted diagrams that locate the gaping exit wound exactly where the Parkland witnesses placed it - at the right rear of JFK's skull.

Despite some 46 medical professionals from two different settings all agreeing that they observed an unmistakable gaping exit wound at the back of Kennedy's head, all of their identical testimonies and supporting diagrams were ignored and suppressed by major government investigations into the murder of the President of the United States!

Instead of accepting the multitude of identical expert medical testimony, the HSCA decided that a single photo showing no such wound at the back of the victim's head would represent the official record of how JFK died.

A COVER-UP FROM WITHIN

A cover-up of the medical evidence, the ARRB investigation of the mid 90's discovered, included a deliberate scheme by the HSCA 20 years earlier to dupe its own forensics panel into officially affirming the original autopsy findings that shaped the Warren Commission's conclusion that Oswald fired all the shots from above and behind the limousine.

Dr. Aguilar was shocked to learn of how the HSCA handled the evidence provided by the 26 autopsy witnesses, all of whom were medical professionals of varying degrees:

"The HSCA not only withheld the statements (of the autopsy witnesses) *from the public, they also withheld them from their own forensic consultants whose job it was to assess the medical/autopsy evidence,"* Dr. Aguilar notes.

And since the testimonies of the Parkland Hospital medical professionals who observed the fist-sized exit wound at the rear of Kennedy's skull were likewise not included in the Warren Report, the HSCA forensic panel was unaware of the abundance of evidence of such a wound that supported the kill shot as coming from in front of the car.

The consequence of this double suppression of critical expert eyewitness testimony?

When the HSCA forensic panel examined the official autopsy materials, they had little reason to question the photograph of the back of Kennedy's head that showed the crown area as the entry point for the fatal shot.

I say little reason rather than no reason because another discrepancy mysteriously escaped them. HSCA medical illustrator Ida Dox drew the diagram at the top of the next page that places the bullet entry even higher than the cowlick are indicated in the autopsy photo.

A post mortem examination fraught with such inconsistencies and inaccuracies would have been easily discredited at trial by a capable defense team's forensic expert witnesses on behalf of Oswald.

This is particularly true of the eye-witness account of Tom Robinson, the mortician who prepared JFK's body for burial after the autopsy was completed.

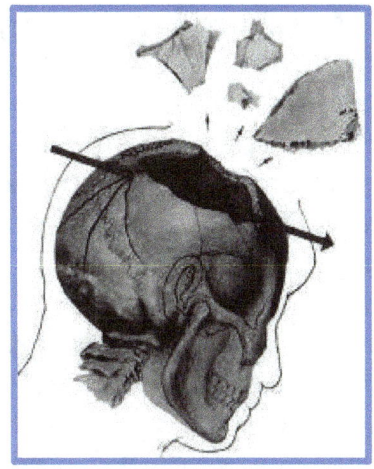

It is amazing to discover that drawings from two medical illustrators do not match purported autopsy photos which in turn do not match autopsy x-rays.

Other than the autopsy surgeons themselves, there is no other man who had more time to view JFK's body than Robinson.

Drawing by mortician Tom Robinson shows the gaping exit wound at the rear of JFK's head he had to repair for a private viewing by the family.

Even more important, Robinson was not surrounded by a horde of military superiors barking instructions on how to do his job.

In preparing JFK's body for burial, which included a private viewing of the body by the Kennedy family, it was Robinson's job to meticulously hide all wounds and make the fallen President presentable.

This included him carefully positioning scalp and hair to cover-up a fist-sized exit wound at the rear of Kennedy's head, which he noted by providing the diagram on the previous page to the HSCA. This diagram was not only kept from the HSCA public record, it was not shown to the HSCA's forensics panel assembled to evaluate all the medical evidence.

While Robinson's key observations of the wounds he had to professionally conceal for a private family viewing was ignored by the HSCA, Robinson wasn't even called before the Warren Commission.

As Dr. Aguilar learned when he had his own eye-opening encounter with members of the duped HSCA forensic panel:

"Not long after I discovered that the HSCA had misrepresented what JFK autopsy witnesses said, I spoke in Washington, D.C. at a conference. On the stage speaking with me were Drs. **(Michael)** *Baden and* **(Cyril)** *Wecht* **(both HSCA medical panel members).**

"I projected a slide of HSCA V.7:37 which showed the HSCA reporting that all the autopsy witnesses had refuted the Parkland doctors about a defect in the back of JFK's head.

"I then showed slides of the actual statements and diagrams that the autopsy witnesses had given the HSCA, and which the HSCA had suppressed in 1979. I then asked Baden and Wecht if they'd ever seen these testimonies, statements and diagrams that had forensic significance. Neither of them had."

Dr. Aguilar found that his analysis of the medical/autopsy materials and the flawed subsequent reviews by other government panels were exposed by the ARRB investigation in the '90s.

That study revealed troublesome mistakes and omissions during the initial autopsy on 22/11/63 that were never corrected by the government until its own ARRB inquiry three decades later declassified a multitude of documents.

Only then was it ever revealed, for instance, that there was an explosive exit wound at the back of JFK's head observed by a multitude of Parkland medical staff that would be evidence of a second sniper to the President's right-front.

The HSCA 15 years later, as Dr. Aguilar notes, *"clearly understood the implications of the conflict between the witnesses and the autopsy photographs."*

So when the HSCA encountered 26 additional medical professionals present at the autopsy who confirmed the observations of the Parkland personnel, it not only excluded their true testimony from its final report and kept the information from its own medical panel, it blatantly lied by saying the autopsy witnesses strongly disputed what the Parkland witnesses saw.

The truth is that the HSCA could not produce one autopsy witness to dispute the multiple Parkland accounts of the large exit wound at the rear of Kennedy's head.

Just as the Warren Commission excluded the expert

medical eyewitnesses from its public report in 1964, the HSCA suppressed the observations of the 26 autopsy medical witnesses in its 1979 public report.

KEY WITNESS IGNORED

Another blatant example of dismissing or ignoring witness testimony because it did not fit the one assassin scenario is the observations of the only man to view JFK's body up close before Parkland, at Parkland and during the autopsy procedure.

Secret Service agent Clint Hill never wavered on what he observed to whichever investigative body queried him.

In a memorandum from the Secret Service to the Warren Commission, agent Clint Hill made reference to what he saw once he jumped onto the back of the President's limousine and covered JFK's body from potential more gunfire.

"As I lay over the top of the back seat (of the President's limousine), *I noticed a portion of the President's head on the right rear side was missing."*

When Hill appeared before the Warren Commission, he had this exchange with assistant counsel Arlen Spector about his efforts at Parkland Hospital to help transport Kennedy's body into the trauma room:

Specter – "What did you observe as to President Kennedy's condition on arrival at the hospital?"

Hill – *"The right rear portion of his head was missing. It was lying in the rear seat of the car. His brain was exposed...you could not tell if there had been any other wound or not, except for the one large gaping wound in the right rear portion of the head."*

At the autopsy at the Bethesda Naval Hospital, Hill further testified: *"When I arrived the autopsy had been completed and...I observed...a wound on the right rear portion of the skull."*

It should be noted that 'Lone Nut' advocates who dismiss recent medical findings of Drs. Mantik, Chesser and Aguilar have yet to present a single medical professional who can dispute the findings of the three experts featured in this book based on examining the evidence currently kept in the Archives.

Now that we know that Dr. Baden was duped by the HSCA into falsely believing the photo of the crown area bullet entry was authentic, he is the only forensic professional that Lone Nutters rely on in support of their 'Oswald acted alone' claim.

Nor have they produced a person of expertise who can dispute the methodologies or technologies used by the three doctors in arriving at their mutual finding of wound alteration and suppression of the medical evidence in this case.

Clearly, any new official investigation needs to focus on using today's technology to distinguish between altered and authentic autopsy x-rays and photos.

With that achieved, more experts like Mantik, Chesser

and Aguilar need to apply ever evolving technologies to this evidence to remove any bias from its findings.

It should also include medical experts who still agree with the Warren Report. It is time for conspiracy theories to be replaced by scientific fact.

Chapter 14

How Two Medical Illustrators Were Duped into Falsifying Autopsy Photos in Support of a 'Lone' Assassin!

At first glance, it seemed like the right thing to do, but it turns out that even this decision by the Warren Commission was intended to deceive and promulgate a sinister cover-up to frame Lee Oswald as the '**lone**' assassin of JFK.

And 15 years later when the House Select Committee on Assassinations (HSCA) took another look at the events of 11/22/63, it too failed to correct history when it ignored the plethora of evidence that exposed the original deception.

Back in 1964, the Warren Commission rightly decided to not publish the gruesome Kennedy autopsy photos in its report despite their historical importance to the death of a President.

There was no need, it was reasoned, to subject the Kennedy family or the American public to the graphic images of the horrific wounds inflicted on a beloved man.

Medical illustrator Harold Rydberg believed his entire life that he was duped into falsely representing JFK's wounds in his three drawings.

Instead, the Commission decided to have the gruesome JFK autopsy photos dramatically toned down by medical illustrator Harold Rydberg, a Naval corpsman directed to work with autopsy surgeon Dr. James Humes on this task.

Rydberg was directed to remove all graphic details of the damage sustained by President Kennedy, especially to his head, but that would not be a problem since he was not allowed to view the actual autopsy photos on which to base his illustrations.

Instead, some four months '*after*' the assassination, Rydberg was instructed by Humes to prepare schematic drawings based solely on the doctor's recollection of the wounds he saw on the President during the autopsy.

Further, Rydberg was directed to merely indicate in his drawings the points of entry of bullet wounds on President Kennedy per Humes' recollection as well as a sizeable blotchy black mark to denote the exit point of the fatal head shot.

Based on their collaboration, here are the three drawings prepared by Rydberg that would become the official 'visual' account in the Warren Report of the wounds sustained by the President:

JFK Case NOT Closed

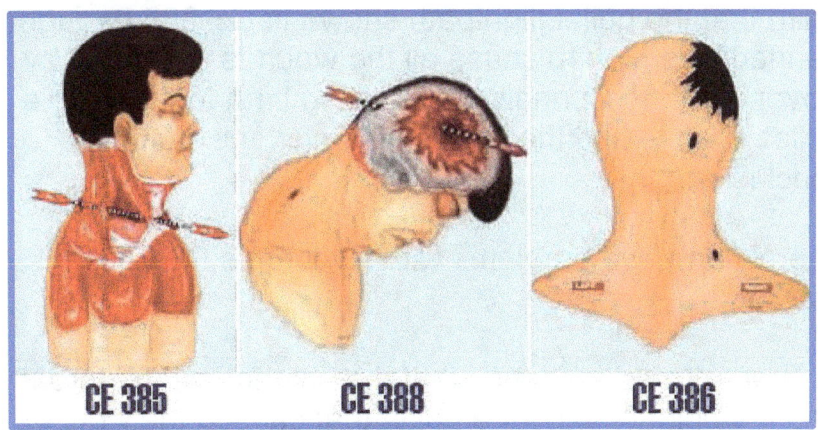

NOT ONE WOUND ACCURATELY DEPICTED?

Through no fault of Harold Rydberg, evidence suggests that, except possibly for the location of the throat wound in CE 385, none of the wounds shown in the above three illustrations are accurately located on the body.

Even more alarming, all the wounds on the illustrations above appear to have been unwittingly drawn by Rydberg to denote that the wounds shown were caused by shots from the rear of Kennedy thereby supporting the Commission's assertion that Oswald was the only shooter that day.

CE 385

Rydberg drawing CE 385 shows a bullet entering the base of the neck and traversing slightly downward to exit at the throat just below the Adam's apple.

The Commission used this illustration by Rydberg to

claim that the bullet flightpath shown in CE 385 through Kennedy went on to cause all the wounds sustained by Governor John Connally, thus giving birth to the 'Single Bullet Theory' and the corresponding 'lone' gunman conclusion.

There's only two problems with Rydberg's CE 385 drawing:

1. There is zero evidence that the tiny hole at the throat was the point of exit for a bullet that caused the wounds on Connally.

2. Chapter 10 clearly outlines the problems with both wounds. Specifically, the rear neck wound in CE 385 does not exist.

Instead, the official autopsy report, the FBI autopsy report, the testimony of Secret Service agent Clint Hill and the President's clothing worn that day, as shown on the next page, all locate the entry wound on his back to be approximately 5 ¾ inches below what is depicted in CE 385. Why the discrepancy?

The Commission, for disturbing reasons discussed in Chapter 10, had to have the entry wound on JFK up higher so it could reasonably say the bullet, coming from above and behind the limousine, travelled downward to exit at the throat and go on to strike Connally.

Without this contrived scenario, the Single Bullet Theory cannot have happened, leaving only one other possibility:

Kennedy and Connally were hit by separate bullets fired almost simultaneous to each other!

CE 388

The middle schematic drawing by Rydberg (CE 388) also falsely shows an entry wound at the base of the neck instead of where all the evidence places it — 5 ¾ inches below the collar line.

JFK's suit jacket shows a bullet hole almost six inches lower than Rydberg diagram CE 385. And his jacket was not bunched up at the time of the first shot.

Just as disturbing is the representation of the kill shot to Kennedy's head, CE 388 shows a bullet entry at the rear of the head and an explosive exit wound at the right side of his head just above the right ear.

As other evidence persuasively suggests, the exit wound in CE 388 is blatantly false!

First, as documented in Chapter 11, more than a dozen Parkland Hospital doctors, nurses and trauma room attendants have gone on record as saying they saw no such exit wound on the President's head.

Instead, all medical professionals, such as Dr. Charles Crenshaw pictured here pointing to where he observed a massive exit wound on Kennedy, reported seeing a fist-sized blow-out wound to the right rear occipital region of the skull.

Rydberg's drawings depict no such trauma at the rear of the skull because it is inconsistent with the kill shot coming from above and behind Mr. Kennedy.

Incredibly, the Commission chose the Rydberg drawing to reflect the exit wound on the President's head. As for the doctors and other medical professionals, none of them were called to testify before the Warren Commission hearings!

CE 386

The final Rydberg diagram (CE 386) at right in the photo panel on page 267 nicely wraps up the three shots fired by Oswald as the solo sniper in Dealey Plaza.

CE 386 shows the entry wound in the neck, which is even more inaccurately placed than CE 385.

It shows a bullet entry wound at the right rear of the head where all other evidence places a large gaping exit wound. Further, as you are about to see, this Rydberg drawing is at odds with black and white sketches done by medical illustrator Ida Dox for the HSCA hearings.

Lastly, the explosive exit wound above the right ear in CE 386 is erroneously placed but necessary to support Oswald being the shooter from the 6th floor Book Depository window.

JFK Case NOT Closed

HSCA – BLUNDER # 2

Are we to believe that when the HSCA convened in 1976 to review the deaths of JFK and Martin Luther King Jr., they were still under the belief that the Rydberg drawings of 1964 represented the official record of the wounds inflicted on President Kennedy?

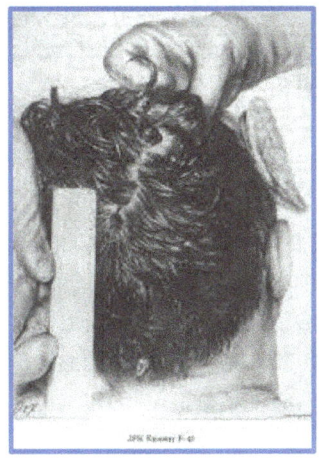

Dox 1

It is highly doubtful given Rydberg's attempts to be given an opportunity to correct his drawings and set the record straight.

Yet, the black and white renditions sketched by Ida Dox strangely mirror the less sophisticated drawings by Rydberg. How are we to explain this?

In a Q&A with Dr. David Mantik for this author's website (see Resources), the radiation oncology expert reports that Ida Dox based her diagrams on extensive discussions with Dr. Michael Baden, who chaired the medical panel for the HSCA hearings.

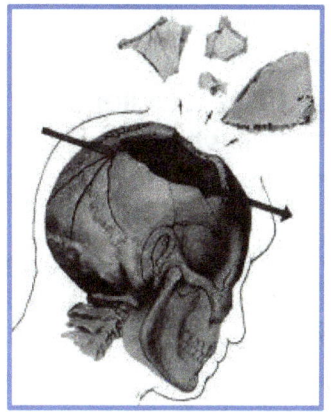

Dox 2

Dox thereby becomes the second medical illustrator to go by the verbal direction of a doctor rather than be allowed

271

to examine the original autopsy photographs in order to craft drawings of the wounds that would be presented by a government investigation as factually accurate.

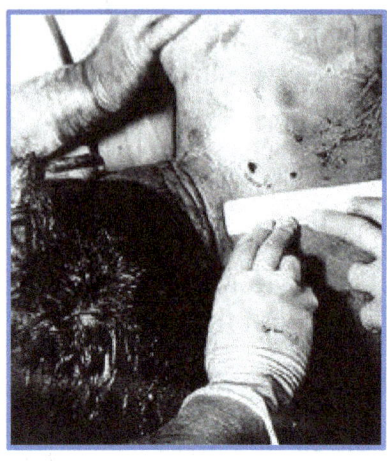

Dox 3

This is even more problematic for Dox than it was for Rydberg in 1964 since, as Dr. Cyril Wecht puts it, *"the autopsy photographs given to Dr. Baden were forgeries."*

While the information relayed to Dox by Dr. Baden was correct based on what he saw in photos, for the same reasons stated in the Rydberg matter earlier, the JFK wounds depicted in the three Dox diagrams are mistakenly located as follows:

Dox 1

In the Dox 1 diagram on the previous page, the ruler measures a bullet entry wound at the rear crown area of the skull whereas Rydberg places this wound noticeably more lower and to the right.

Even if there was a bullet entry wound at the back of Kennedy's head where Rydberg places it, such a wound would not have been visible because of the extensive 'blow-out' damage to the rear of his head in the same location as reported by all the medical professionals.

Dox drawing #1 fails to show this massive wound to the

back of the skull, instead placing the exit wound above JFK's right ear. No doctor or nurse who saw or treated President Kennedy say they observed a gaping wound at his right temple.

Dox 2

The Dox 2 illustration on page 271 coincides with Dox 1 in that it shows a bullet entry from the rear and an explosive exit wound at the right-top of the head.

However, to be nit-picky, the exit wound depicted in Dox 2 is more toward the top of the head where we see the surgeon's hand in Dox 1.

This is higher than the exit wound drawn in Dox 1 or Rydberg sketch CE 388, which appears to be at the side of the head closer to his right ear. A minor imperfection, you say?

Since both the Warren Report and HSCA Report present these illustrations as evidence of these shots coming from the so-called 'Oswald' window, why shouldn't we expect either set of diagrams to be highly accurate?

Dox 3

The Dox 3 diagram on page 272 further creates doubt about the Single Bullet Theory despite efforts by the HSCA to support it.

Notice that we now have three different versions of the non-lethal bullet entry wound on JFK:

1) **CE 385** – Rydberg sketch shows bullet entry at the collar line of the neck, not the upper back. This makes the 'Single Bullet Theory' possible.

2) **Dox 3** – This diagram shows a bullet entry wound high in the upper back, not the neck. This makes the 'Single Bullet Theory' highly improbable.

3) **Official Autopsy Face Sheet** – The only sketch of this important wound done with the body present shows a bullet entry wound in the back, a full 5 ¾ inches below Rydberg's CE 385 and approximately 4 ½ inches below the entry point shown in Dox 3. The face sheet makes the 'Single Bullet Theory' impossible.

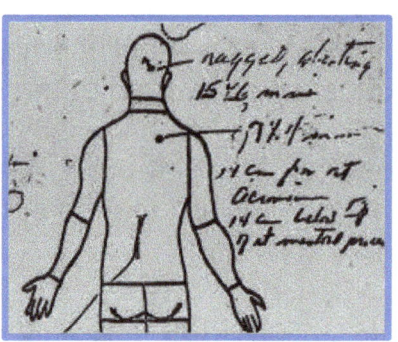

JFK Autopsy face sheet prepared by Dr. J. Thornton Boswell.

Which diagram of this wound do you believe is accurate?

Unfortunately for the historical record, both panels dismissed the actual autopsy report and accepted the diagrams done by their respective hired illustrators, neither of whom were allowed to see the authentic autopsy photographs to guarantee the accuracy of their work.

But there is good news.

As discussed in Chapter 16, JFK autopsy photos still reside in the National Archives, as do altered autopsy photographs.

Modern advancements are making it possible to distinguish between the authentic and fake photos.

Altered photographs can mean only one thing – an effort to cover-up the true nature of the wounds inflicted on President Kennedy.

The evidence is there for an investigative body to examine, which is why such an inquiry on this topic should include experts on the lone gunman and multiple gunmen side of the issue.

Chapter 15

Ghosts of Witnesses Passed:

They May Be Deceased but the Many Ignored Witnesses of 11/22/63 Can Still Tell Us How JFK Was Assassinated!

"I do believe that when at least seven witnesses stated that they saw a puff of smoke on the knoll at the instant the shots were fired and fifty-eight persons state they heard shots coming from that direction, it is reasonable to infer that the puff may have come from a gun fired at the President."

- Mark Lane (1968)

Of the many egregious displays of negligence by the Warren Commission, the blatant disregard of hundreds of witnesses to the crime in Dealey Plaza proves intent to frame Lee Oswald as the '**lone**' assassin of President Kennedy.

At any crime scene involving death by homicide,

investigators routinely search door-to-door if need be in hopes that someone saw something of relevance.

Here, more than 600 people rendezvoused at a small plaza in Dallas and witnessed history they could never have imagined.

The vast majority of witnesses to President Kennedy's murder never got to tell anyone what they saw or heard except family and friends.

Mere dozens of onlookers were interviewed by the Dallas police or FBI in the days following the assassination. For almost all of them, that's as far as it went.

And unless a witness saw or heard the shots come from the upper floor of the Texas School Book Depository building, his or her testimony was of little interest to the Warren Commission.

Granted, eyewitness and earwitness testimony can prove to be unreliable in a court of law. You and I can be standing next to each other as total strangers, witness a crime not far from us and see or hear it differently.

However, upon questioning by prosecution or defense councils, witness testimony can still be integral to conviction or exoneration of the accused.

Lee Oswald never received that staple of jurisprudence in a courtroom and he was most certainly victimized by a Commission investigation that welcomed all witnesses in support of his guilt and virtually ignored almost all witnesses suggestive of his innocence – or at the very least witnesses whose testimony inferred that he was not a 'lone' assassin.

Where the Dallas police, FBI and Warren Commission failed, we can thank local newspaper reporters like Penn Jones Jr. and independent researchers like Mark Lane for getting so many more witnesses on the public record.

As you will later read, their collective recollections do not support the Warren Report findings about the events of 11/22/63.

STAR WITNESS?

The Commission concluded that Oswald was the 'lone' assassin despite the shaky testimony of its 'Star' witness.

Howard Brennan testified that as he heard the shots, he looked up at the Book Depository building and saw a man with a rifle at the southeast sixth-floor corner window whom he waveringly identified later that day as Lee Harvey Oswald.

The Commission accepted Brennan's account of the shooting despite the following problems:

* **Eye Sight Challenges** – Howard Brennan, age 44 at the time, was never asked to demonstrate that he was capable of recognizing the facial features of a person standing almost 100 feet away, never mind having to look sharply upward in bright daylight to see a man mostly in the shadows of a window that wouldn't open more than three feet.

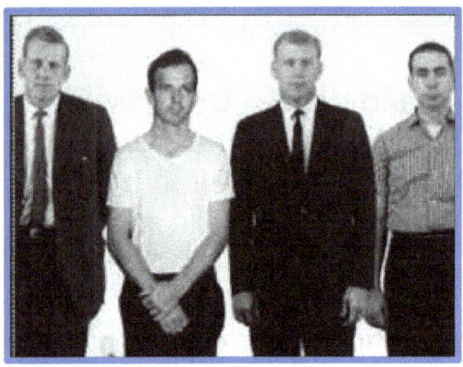

Although Lee Oswald stood out in this police lineup, 'star' witness Howard Brennan could not ID him as the man he saw in the Book Depository assassin's window.

* **Assassin on TV** – Upon identifying Oswald as the man he saw in the sniper's nest window, when asked if he had ever seen the suspect before, Brennan replied that he had seen Oswald in police custody earlier that day on TV.

* **Police Lineup** – When Oswald was paraded in front of Brennan as part of a police lineup, he was not able to pick out Oswald as the man he saw at the window holding a rifle.

How do you think Howard Brennan would have stood up as a 'star' witness to cross examination by Oswald's defense attorney?

In his book The JFK Assassination File, former Dallas Police Chief Jesse Curry glumly conceded that while witnesses like Brennan, Amos Euins and Robert Jackson saw a shooter at the 6th floor window at the time of the assassination, it could not be established that it was Lee Oswald who was at that window at 12:30 p.m.

As detailed in my first book Through The 'Oswald' Window, Dallas police officer Marrion Baker said he confronted Oswald in the second-floor lunchroom no more than 90 seconds after the shots rang out but did not detain him since he looked calm and collected and had the right to be in the building as an employee.

When I re-enacted Oswald's alleged descent down four flights of stairs to the lunchroom, I was able to do it in 90 seconds, but I was noticeably winded, slightly sweaty and flushed of face – nothing like cool, calm and collected Oswald.

Brennan's testimony is countered by a second witness, Oswald's fellow Book Depository employee Carolyn Arnold, who says she saw Oswald down on the first floor mere minutes before the shooting began.

Are we to believe that Oswald managed to rush up to the sixth floor sniper's nest just in time to murder JFK and then rush back down to the second-floor lunchroom to grab a Coca-Cola from the vending machine rather than escape the building immediately?

MAJORITY DOESN'T RULE?

While there are NO witnesses who can place Oswald at the Book Depository sniper's nest at 12:30 p.m. that day, even the circumstantial evidence cited by the Commission to name him the assassin at that window is overwhelmingly debunked by fellow researcher Johnny Cairns in chapters 4,5,6 and 7.

As it relates to eyewitnesses and earwitnesses to the murder of Jack Kennedy, it is equally disturbing to learn that the vast majority of them were dismissed or ignored completely in the Warren Report.

There are dozens of witnesses who place a gunman to

the right-front of the JFK limousine as the shots sounded, including as many as 21 on-duty cops who are trained to distinguish, for instance, motorcycle backfires from gunshots.

It is shocking to learn how many witnesses saw a puff of smoke or heard a shot come from this picket fence on the grassy knoll but were never called before the Warren Commission.

As Mark Lane discovered while interviewing several witnesses the Commission ignored, at least seven people not only heard a sharp report come from the west end of the picket fence atop the grassy knoll, they also saw a corresponding puff of smoke emanate from the trees at that spot.

Two of these witnesses, Sam Holland and Ed Hoffman, did get to report their grassy knoll observations to the Warren Commission, but both were dismissed as not credible.

Had the Commission taken the time to interview the 21 cops in Dealey Plaza who claim a shot came from the knoll or any of the several eyewitnesses and earwitnesses listed below, it could not have as easily dismissed the testimony of Holland and Hoffman.

Not only that, in dismissing Holland and Hoffman, the Commission also decided to ignore a growing list of

JFK Case NOT Closed

From Sam Holland's position on the triple overpass, he heard a shot and saw a puff of smoke come from the fence and trees to his left.

witnesses interviewed by Dallas police, the Sheriff's office or the FBI who reported at least one shot as having come from the knoll to the right-front of the car.

Thankfully, here are several of these witness accounts as well as others tracked down by reporters and researchers in the few short months and years following the assassination:

SILENCED EYE AND EARWITNESSES

Much like Holland and Hoffman, several witnesses heard or saw an indication of a shot fired from the grassy knoll area as follows:

James Leon Simmons – Heard a shot from the picket fence on the knoll and saw a puff of smoke.
Cheryl McKinnon - Heard shots coming from behind her. She hit the ground and looked back and saw smoke lingering in the air in the trees on the knoll.
Thomas Murphy - Heard 4 shots. Thought they came from his left by the trees. Saw smoke there.
Walter Winborn - Saw smoke rise up from under trees on knoll.

Austin Miller - Saw puff of smoke by the trees along picket fence.

The grassy knoll didn't just attract the attention of witnesses in the area like those mentioned above. J.C. Price was sitting on the roof of the Terminal Annex Building overlooking Dealey Plaza.

He told Mark Lane that he thought the shots came from the area of the triple overpass and he then saw a man run along the fence on the knoll toward the Book Depository building. Price talked to the Dallas police but like almost all other witnesses about a possible grassy knoll shooter, he was never called before the Commission.

WITNESS INTIMIDATION

Witnesses who spoke to the FBI or appeared before the Warren Commission whose testimony challenged its 'lone' gunman scenario described their session as anywhere from unpleasant to hostile and intimidating.

Noted reporter for the Dallas Morning News Earl Golz spoke to several witnesses who claim the interrogators challenged their stories and even tried to get them to alter some of the facts.

These included Ronald Fischer, who was standing on the street and looked up just prior to Kennedy arriving. He saw a man in the 6th floor window. Golz reports this run-in with Commission counsel David Belin over his description of the man he saw:

"*He* (Belin) *and I had a fight almost in the interview room over the color of the man's hair. He wanted me to tell him that the man I saw was dark-headed but I wouldn't do it.*"

The spat started when Fischer was shown photos of Oswald's hair; "*The hair doesn't appear to me in the photographs to be as light as the man I saw and that's what Belin was upset about.*"

Belin also seemed agitated when Fischer noted that the man he saw in the window "*seemed transfixed on the triple underpass*" while most people were looking the other way for the motorcade. Not all witnesses who placed a shooter in the 6th floor Book Depository window incriminated Oswald as a **'lone'** assassin.

Both Ruby Henderson and Carolyn Walther told Commission investigators that they saw TWO men in the 6th floor window only a few minutes before the cavalcade arrived.

Their account would later be affirmed by the Charlie Bronson film that showed more than one figure in and around the sixth floor window. If Oswald was one of those men, it appears he had an accomplice.

When both women described the men's clothing, neither matched what Oswald was known to be wearing that day. That's when things got a bit testy.

"*The FBI tried to make me think that what I saw were boxes,*" stated Walther. "*They were going to set out to prove me a liar and I had no intention of arguing with them and being harassed.*"

SELECTIVE TESTIMONY

Golz also located a witness whose testimony went from potential bombshell to suppressed. Carolyn Johnston worked on the second floor of the Book Depository. Just five minutes before the shots started at 12:30, as she was heading out to watch the parade, Johnston says she saw Lee Oswald on the second floor near the lunchroom.

Despite being interviewed twice by the FBI, when the Warren Report was released, she was surprised that her testimony made no mention of her seeing Oswald on the second floor minutes before the shooting.

This validates the testimony of Carolyn Arnold, who says she saw Oswald on the first floor of the Book Depository only a few minutes before the shots rang out. While Johnston's testimony was suppressed, Arnold's testimony was merely dismissed as incorrect.

However, with the support of Johnston's claim of seeing Oswald on the second floor just before Kennedy passed by the Book Depository, we may have a bombshell after all.

Noted researcher Robert Groden found a witness who potentially destroys the notion of Lee Oswald being the assassin at the window named after him.

In his 2013 book JFK: Absolute Proof, Groden presents a witness who verifies Oswald's alibi that he was in the second-floor lunchroom at the time of the shooting.

Groden calls Geraldine Reid *"the single most important*

witness in the Kennedy case." He promised to keep her story a secret until her death because after testifying before the Commission, what she said was so damaging to the Commission's conclusion that Oswald acted alone, "*I was threatened to keep my mouth shut, or else.*"

Robert Groden's work as a film expert and researcher has seriously shattered the credibility of the Warren Report.

As Groden tells it, "*About one minute before the fatal shots were fired at the motorcade, Lee Oswald walked into the office across the second floor hallway from the snack room where he had been eating his lunch. He wanted to buy a bottle of soda and did not have the required change for the machine. He walked up to Geraldine Reid at her desk and handed her a dollar bill and asked her for change.*"

Reid recounts their exchange as follows – "*As I was counting out the change, I heard what I later learned were gunshots. Mr. Oswald and I looked at each other quizzically for a moment, but neither of us said anything about the sounds. I did not know that they were shots at the time. I gave Mr. Oswald the change and he turned and walked back into the hallway toward the snack room. That's the last time I saw him until he passed by me a few minutes later as he was leaving the building.*"

Good luck finding any word of Reid's ill-timed encounter with Oswald in the Warren Report, but Groden says that he has verified that her account appears in still classified documents.

The Commission quickly learned that another effective way to control the narrative of witnesses to the Kennedy assassination was to take the position that they didn't exist.

One example is Johnny Powell, an inmate at the county jail who watched the parade pass by below him. His position was identical to the height of the 6th floor Book Depository window, directly adjacent to where the shots are said to have been fired.

Powell and several other inmates in a cell overlooking Houston and Elm Streets, were waiting for the motorcade to arrive. At 12:24 p.m., Powell said he saw 'two' men with a rifle in the 6th floor Book Depository window.

One of the men seemed to be adjusting a scope on the rifle. Although several other inmates witnessed the assassination and could verify Powell's account, when authorities were told about the vantage point of Powell and his fellow inmates, none of them were ever questioned by the Dallas police, FBI or the Commission.

THE SOUNDS OF MULTIPLE GUNMEN!

The much disputed police dictabelt tape recording of four apparent shots in Dealey Plaza has been re-authenticated in first generation researcher Josiah Thompson's 2021 book Last Second in Dallas.

The police dictabelt tape turned over to the HSCA by

famed researcher Mary Farrell caused the 1978 panel to conclude that a shot came from the grassy knoll to the right-front of the car but missed JFK.

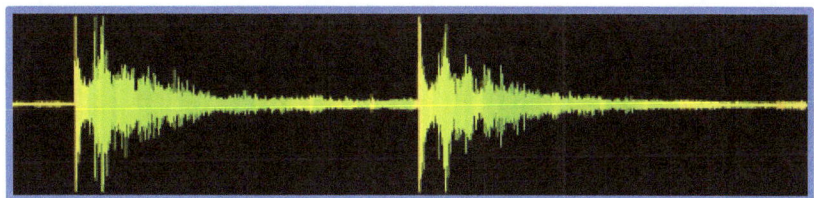

Since the HSCA report, experts have debated the authenticity of the dictabelt recording. Thompson's latest study will surely add to the controversy despite claiming to be definitive proof of the shots fired in Dealey Plaza.

Any new official inquiry will have to re-visit the dictabelt recording evidence, given its relevance to the claim of more than one gunman, but what about the sounds of the shots heard by dozens of earwitnesses at the scene of the crime?

Although much less scientific than the acoustical evidence of the dictabelt recording, the sheer volume of earwitnesses reporting a common audio observation cannot be ignored even though virtually all of them are now deceased.

Very few of these witnesses talked to the Dallas police, the Dallas County Sheriff's Office, the FBI or the Warren Commission, but what they heard was not allowed to be ignored thanks to newspaper reporters and independent researchers like Thompson and Mark Lane.

After the Warren Report release in 1964, several

witnesses to the Kennedy assassination were tracked down and given a voice for the first time by investigative reporters and researchers.

A BIG HEARING PROBLEM
FOR WARREN COMMISSION

The major issue of earwitnesses in Dealey Plaza isn't just the number of shots or where they came from. Witnesses reported as few as two shots and as many as nine shots in those history-changing seconds.

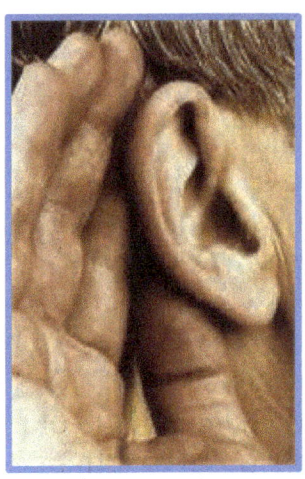

A majority of earwitnesses heard three shots, which the Commission was quick to embrace since it confirmed their assertion that Oswald fired a total of three shots from the Book Depository window.

However, even for those earwitnesses who thought the shots they heard came from the Book Depository 6th floor window, their testimony proved to be extremely problematic for the Commission.

It is the spacing of those three shots heard by the majority of earwitnesses that, in fact, prove that the 6th floor Book Depository gunman could NOT have fired those shots on his own!

Collectively, here's how a high percentage of earwitnesses heard those three shots in Dealey Plaza when JFK was assassinated:

BANG - - - - BANG - BANG

With each dash representing one second of elapsed time, we now realize why the Commission chose to disregard the earwitness testimony of virtually everyone at the scene.

The second and third shots could not possibly have come from the same rifle, namely the 'Oswald' Mannlicher-Carcano found near the 6th floor southeast corner Book Depository window. Why?

The FBI test-fired the Mannlicher and determined that the 'minimum' firing time between shots was 2.3 seconds. Yet, the sounds of gunfire reported by most of the earwitnesses have the second and third shots being no more than one second apart – a physical impossibility for Oswald or anyone using the rifle found near the Book Depository sniper's nest.

A possible fourth shot is a different argument but does not change the fact that shots two and three were too close together to have been fired from the same 'Oswald rifle.'

The Warren Commission and it's chief investigative arm, the FBI, were not choosy in ignoring earwitness testimony. Kennedy special assistant Kenneth O'Donnell, riding in the Secret Service car, told the FBI the shots come from *"in front of the car."*

Let's start with other people you may be familiar with. Some got to testify before the Commission only to have their testimony dismissed as not credible (see chapter 15 in Resources):

BILL GREER – (Secret Service agent driving JFK limousine) – "*It seemed like the first one, and then there was, you know, bang, bang, just right behind it almost. The two seemed, the last two seemed, closer to me than the other.*"

BONNIE RAY WILLIAMS – (On the fifth floor, directly below sniper's window) – "*I remembered three shots, because there was a pause between the first two shots. There was two real quick. There were three shots.*"

EARLE CABELL – (Mayor, four cars behind the Presidential limousine) – "*There was a longer pause between the first and second shots than there was between the second and third shots. They were in rather rapid succession.*"

FORREST SORRELS – (in front of JFK in the lead Secret Service car) – "*On the first shot, it was too sharp to be a backfire of an automobile. It just didn't sound like that at all. And then, of course, the other two coming as quickly as they did.*"

JAMES TAGUE – (Near the triple overpass. After the first shot) "Then there was a pause and then the crack-crack of two rifle shots."

LADY BIRD JOHNSON – (in the Vice-Presidential car, two cars behind the Presidential limousine) – "*And suddenly there was a loud report - a shot... Then a moment and two more shots in rapid succession.*"

LEE BOWERS – (in tower in railroad yard behind the grassy knoll) - "*I heard three shots. One, then a slight pause, then two very close together.*"

RALPH YARBOROUGH – (Senator in the Vice Presidential car, two cars behind the Presidential limousine) – "*To me there seemed to be a long time between the first and second shots, a much shorter time between the second and third shots.*" Yarborough further stated: "*I smelled gunpowder as the car drove away through the underpass.*"

ROBERT JACKSON – (In the press car on Houston Street) – "*The second two shots seemed much closer together than the first shot.*"

ROBERT MACNEIL – NBC News journalist on the press bus – "*There was a bang and we asked was that a shot? We had time for that exchange and then there were two shots close together.*"

ROY KELLERMAN – (Secret Service agent in JFK limousine describing the second and third shots) – "*It was like a double bang: Bang,Bang.*"

Here are other witnesses in Dealey Plaza whose testimony was ignored by the Commission:

CAROLYN WALTHER – (on the east side of Houston Street, near corner of Elm Street) – "*There was a pause after this first report, then a second and third report almost at the same time.*"

CLYDE HAYGOOD – (motorcycle policeman on Houston Street at the time of the shots) – "*The last two were closer than the first. In other words, it was the first, then a pause, and then the other two were real close.*"

GARLAND SLACK – (on Houston Street, between Elm and Main Streets) – "*Heard two shots in rapid succession.*"

GEORGE HICKEY – (Secret Service agent in the follow-up car) – "*I heard two reports which I thought were *shots and that appeared to me completely different in sound than the first report and were in such rapid succession that there seemed to be practically no time element between them."*

JAMES CRAWFORD – (on the south-east corner of Elm and Houston streets) – *"The second shot followed some seconds, a little time elapsed after the first one, and followed very quickly by the third one."*

LINDA WILLIS – (on the south side of Elm Street, opposite the Stemmons Freeway sign) – *"I heard one. Then there was a little bit of time, and then there were two real fast bullets together."*

LUKE MOONEY – (Deputy Sheriff, at the corner of Main and Houston Streets) – *"The second and third shot was pretty close together, but there was a short lapse there between the first and second shot."*

MARY MITCHELL – (on the southeast corner of Elm and Houston Streets) – *"After a short pause of four or five seconds, there were two more rapid explosions."*

PEARL SPRINGER – (near Houston and Elm intersection) – *" After the first shot, there was a pause, then two shots fired close together."*

RUTH THORNTON – (from a window in the Criminal Courts Building) – *"Two more reports followed* (the first shot) *in quick succession."*

SEYMOUR WEITZMAN – (Dallas police officer, on the corner of Main and Houston Streets) – *"First one, then the second two seemed to be simultaneously."*

WILLIAM MCINTYRE – (Secret Service agent in the follow-up car) – *"The Presidential vehicle was approximately 200 feet from the underpass when the first shot was fired, followed in quick succession by two more."*

WINSTON LAWSON – (Secret Service agent in the lead

car ahead of the President's car) – *"There was one report, and a pause, then two more reports closer together, two and three were closer together than one and two."*

There are at least another 20 eyewitnesses and earwitnesses in addition to the 35 witnesses named above who place at least one shot coming from the grassy knoll area to the right-front of the limousine.

Some were interviewed about what they saw or heard by the Dallas Police Department and it went no further than that.

Others gave sworn statements to the FBI, which did the majority of investigative work for the Commission. For almost all of them, their next contact came from local newspaper reporters or independent researchers.

Only a handful of these witnesses ever got to tell their story to the Warren Commission and EVERY ONE of them were dismissed as mistaken or were blatantly ignored.

Two key witnesses never called before the Commission were Gayle and Billy Newman who were mere feet away from JFK when the fatal shot was fired.

Along with their two young children, the Newman's were standing near the curb on Elm Street as the limousine drove past them.

Both parents report hearing a shot come from behind them (in the vicinity of the grassy knoll) and seeing the bullet strike President Kennedy in the side of his head.

JFK Case NOT Closed

Billy Newman actually heard the bullet whiz by his ear and instinctively told his wife to grab the kids and hit the ground because he feared his family was in the line of fire.

When the Newman family instinctively hit the ground after believing a shot from behind them killed JFK, their reaction drew the attention of news cameramen.

The Newman family were the closest witnesses to President Kennedy when the fatal head shot missed them en route to him. They were independently interviewed by the FBI and gave a sworn affidavit to the Dallas County Sheriff's Office but were never called to testify before the Commission hearings!

New Orleans District Attorney Jim Garrison didn't ignore them when he called Gayle and Billy Newman to testify at the Clay Shaw trial in 1969 as he tried to show a conspiracy to kill President Kennedy on 11/22/63.

WEIGHING THE WITNESS TESTIMONY

So, the question becomes: All these years later, must any new official inquiry into the JFK assassination ignore these witnesses as the Warren Commission did almost 60 years ago?

It is easy to say yes because almost every one of them is deceased and took what they witnessed to the grave...or did they?

Almost every witness named here either:

- A) Gave testimony under oath to the FBI.
- B) Made a sworn affidavit before the Dallas County Sheriff's Department.
- C) Freely put what they saw or heard on the public record of a newspaper, TV station or radio station.
- D) Gave an audio or video recording interview of what they saw or heard in Dealey Plaza on 11/22/63.

A rare few had their account of what happened to President Kennedy accepted into the Warren Commission record only to have their testimony, at odds the eventual findings, ignored, dismissed or suppressed.

What makes the testimony of the above witnesses so compelling is that what they saw or heard that tragic day in Dallas didn't die with them.

Their testimony is on the public record be it government files, police files, news media reports and even taped interviews by respected historical researchers.

How can we dismiss, even all these years later, the overwhelming consistency of what they saw or heard – a shot that came from the right-front of the car?

We know why they were ignored in 1963. To believe them back then would have, at the very least, helped prove that Lee Oswald was not a '**lone**' assassin that day.

Nothing less than history as we know it would be different.

Can these witnesses speak from their graves in any effectual way to a new formal investigation?

Perhaps it's just as effective to validate their testimony as factually correct, which the next two chapters just may do.

Using modern technologies, what if it can be established that the kill shot these witnesses heard, and the result they saw, had to have come from exactly where they believed it came?

Chapter 16

How Advancement in Imaging Proves JFK Autopsy Photos and X-Rays Were Altered to Frame Oswald as a 'Lone' Assassin!

Technology is the truth's best friend when applied to the JFK assassination.

Radiation oncologist Dr. David Mantik applied an optical densitometry technology not available in 1963 to the JFK autopsy X-rays and discovered history-challenging results.

With almost all of the witnesses, investigators of the crime and others associated with the Kennedy murder in 1963 now dead, must we finally accept the Warren Report as the official explanation of what happened in Dealey Plaza?

Absolutely not! Thanks to advancements in technology, nearly 60 years later, we might be closer to learning the truth than ever before.

This chapter, as well as the next, highlight modern

technologies that were not available in 1963. This chapter details an imaging technique performed on the Kennedy autopsy x-rays three decades later that has revealed a sinister attempt by the U.S. government to frame Lee Oswald as a 'lone nut' assassin.

Chapter 17 chronicles new technologies being applied to the crime scene in Dealey Plaza precisely as it existed on November 22, 1963, that promises shocking revelations about the murder of JFK when the project becomes public in and around the 60th anniversary date.

The point of these two reports is to demonstrate that emerging technologies are our best bet to one day discover the truth about the events of 11/22/63.

Thanks to the visionaries and experts who applied these advancements to the JFK assassination evidence, it may be such independent researchers who correct the history books.

One example of technology in medicine created after 1963 involves applying a technique called optical densitometry to existing x-rays.

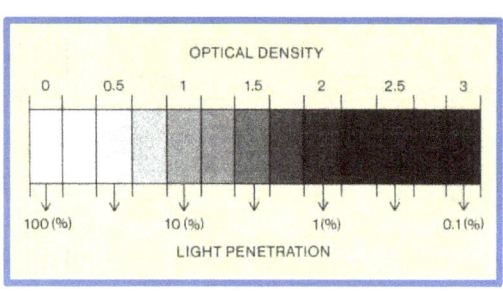

Dr. David Mantik, a board-certified radiation oncologist based in Rancho Mirage, California who has treated thousands of cancer patients, was the first specialist to apply optical densitometry to the JFK autopsy x-rays during nine separate visits to the Archives.

As one of the expert contributors in the book Assassination Science, Dr. Mantik explains the Optical Densitometry technique as follows:

"It measures the transmission of ordinary light through selected points of the x-ray film. If I had measured thousands of points (using a densitometer), *I could construct a three-dimensional topographic map of the x-rays...*

"In a way, therefore, the information contained in an x-ray film is converted from two dimensions into three dimensions and is that much richer in detail.

"The range of peaks and valleys on such a topographic map would be expected to fall within a well-defined range for a normal human skull. Any values which lie unnaturally far outside – would not be consistent with ordinary skulls and would raise questions of authenticity."

The Optical Densitometry (OD) measurements Dr. Mantık performed on the lateral (side view) JFK x-ray in the Archive were not only far greater than what he was accustomed to seeing in thousands of his own cancer patients, he was able to compare apples to apples by viewing a quality photo print of a lateral x-ray taken of JFK's head before 11/22/63.

The Kennedy lateral x-ray taken prior to November of 1963 showed normal OD readings whereas the post mortem x-ray showed obvious evidence of being physically altered.

As Dr. Mantik notes in Assassination Science, *"In an x-ray, the whiter areas represent denser tissue such as* bone. *This is because fewer x-rays strike the film, and during the development process, this area turns relatively lucent.*

"On the other hand, less dense tissues permit more x-rays to pass through to the film and these areas then become dark.

"With that in mind, I shall turn to the JFK autopsy x-rays. On the skull x-rays taken from the side – they are called lateral x-rays – in the rear portion, there is an obvious large white area that is easy to see on both the right and left skull x-rays.

"By contrast," Dr. Mantik continues, *"In the frontal area, the x-ray is usually dark. When I first saw these two areas, I was struck both by how extremely white and how extremely black they looked.*

"Both areas looked very different from what I was used to seeing in my own patients," noting that the differences in optical densities between the front and back is almost always very small.

However, in the JFK autopsy lateral x-ray Dr. Mantik observed, the posterior white area transmits almost 100 times more light than the dark area.

Whereas the Kennedy autopsy x-ray showed extreme differences in whiteness and darkness, the photo of the earlier Kennedy x-ray, which can't be subjected to OD measurements because it is a photograph of an x-ray, appeared normal with very little variance between the back and front segments of the skull, much like normal x-rays of his patients.

STUNNING EXPERT OBSERVATIONS

What do hundreds of optical densitometry measurements on the JFK autopsy x-rays by Dr. Mantik tell us? The Warren Commission's account of the fatal head wound sustained by President Kennedy was wrong!

Dr. Mantik was also able to establish that the 'official' autopsy photos and X-rays had been *"critically altered"* in the hours after the body left Parkland Hospital.

The radiology expert's bombshell observations provide a viable explanation as to why JFK's body was forcibly and illegally removed from local authorities and subjected to a post-mortem examination by unqualified military pathologists at the Bethesda Naval Hospital in Maryland.

Had local laws been adhered to, Dallas County Medical Examiner at the time, Dr. Earl Rose, would have conducted a professional forensic post-mortem examination of the President's body with no outside influence.

Tragically for history, we now know that three military "general hospital" pathologists who had never before conducted an autopsy involving death by gunshot submitted a seriously flawed and incomplete autopsy report which became the official record.

Dr. (Colonel) Pierre Finck, one of the three attending pathologists, would reveal to the House Select Committee on Assassinations (HSCA) that there was more hampering the team's post-mortem examination than inexperience.

When Dr. Finck went to dissect the President's back to ascertain the trajectory of a possible bullet that struck the victim 5 ¾ inches below the collar line and slightly to the right of the spinal column, his procedure was abruptly halted by a military superior present at the autopsy.

Civilian pathologist Dr. Earl Rose, if he had conducted a thorough post-mortem procedure per Texas state law, could not have been halted by such a military directive.

The consequence of this order by a military superior at the autopsy was the unfounded fabrication of the 'Single Bullet Theory' that the Commission relied heavily upon in naming Lee Harvey Oswald as the 'lone' assassin of JFK.

X-RAYS DEBUNK
SINGLE BULLET THEORY!

To attribute the assassination to one individual, the bullet that apparently entered Kennedy's upper back is required to have exited his throat and travelled on to cause all the non-fatal wounds suffered by Governor John Connally.

This scenario was necessary because Connally is seen in the Zapruder film physically reacting so soon after Kennedy reacts to his non-fatal wounds, only two possibilities exist:

1. **Same Bullet** – All seven non-lethal wounds on the two men were caused by the same bullet (CE 399) or…
2. **Separate Bullets** – Governor Connally was hit by a second separate bullet fired almost simultaneously to the first shot.

The Commission, based mainly on the autopsy findings, had to adopt point #1 or admit that at least two gunmen fired at the President, hence a conspiracy.

However, over the years, Dr. Humes changed his testimony from what he gave to the Warren Commission in 1964.

After defending the Single Bullet Theory (SBT) less enthusiastically before the HSCA hearings in 1977 and 1978, by the time he appeared before the Assassination Records Review Board in 1996, he conceded the implausibility of the SBT because the entry wound in JFK's back was at least five inches lower than the supposed exit wound at the throat.

As Dr. Mantik points out in his Future of Freedom webinar on April 27, 2021, which couldn't have escaped Dr. Humes in preparing his autopsy report, the 'upward' flightpath of the bullet while inside JFK's body, in order for the SBT to be possible, would have caused damage to Kennedy's upper right lung and fractured his spinal cord, neither of which happened!

Not only does Dr. Mantik, based on his expert findings rather than speculation, call the Single Bullet Theory *"utter nonsense,"* he says the JFK autopsy X-rays reveal a much more sinister attempt by high authorities to place sole blame on Oswald.

DELIBERATE ALTERING OF X-RAY EVIDENCE

The application of Optical Densitometry establishes that some X-rays were altered, thus enabling the Warren Commission to pin the murder solely on Oswald who was above and behind the limousine.

Dr. Mantik discovered proof of a cover-up to hide a wound that would have established, with certainty, a gunman to the front of the President.

While Dr. Mantik notes that an autopsy x-ray does not show this particular "*entry wound,*" it does show an incision at the left forehead which obscures the actual wound.

"*We know with certainty, based on eyewitnesses, that this incision did not exist in Dallas. So, somewhere after Parkland, this incision was deliberately created,*" reveals Dr. Mantik. "*Only one possible reason exists for this: It was intended to obscure the entry wound at this site. Even Boswell* (one of the three autopsy surgeons) *admitted that the forehead contained an 'incised wound.' It does not get much clearer than that.*"

This history-changing discovery was verified by noted neurologist Dr. Michael Chesser who also examined the JFK autopsy materials extensively.

Dr. Chesser found evidence of an "*incised wound*" on JFK's right forehead at his hairline that was not discovered by any of the doctors and nurses at Parkland

Hospital, thus indicating that the surgery took place 'after' the body left Dallas.

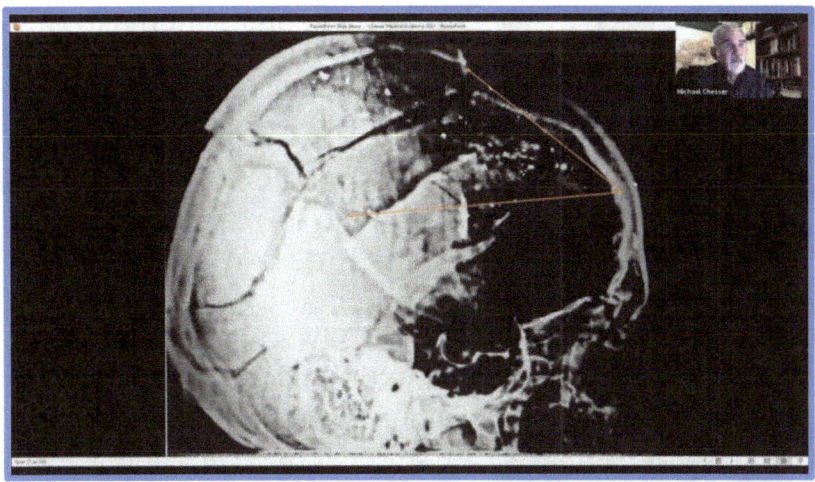

When a trail of metallic fragments in JFK's head was noted by the autopsy surgeons (inside orange arrow), Dr. Chesser says the Commission erroneously claimed the debris came from a shot from behind.

On a head x-ray, Dr. Chesser found a corresponding flightpath of a projectile that almost traversed the entire length of the skull that shows a trail of fragments discarded along its path.

The debris deposits, Dr. Chesser notes, had to have come from a bullet transiting Kennedy's head on a front-to-back trajectory.

SCHEMATIC DRAWINGS TO HIDE WOUNDS

The most glaring examples of a conspiracy to cover-up certain shots in Dealey Plaza to frame Oswald as the '**lone**' assassin of JFK is the Warren Commission and

HSCA's use of medical illustrators to unwittingly misrepresent the wounds on JFK (see chapter 14).

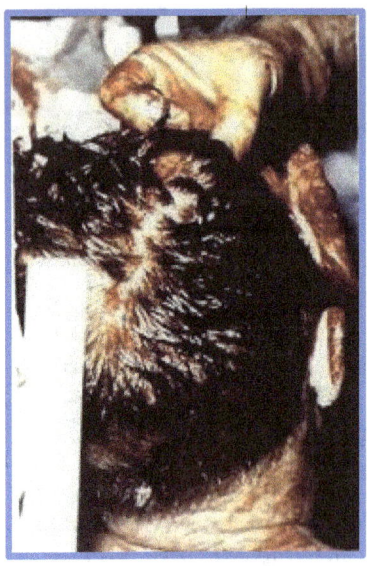

This drawing by Ida Dox for the HSCA shows a bullet entry wound near the top of the ruler and an exit wound above the right ear that does not match an autopsy photo shown below.

One particular schematic drawing for the HSCA by Ida Dox (at left) was presented by the HSCA as an accurate representation of a bullet entry wound to the rear crown area of the President's head.

This drawing not only infers that the bullet that caused this wound came from above and behind, it depicts a large exit wound above the right ear to denote that the President was killed by this one shot.

However, the black and white autopsy photograph on the next page, showing a massive blow-out wound at the back of Kennedy's head, is not only verified by more than a dozen medical professionals in Trauma Room 1, Dr. Mantik says the autopsy X-rays subjected to Optical Densitometry show an attempt to hide this exit wound entirely.

Is it really possible that a gaping exit wound the size of a fist at the right rear occipital region of Kennedy's head as reported by several medical professionals is nothing more than a collective fabrication?

Not only does Dr. Mantik refer to the X-rays as factual proof of the rear head exit wound, he reveals physical tampering associated with the critical X-rays and photographs:

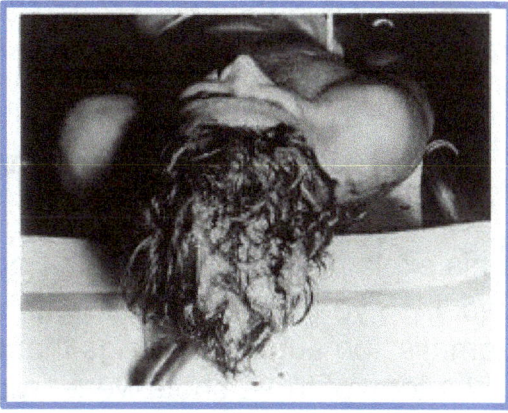

"The X-rays are in excellent agreement with the eyewitnesses, including Dr. McClelland (below).

Drawings by two different medical illustrators fail to show this massive wound to the top and back of JFK's head. Why?

"The photographs of the back of the head show no occipital wound. Of course, they (photos) can only show scalp and therefore they can tell us nothing about underlying bone, which McClelland says was missing. (The X-rays agree with McClelland).

Dr. Robert McClelland points to where he observed a gaping exit wound on the President's head.

"In any case, the image pair of the back of the head yields only a 2D image (precisely where the medical witnesses observed a large hole), so we know that the images are not trustworthy.

"Furthermore, the HSCA discovered that the images could not be matched to the camera/lens combination actually used at the autopsy, so the Forensic Pathology Panel was misled about the reliability of the photographs."

CONTINUING COVER-UP!

This explains why the HSCA's Forensic Pathology Panel, 15 years later, agreed with the Warren Commission autopsy findings that led to the conclusion that a total of three shots were fired by Oswald from above and behind.

The panel of medical experts, headed by Dr. Michael Baden, was duped into believing that the fake autopsy photographs and altered X-rays given to them by the HSCA were authentic. They weren't!

With no imaging evidence to support the large gaping exit wound at the right rear of JFK's head, Dr. Badan unknowingly used the doctored photographs to guide Ida Dox into drawing the erroneous image you see on page 308 as well as others.

This is what Dr. Mantik and photography expert and famed JFK assassination researcher Robert Groden discovered when they conducted stereo viewing of the photograph of the back of the skull. This doctored photo is what Dr. Baden referenced in having Dox re-create it as a more tasteful illustration for publication in the HSCA Report.

"The chief candidate for alteration, of course, is the back

of the head photograph," says Dr. Mantik. "*Stereo viewing of this site shows that the expected 3D image does not result.*

"*This can only mean that two 'identical' images were pasted onto both members of the photographic pair,*" says Dr. Mantik. "*The schemers, instead, should have inserted a slightly different image into each member of the pair – this would have yielded a genuine 3D image via stereo viewing.*"

Further, Dr. Mantik argues that the photograph in the Archives of the back of JFK's head is "*embarrassing*" in its lack of accuracy.

He bases that on a photograph of the back of JFK's head taken that same morning in Fort Worth, which he presents in the Conclusions section of his JFK Assassination Survey.

The altered photos and X-rays of the exit wound at the right rear of Kennedy's head examined by Drs. Wecht, Mantik, Chesser and Aguilar is conclusive evidence of multiple gunmen, conspiracy and the resulting cover-up, especially when combined with affirming eyewitness testimony of multiple medical experts at Parkland.

What is also coming to light is just how quickly the alteration of evidence began on 11/22/63. Lead autopsy surgeon James Humes may have been an unwitting facilitator at the beginning, but in the days that followed the Kennedy post-mortem, he was knowingly providing investigators with false and misleading evidence and testimony.

At the autopsy, Dr. Humes noted that the cerebellum at the rear of the President's head was damaged, which is affirmed by the observations of more than a dozen medical professionals at Parkland.

Dr. Robert McClelland, a highly skilled surgeon who stood at the end of the gurney with Kennedy's head directly below him, not only identified a large gaping exit wound at the right rear occipital region of the skull as he indicates in the photo on page 309, he witnessed damaged pieces of the cerebellum oozing out onto the gurney.

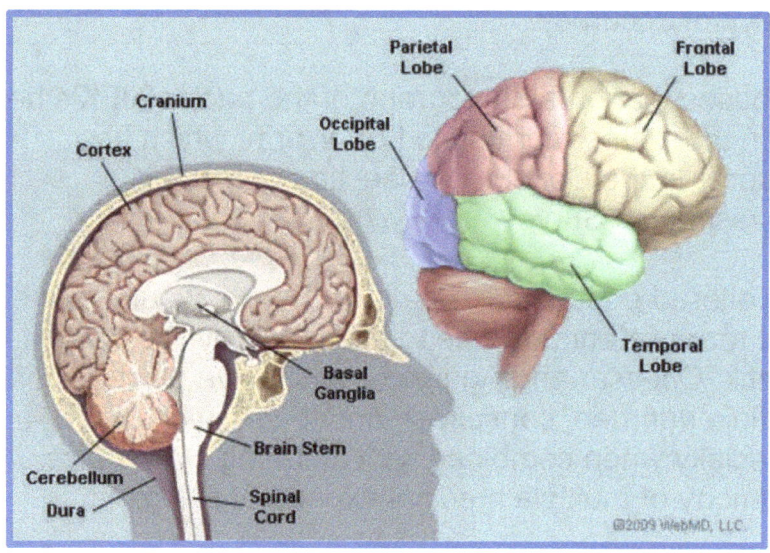

At left, note the Cerebellum at the low end of the brain which was observed to be badly damaged by several Parkland doctors and the autopsy surgeons, yet in the Ida Dox drawing above for the HSCA, the back of the head is completely intact, showing no damage to the Cerebellum or Occipital Lobe. Mysteriously, lead autopsy surgeon James Humes later changed his observation to match the Dox drawing.

What would cause Dr. Humes to change his testimony before the HSCA hearings 15 years later to concur with the fully intact back of JFK's head as drawn by medical illustrator Ida Dox?

TALE OF TWO BRAINS

As the lead autopsy surgeon and author of the official post-mortem report, Humes' official duties did not end on the night of 11/22/63.

Per standard procedure, the President's brain was removed from the skull and placed in a formalin solution intended to preserve the brain and harden it so that at a later date, usually a couple of weeks, the brain can be cut into thin slices to enable the tracking of bullet and/or fragment trajectories.

Obviously, since President Kennedy died as a result of a gunshot or gunshots to the head, results from this examination would have been critical had Oswald lived to stand public trial.

This customary examination never happened. It has been rumored that Robert F. Kennedy had family physician George Burkley take possession of the brain and placed in the coffin with the body for burial at Arlington National Cemetery.

When Dr. Humes went to do the post-autopsy procedure, the brain he was given was fully intact. For reasons only he can explain, the replacement brain formed the basis of his testimony before the HSCA, causing a ripple effect.

The testimony of Dr. Humes of there being no damage to the rear of Kennedy's head other than a small entry wound affirmed the illustration by Ida Dox, which is what the forensic panel accepted as fact in concluding that the President died as a result of a single gunshot to the back of the head. Accordingly, the Commission concluded that the kill shot was fired from the 6th floor southeast corner Book Depository window.

MORE SHOCKING EVIDENCE OF ALTERED PHOTOS AND X-RAYS

Much more damning evidence emerges from Dr. Mantik's multiple visits to the National Archives. Here are some of the astonishing revelations he shared with this researcher:

TARGETED ALTERATIONS – From a small incision at the President's upper forehead to more extensive tampering of head X-rays and photos, Dr. Mantik cites these as the most critical aspect of the JFK cover-up, stating *"Had the X-rays shown clear evidence of a frontal head shot, the game would have been over."*

EVIDENCE STILL RELEVANT – Like his application of Optical Densitometry, DNA testing did not exist in 1963 and may now yield benefits in solving this case.

"The Magic Bullet (CE 399) could be assessed for JFK's and Connally's DNA. So could the fragments found in the limousine," suggests Dr. Mantik.

BEST EVIDENCE BURIED FOREVER? – Dr. Mantik says the exhumation of the President's body, which he believes will never happen, would answer key questions.

"CT scans of his body and head would be enormously useful," he offers. *"We could quite precisely evaluate the SBT and we would clearly see where skull bone was missing."*

When this researcher contacted CT manufacturing Research & Development people in Europe, two would only comment off the record that they foresaw a possibility of CT scanners becoming much smaller and mobile in the future.

This would allow a body to be exhumed and remain on site where CT scans could be performed on the body with virtually nothing invasive about the process.

The question becomes: Would this be acceptable to the Kennedy family?

SINGLE BULLET BULLSHIT! – Dr. Mantik agrees with my argument in Through The 'Oswald' Window that the small hole in JFK's throat was neither a bullet entry wound nor exit wound.

His extensive study of the X-rays provides an interesting hint as to what may have caused the controversial throat wound:

"The throat wound was not due to a bullet entry and it was not an exit wound, so no through-and-through trajectory applies here. The throat wound was most likely caused by a glass fragment from the windshield, which did not exit (JFK) *but rather caused the contusion at the top of the **right lung**."*

CHANGING HISTORY?

Dr. Mantik's findings within the National Archives medical evidence could very well help to re-write the history books.

His decades of work are proof that a single advancement in medicine or science can provide new evidentiary tools that could not be applied in 1963.

Whether we believe the Warren Commission was the key instrument in a cover-up or just incredibly incompetent, Dr. Mantik's work, as well as that of fellow scientists like Dr. Gary Aguilar and Dr. Michael Chesser, give us hope that new technology in the right hands will one day solve America's ultimate cold case.

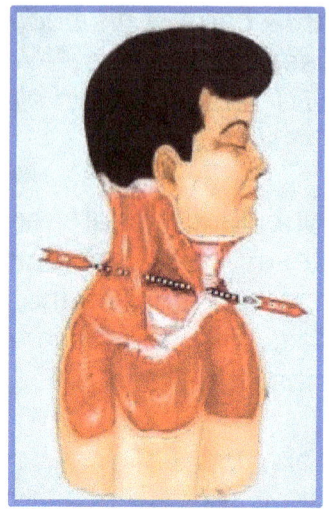

Medical illustrator Harold Rydberg spent the rest of his life trying to correct this diagram he did for the Warren Commission (CE 388) after realizing he was duped into misrepresenting wounds to fit the Single Bullet Theory.

JFK Case NOT Closed

Chapter 17

From Cartoons to Modern 3D Realism: These Evolving Technologies Seek to Finally Tell Us How JFK Was Assassinated

John Orr never could understand why the events in Dallas on 11/22/63 have become more perplexing as the years have passed.

After all, the assassination of President John F. Kennedy was witnessed by hundreds of bystanders in Dealey Plaza.

Dozens of professional and amateur photographers captured virtually every moment with hundreds of clicks of their cameras.

And several home movies visually documented the historic tragic day on everlasting film, none more

317

horrifying than the images we see on the motion pictures taken by Orville Nix and Abraham Zapruder.

With so many ear and eyewitnesses and all the still photos and film images of those few seconds that changed American history forever, why does the Kennedy assassination remain as America's ultimate cold case as the 60th anniversary nears?

As Orr puts it: "*The actual solution is simple. It is straightforward. What got me going as a former prosecutor was that I found it odd that after decades, there was still huge controversy over a very small number of gunshots.*

John Orr and his associates are applying new technologies to accurately capture the fatal moments in Dealey Plaza that took the life of President Kennedy.

"It should have been easy and I found it was easy if you don't get your initial facts wrong. The Warren Commission got many key facts wrong in arriving at its conclusions."

In 1995, while serving as a senior official in the Department of Justice Antitrust Division, Orr submitted a detailed visual reconstruction of the shots in Dealey Plaza to Attorney General Janet Reno in an effort to have her order a new official investigation into the assassination of

President Kennedy.

Orr's report, based on evidence found in the official records, prompted the FBI to conduct some updated scientific testing of certain evidence, but Reno, in essence, buried it.

"As I mentioned in my letter to Janet Reno, about 82% of the American people trusted their government on November 22, 1963 and after that, it went down into the teens at times," **says** Orr. *"This was a true watershed event in American history."*

GROWING TEAM OF TRUTH SEEKERS

It was 2017 when Orr crossed paths with another unstoppable force, both sharing serious doubts about the flawed findings of the Warren Commission Report.

Larry Schnapf, then a Board member with Citizens Against Political Assassinations (CAPA) and Chairman of its Legal Committee, invited Orr to Houston where an Oswald mock trial was taking place.

When the mock trial proceedings had concluded, Orr presented his study of the public execution of JFK as he had detailed in his report "Analysis of Gunshots in Dealey Plaza on November 22, 1963." (See Orr's Houston presentation on YouTube link in Resources section).

Schnapf, independent of CAPA, would join Orr in a non-profit arrangement, bringing his legal expertise and JFK assassination insider knowledge to the project.

Former Chair of the legal committee for CAPA, Larry Schnapf is still working to uncover what happened in Dealey Plaza with John Orr and is trying to have still sealed documents released via court order.

Knowing that the Dealey Plaza project would require the latest, most sophisticated technologies in several fields relative to imagery, Orr reached out to Knott Laboratory Director of Visualization Angelos Leiloglou, who stayed on with this project while starting his own company, Forensic Viz.

Using the latest laser scan technology combined with advancements in photogrammetry and animation, the finished 3D project will precisely document all gunfire trajectories at the crime scene that caused all the wounds sustained by President Kennedy and Governor John Connally.

The visual end result has to be just as exact, so the team recruited the 3D imaging expertise of Visual Law Group CEO Mark Johnson.

Collectively, the project team has poured thousands of their own dollars and countless hours of free time into building a highly accurate and detailed 3D model of every aspect of Dealey Plaza.

To make things official, Orr established DP3D (LLC) as a formal commitment to seek the truth about the shots in Dallas that haunt us to this day. In essence, this group's mission, as paraphrased on Mark Johnson's website jfkforensics.com, is:

Fortunately, today we have forensic tools, techniques and software that did not exist for prior investigations. We have assembled an independent team of experienced and respected forensic technicians and medical experts with the sole mission of applying those tools objectively to the facts of the JFK assassination to derive factual conclusions without bias or prejudice.

The famous Hertz sign atop the Book Depository building, shown here in a temporary generic setting, shows the detail Mark Johnson and the DP3D team is devoting to re-create those fatal moments in Dealey Plaza.
- © DP3D (LLC)

Ever since, the group has worked to construct a visual model of the events in Dealey Plaza down to a few millimeters in painstakingly accurate detail.

With the targeted release date for their documentary set for the 60th anniversary in 2023, the DP3D team is open to other research enthusiasts becoming involved in its project on a not-for-profit or for-profit basis.

Mark Johnson sees an exciting application for the general public – "One objective is to create a truly accurate version of one of this nation's very important historical sites," he says.

"Our model will allow other researchers to test various theories and hypotheses while also providing the opportunity for anyone to experience any view from within Dealey Plaza as it appeared on that fateful afternoon. Our hope is that our model will eventually be incorporated into an exhibit or online display that the public can access."

SEE THE DIFFERENCE

When it was pointed out to John Orr that there is already a plethora of animated videos on YouTube that purport to accurately depict the Single Bullet Theory as well as all the shots fired in Dealey Plaza that day, he was resolute to distinguish his project from the crowd.

"All the other animations I have seen over the last 20 plus years are what I call cartoons. They are animations created out of the mind of the cartoonists. They make the figures the way they want to make them and place them where they want them to be," **says Orr.**

The DP3D project, by comparison, uses the latest technologies in several fields to create a state-of-the-art reconstruction of Dealey Plaza that allows the creators to accurately document the origin of the gunshots based on the wounds sustained by Kennedy and Connally as well as the multitude of film and photographic evidence.

"Our model is based purely on science," states Orr matter-of-factly, ignoring all speculation and the plethora of conspiracy theories.

In the pursuit of perfection, the team has spent considerable time in Dealey Plaza, even making sure to film and apply their technologies and techniques at 12:30 p.m. on November 21 of 2020, exactly 24 hours before the 57th anniversary moment.

Attempts by researchers like this author to recreate the shots in Dealey Plaza via animation fall way short compared to the advanced techniques used by the DP3D team to create incredibly accurate trajectories and images.

Unable to do its work on the actual anniversary date because of the large crowds that gather to mark the occasion, the team was technically able to accurately capture the lighting and shadows as to what it was at 12:30 pm on 11/22/63. How's that for attention to detail?

"We use laser scan technology on a tripod. Dozens of scans in Dealey Plaza – accurate to a few millimeters. For instance, the entire dimensions of the Book Depository building or even the 6th floor window, which haven't changed over the years, can be measured and recreated to within a fraction of an inch in a 3D image.

"We also use photography from drones that can be combined into the laser scan work to add realism and check from elevation angles for dimensions and the *geometry of everything.*

As for the application of photogrammetry, Leiloglou states: *"We take photo evidence (2D) and extract 3D info from the photos using the science of photogrammetry."*

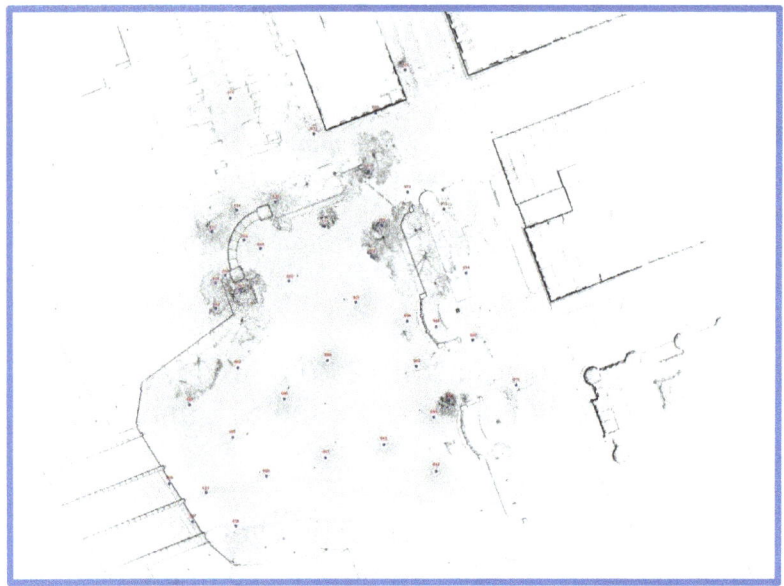

Mark Johnson and his DP3D team are recreating a 3D model of Dealey Plaza as precisely as possible to what it was on Nov. 22, 1963. An example of the attention to detail is this orthographic view of most of the laser scanning stations they used to take thousands of key measurements of the plaza. New laser scan technology generates a three dimensional 'point cloud' that precisely captures every detail of the crime scene.   - © DP3D (LLC)

Johnson explains the end result: *"In combining all this latest technology, we are trying to build a 3D model down to a fraction of an inch of all the films and all the still photos.*

"We have all the photo work we need to make any section of the Plaza photo realistic. We can recreate the

shadows exactly as they were that day, even the reflections off the chrome. We can do amazing things with photo realism so that we will be able to create what appears to be a high definition video of a real scene."

THE BIGGEST CONTROVERSY DEBUNKED!

Starting with the Warren Commission's essential finding that one bullet (CE 399) fired from the so-called 'Oswald' window above and behind the limousine caused all seven non-lethal wounds sustained by Kennedy and Connally (Single Bullet Theory), Orr's group put any skepticism aside, knowing the soundness of their applied technologies not available in 1963 would yield factual results.

Nonetheless, the enormity of their findings of this one key bullet trajectory has the potential to change the history books.

If their 3D model scientifically verifies that both men could have been hit per their actual bullet entry and exit points by a single shot from the 6th floor southeast corner Book Depository window, the Commission's single bullet conclusion is validated.

If their 3D model scientifically proves that a single shot from the 'Oswald' window could **NOT** have caused **ALL** the known survivable wounds on the President and Governor, there had to be multiple gunmen, hence a conspiracy to kill the POTUS.

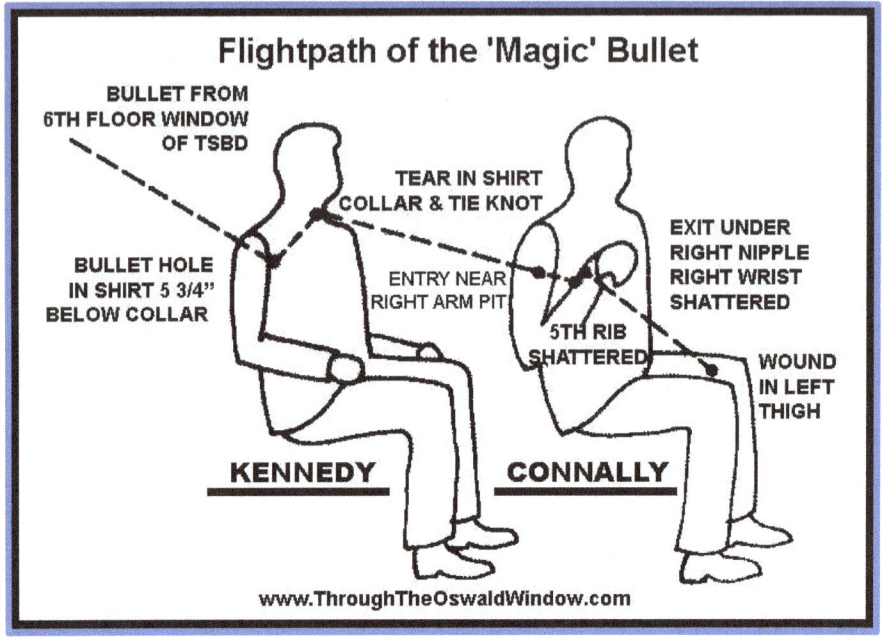

Can new technologies prove or disprove the JFK Single Bullet Theory as presented by the Warren Commission Report?

Leaning on modern technology to prove or disprove this critical theory requires accurate measurements of bullet trajectories from multiple potential sniper positions to the limousine, including the Commission's 6th floor southeast corner window conclusion.

Then there's the exact distance between the two seated men and position of them in relation to each other in the Presidential limousine, as well as each man's precise posture at the moment the Commission says CE 399 allegedly struck them.

On this one point alone, the DP3D model avoids all the speculation and controversy over the years, instead applying their modern technologies to dozens of film and photo images until the precise position of the two men at the bullet's impact is calculated and verified from multiple different angles.

Further, the entry and exit wounds on the two men, as documented by the Commission's own medical records in the National Archives, had to be considered as well as countless other meticulous variables.

As you can imagine, virtually every moment, from the first shot to the last shot as well as each bullet's flightpath from origin to the wounds inflicted on both men, requires painstaking attention to a multitude of details.

The DP3D model, unlike the Warren Commission, did not start with the pre-determined conclusion that the 'Single Bullet Theory' shot came from the 6th floor southeast corner Book Depository window. Instead, they conducted extensive analysis and let science prove or disprove where all the shots came from as well as the resulting wounds sustained by the two victims.

Beyond that, the DP3D team let all the consistent evidence, cross-referencing images and laser measurements, dictate bullet trajectories and corresponding wounds on the two victims.

THE FIRST SHOCKING REVELATION

The result of all those tedious calculations?

"***The Warren Commission's straight-line theory does not hold up***," exclaims Orr, thereby destroying the validity of the Single Bullet Theory!

Having scientifically established that all seven non-fatal wounds suffered by the two men could **NOT** have come from one bullet fired from the 6th floor southeast corner Book Depository window or one bullet fired from any location for that matter, the lone gunman theory takes its rightful place in the trash-heap of historical lies.

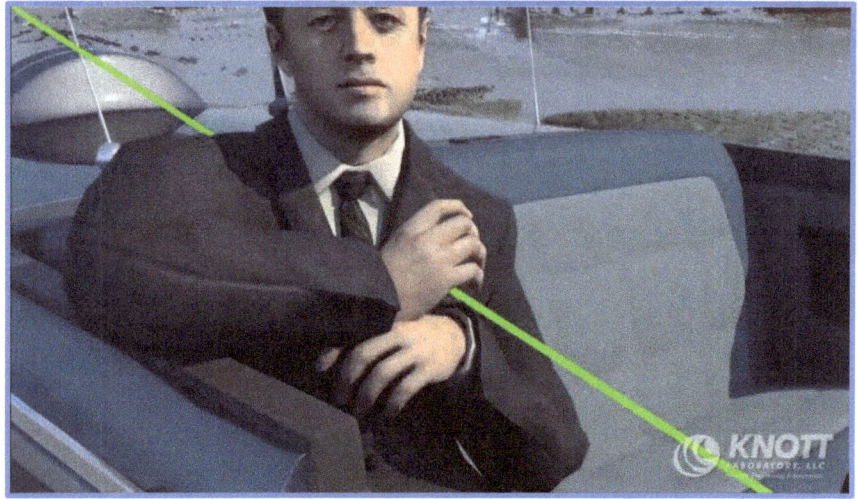

When the DP3D project combined evidence on record with modern technologies to include hundreds of other measurable calculations, its model shows there was a bullet wound below the Adam's apple on JFK's throat but it could not have been caused by CE 399, thereby debunking the 'Single Bullet Theory' as put forth by the Warren Report.   *- © DP3D (LLC)*

"Angelos has rather effectively and impressively destroyed the SBT," emphatically states Johnson.

"CE 399 did strike Connally near the right armpit but did not strike Kennedy first," reveals Orr. How's that for a shocker?

Orr's analysis establishes that CE 399 went through Connally's chest and ended its flight in his left thigh but did **NOT** strike his right wrist.

The stunning revelation that Connally was hit by two separate bullets will become even more shocking when the completed DP3D visualization reveals the flightpath of the bullet that shattered Connally's wrist.

Did the shot that inflicted the non-fatal wounds on JFK go on to cause all the wounds on Governor Connally? The DP3D model not only dispels the single bullet trajectory put forth by the Warren Report, it provides a shocking revelation about the wounds suffered by Connally. - © DP3D (LLC)

"*So, the Commission's straight-line single bullet theory is not correct,*" re-emphasizes Orr. "*Our finished DP3D visualization will show that for the straight-line theory to be correct, the bullet would have hit Connally to the left of his spine down near the car seat.*"

On a lighter note, when all the meticulous work put into the DP3D model revealed the controversial Single Bullet Theory to be hogwash, Larry Schnapf quipped to partner John Orr; "*It looked to me that if the single bullet theory *was correct, then John Connally would have been circumcised by the bullet."*

In addition to scientifically proven bullet trajectories to account for all the wounds on the two men, the last phase in the interest of realism will be to make the human subjects in the limousine as realistic as possible, which is where Johnson's expertise comes in.

"When we complete our work, we will be replacing the models with very realistic versions of the figures matching their true kinematic dimensions," **assures Johnson.**

One teaser Orr is willing to share is that the technology shows Connally's wrist wound was caused by a left-to-right shot whereas the 6th floor Book Depository sniper was right-to-left in relation to the limousine while on Elm Street!

Does this open up the possibility that not all of Connally's wounds were caused by one bullet? One thing is certain; When the DP3D animated documentary is complete, you won't find even a hint of speculation. All findings will be based on the latest applied sciences and technologies.

With revelations like the debunking of the Single Bullet Theory, the DP3D model analyzes something the Warren Commission didn't even contemplate: How many other gunmen were in Dealey Plaza and where were they positioned?

To scientifically account for the shot that completely missed the limousine, all the wounds on JFK and Connally and the bullet trajectories that caused them, the 3D model avoids conjecture and instead relies on

JFK Case NOT Closed

consistent evidence such as damage to the car windshield and damage to each man's clothing.

Was there a shooter in the Dal-Tex building? Was there one or more gunmen on the grassy knoll? Could a shooter have been positioned in the storm drain along the north curb side of Elm Street?

Will the coming DP3D model prove that a shot came from behind this fence on the grassy knoll that struck JFK? One thing is certain: Modern science will one day tell us the truth about the events of 11/22/63.

Sorry folks, but like a good Hollywood movie teaser, you'll have to wait until the finished documentary comes out to mark the 60th anniversary.

And in case you are wondering, the tantalizing answers to these questions, as documented in the upcoming DP3D project, will astound you!

All this leaves John Orr and his colleagues with quite the challenge.

NOT JUST ANOTHER CRAZY CONSPIRACY THEORY

Although the DP3D visualization may provide us with the most scientifically sound account of how JFK was murdered, how does it distinguish itself from the likes of extreme Q-Anon conspiracy theories?

Perhaps such radical conspiracy thinkers can be ignored, but even in the mainstream world of conspiracy theorizing, as evidenced by the many Facebook pages that indiscriminately post JFK assassination information and misinformation, people are usually entrenched in their favorite conspiracy theory.

They not only show contempt for 'lone nut' advocates, who respond in kind with like venom, people of differing conspiracy beliefs tend to cannibalize each other even though they are all on the same side.

John Orr's biggest challenge, he believes, is the "*numbness*" to new information coming to light after years of misinformation that is out there in cyberspace. Can his team's 3D visualization project avoid being perceived as just another "*crazy, off the wall theory.*"

Orr's team believes its end project has a shot at being critically accepted because they are based purely on science and not speculation, conjecture or theory.

"*I have found the conspiracy theory community is far worse than the single bullet Warren Commission community. There are far more nutty off-the-wall things on the conspiracy side than there are on the mainstream Warren Commission side.*"

Orr claims conspiracy theorists apply "*sloppy thinking*" to their claims whereas his scientific-based project is very methodical and logical in linking point A to point B to what happened in Dealey Plaza. "*I don't know anyone else who has done that,*" he opines.

Orr is not trying to directly get the government to re-open the case, leaving that to Robert F. Kennedy Jr. and others. Instead, he hopes the DP3D documentary will affect public opinion about what happened in Dallas, which he believes will eventually cause a new investigation to be launched.

"History has shown over the years that the only thing that has caused change relative to JFK is a public outcry. Dick Gregory, Geraldo and Robert Groden created public outcry (1975) which led to the House Select Committee and the Oliver Stone movie (1991) led to public outcry that led to the JFK Records Act," notes Orr. *"Every time the public gets fired up and realizes it has been misled, things happen."*

Orr admits that for his group's Dealey Plaza 3D animated model to create public outcry, it would have to become a network, Netflix or Prime Video documentary or become viral on a major social media platform, a long shot he acknowledges, but worth a try.

So, the question becomes: Can modern technologies like Dr. David Mantik's application of Optical Densitometry (chapter 16) combined with the DP3D state-of-the-art use of laser scanning, photogrammetry and 3D imaging technologies prompt the next public outcry that could result in a new official investigation into JFK's murder?

While not as sexy or seemingly impactful as a Hollywood movie or even the actual visual recording of a President's execution, here is where the passage of time can be the servant of truth.

Research dinosaurs like me are stuck in our old-fashioned gumshoe ways of reading, researching and questioning what the existing evidence says happened.

Contemporary researchers like this book's contributor Johnny Cairns, as well as the younger audience they appeal to, are much more in tune with technological advancements and they are open to applying them to the JFK assassination.

Not only did Donald Trump not release all the classified files he promised, his controversial presidency introduced millennials to a mistrust in government just as assassinations of the 60's and Watergate did as I grew up.

For the new generation of skeptics, what will be the technological breakthrough that will create the public outcry needed to prompt another formal investigation into the events of 11/22/63?

If a new investigation happens, this chapter and the previous chapter present two examples of technologies that did not exist in 1963, as well as other yet to be announced advancements in technology that will benefit a renewed search for the truth.

Footnotes:

John Orr's website chronicles his study of the shots in Dealey Plaza going back to his days in the Justice Department – mountainrivercabins.com/JFK

Project partner Angelos Leiloglou has parted ways with Knott Laboratory to form his own company, Forensic Viz. He remains a valued member of the DP3D team.

Project partner Mark Johnson has created a website (jfkforensics.com) in which project updates will be posted. It will offer a private forum *"to keep the nuts out"* as Orr puts it. Orr and Johnson are looking to get serious researchers plugged into the project to welcome their input or possibly get involved on a profit or not-for-profit basis.

Project partner Larry Schnapf is leading an effort to lobby the Senate Committee on Homeland Security and Governmental Affairs, as well as the House Committee on Oversight and Reform (see next chapter).

He is asking the committees to force the U.S. government to comply with the President John F. Kennedy Assassination Records Collection Act of 1992 which it failed to do by not releasing all remaining classified documents by the date set by law. How you can support this effort is detailed in the concluding chapter.

Chapter 18

Top Researchers Weigh In on How Best to Formally Re-Investigate the JFK Assassination and the Key Evidence that Needs to be Examined

Having established reasonable doubt in this book for the accused as would have been required in a courtroom for the State of Texas versus Lee Harvey Oswald:

And having demonstrated that relentless researchers and modern technology can rescue truth from the passage of time, we still have one critical task to accomplish:

How best do we officially re-investigate the JFK assassination to avoid another Warren Commission? To begin this process, such a mandate would require:

1. **Viable Evidence** – There remains on record in the National Archives considerable physical evidence that can be subjected to methods of examination either not applied or available in 1963.

It must be determined why much of this evidence was dismissed, ignored, altered or suppressed by the Warren Commission in naming Lee Harvey Oswald as the '**lone**' assassin of John F. Kennedy.

2. **Power of Subpoena** – Any new investigative body must have power of subpoena to summon available witnesses and applicable experts under oath and compel government agencies to turn over still classified files.

3. **Objective Fairness** – Every effort needs to be made to conduct a new inquiry without bias or predetermined outcome of any kind, thus avoiding another Warren Commission.

Such an investigative panel should therefore be comprised of researchers and experts from both sides of the debate of Oswald's guilt or innocence.

REACHING OUT TO THE EXPERTS

At this organizing stage in support of Robert F. Kennedy Jr.'s efforts to have the murders of his uncle and father formally re-investigated, this researcher and author asked several distinguished JFK assassination researchers to participate in a two-question survey as follows:

Question #1

In your opinion, what would be the best way to formally conduct a new investigation into the JFK assassination in order to avoid another Warren Commission?

A) Another House Select Committee on Assassinations
B) District Attorney (New Orleans or Dallas)
C) Special Counsel (e.g. Robert Mueller)
D) Truth and Reconciliation Committee
E) Other – Please specify

Robert F. Kennedy Jr. seeks justice for the murders of his father and uncle all these years later.

Question #2

What one single area or piece of evidence would you most want a new inquiry to examine in search of the truth and why?

THE MAIN INVESTIGATIVE OPTIONS

Before revealing how the panel of great researchers answered these two questions, here is a synopsis of the most viable formal investigative options to consider:

9/11 Commission

Following the September 11, 2001, aerial assault on the twin towers in New York City, President George W. Bush ordered the assembly of a panel, which became known as the 9/11 Commission, to ascertain the facts of a foreign-based terror attack on U.S. soil.

With the help of uncontested subpoenas, the completed

report was delivered to President Bush and Congress 442 days after it commenced hearings.

Like the Warren Commission Report of 1964, controversies and conspiracies theories endure despite its findings.

Although somewhat identically functional as the Warren Commission, there was one effective difference that ought to be adopted if such a Commission is formed to re-investigate the JFK assassination:

Whereas the Warren Commission was comprised of mostly active politicians and a myriad of lawyers, the 9/11 Commission featured a number of 'former' intelligence and justice officials, scholars and experts from industries germane to the tragic event.

Any new formal inquiry into the events of 11/22/63 should mirror the make-up of the 9/11 Commission to include noted experts in forensic medicine, ballistics, foreign and domestic intelligence and historians of that era, to name but a few.

HSCA (Version 2)

The House Judiciary's Select Committee on Assassinations (HSCA, 1976-1979) re-examined both the JFK and Martin Luther King Jr. murders and produced some startling findings.

While concluding that Oswald shot and killed Kennedy and James Earl Ray shot and killed Reverend King, it

G. Robert Blakey, Chief Counsel for the HSCA, named Oswald as the shooter but says he didn't act alone.

concluded that both men likely acted as a result of a conspiracy but could not identify others involved in either murder.

While a new HSCA would have the necessary subpoena power, skeptics believe the same approach would require some strategic changes to avoid a failure to uncover the truth about Dallas.

As some of the experts point out in assessing this method of investigation, less lawyers need to be involved. Additionally, both 'lone assassin' and 'conspiracy' advocates need to be part of the panel overseeing the full inquiry.

The idea is to make a second HSCA investigation somewhat akin to a courtroom proceeding where both sides of the debate get to review and question the evidence and testimony by experts.

Additionally, all exculpatory evidence must be accepted as part of the case record instead of being indiscriminately dismissed or ignored as was routinely done by the Warren Commission.

Such hearings need to be broadcast live to the public on a social media platform to ensure integrity and at least provide Oswald with the legal representation he was denied in life and death.

Dallas/New Orleans District Attorney

The murders of John F. Kennedy, police officer J.D. Tippit and their accused killer Lee Harvey Oswald aren't even considered 'open' cases by the Dallas County District Attorney's office.

Yet in the aftermath of the Jim Garrison probe of assassination-related characters and activities in New Orleans, the current District Attorney there still has some lingering mysteries to solve, such as Oswald's association with David Ferrie going as far back as 1955 in the Civil Air Patrol, his uncle Charles 'Dutz' Murret, a bookie for Louisiana crime boss Carlos Marcello and former FBI agent Guy Bannister, whose nefarious activities were run out of the same office building as Oswald's Fair Play for Cuba Committee.

Embattled New Orleans District Attorney Jim Garrison was the first prosecutor to bring charges in the murder of JFK.

So far, the New Orleans District Attorney's office has shown no appetite to go down the same path as Garrison's late 1960's investigation that failed to prove Clay Shaw was part of a conspiracy to murder President John F. Kennedy.

CRITICAL MONTHS IN DALLAS

Lee Oswald's time in Dallas leading up to Kennedy's fateful visit also has mysteries to be solved such as how Marina and Lee Oswald were under surveillance by the FBI prior to the visit but no alarm bells went off even though the motorcade's route would take the President directly in front of the building where Oswald was employed.

Current liberal democrat District Attorney John C. Creuzot does not seem interested in taking a leading role in re-opening any aspect of America's ultimate cold case, which he made clear in an e-mail response to my inquiry (see appendices section).

As researcher William Kelly pointed out in our Facebook post exchange in early 2021, DA Creuzot could convene a Dallas County Cold Case Grand Jury to investigate the nearly 60-year unsolved crime.

Rather than take any initiative, it's more likely that the District Attorney offices in New Orleans and Dallas would cooperate with a formal Congressional inquiry.

The same can be said of the Dallas Police Department, which wouldn't have the authority or ability to carry out such an expansive investigation on its own, never mind examining the department's gross incompetence in 1963-4.

In the Appendices section, you will find a similar e-mail response to my inquiry from the Dallas Police Department after current Chief Renee Hall delegated the matter to

Assistant Chief Avery Moore's office.

It is more likely that the Dallas Police Department would, by law, assist any new inquiry by the Dallas County District Attorney, a Grand Jury investigation or Congressional committee probe.

Special Counsel

Robert S. Mueller - Special Counsel investigator into possible Russian influence in the 2016 Presidential election.

Most recently in 2017, former FBI Director Robert Mueller was appointed as Special Counsel to investigate possible unlawful Russian government influence in the 2016 Presidential election and potential collusion with members of the Trump campaign staff.

Special Counsels are normally appointed by the Attorney General of the United States or the assistant Attorney General when the Attorney General has recused him or herself due to a potential conflict of interest.

This was the case in the Trump administration when Attorney General Jeff Sessions recused himself, handing assistant Attorney General Rod Rosenstein the authority to appoint Robert Mueller as Special Counsel.
Typically, a Special Counsel, also known as a Special Prosecutor or Independent Counsel, is appointed to investigate matters of alleged government wrongdoing.

A DIFFERENT APPROACH?

This presents an intriguing possibility for those of us leary of another Warren Commission.

Does a panel need to be assembled like the Warren Commission (1964) or the House Select Committee on Assassinations (1976) to investigate the entirety of the JFK assassination?

Alternatively, can several more focused investigative methods be employed to probe specific aspects of this case?

For instance, a Special Counsel might be tasked to only investigate:

- **Top Secret** – Why the U.S. government sealed thousands of 'classified' documents for 75 years if Oswald was a 'lone nut' assassin.
- **Withholding Evidence** – Why government agencies like the FBI, CIA and Office of Naval Intelligence (ONI) either altered documents submitted to the Warren Commission or did not provide them at all.
- **Ignoring the Law** – Why administrations up to Joe Biden's inauguration continue to suppress classified files in violation of the JFK Records Act of 1992 that lawfully required public release of all government records of the assassination by October 26, 2017.

William Kelly, historian and the owner/operator of jfkcountercoup.blogspot.com, offered a similar method to investigate government wrongdoing in a response to a Facebook post by this researcher when he stated:

> "A DC federal grand jury that would be limited to investigating destroyed, stollen, missing, forged and illegally withheld evidence and records."

On this premise, might it be more effective to segment any new JFK assassination inquiry to probe targeted aspects of the case rather than a far-ranging investigation?

Such laser-focused separate investigations might include:

* **Lee prior to 11/22/63** – Oswald's time in the Marine Corp, his defection to the Soviet Union and unorthodox return to the U.S., his time in New Orleans before moving to Dallas and his time in Dallas leading up to the assassination.
* **Lee and J.D.** – Oswald and the Tippit killing.
* **Mobster Jack?** – Jack Ruby's connection to organized crime and its possible connection to Oswald's murder.
* **Medical Mismanagement** – An independent study of all the medical evidence, from Parkland Hospital to the autopsy at the Bethesda Naval Hospital.
* **Bungled Ballistics** – An independent ballistic study of Oswald's rifle, ammunition attributed to his rifle and handgun and all bullet fragments recovered from Kennedy, Connally, the limousine and the scene of the crime.

The evidence can be broken down into several other separate probes, such as an investigation into the handling of the physical evidence in this case as expertly presented by colleague Johnny Cairns in chapters 4,5,6 and 7.

Such independent committees could file a report to a co-ordinating Chairman charged with assembling a final report of what happened before and on 11/22/63, as well as the flawed investigation into the history-changing event.

Truth & Reconciliation Committee

The Kennedy and King families have called for a Truth and Reconciliation Committee, based on a 1995 panel assembled in South Africa to study the social consequences of apartheid, such as human rights abuses.

In a joint statement released by the Kennedy and King families:

"We call for a major public inquest on the four major assassinations of the 1960s that together had a disastrous impact on the course of American history: the murders of John F. Kennedy, Malcolm X, Martin Luther King Jr. and Robert F. Kennedy."

As reported in Politico.com, *"The inquest -- which will hear testimony from living witnesses, legal experts, investigative journalists, historians and family members of the victims -- is intended to show the need for Congress or the Justice Department to reopen investigations into all four assassinations."*

It is believed that a successful truth and reconciliation committee could not only repair the mistrust in government born in the 1960's, it could pave the way for other social fabric investigations in the U.S. such as heightened racial tensions between police and blacks in 2021 and the rise of right-wing extremist groups that played a key role in the January 6, 2021, insurrection at the Capitol Hill building in Washington.

The namesake sons of Bobby Kennedy and Martin Luther King Jr. are calling for new investigations into the murders of their famous fathers. This book supports that effort.

COURTING JUSTICE

While this book extends a welcoming hand to the next generation of JFK assassination researchers, Larry Schnapf proves that we older dogs can still hunt.

The veteran New York Lawyer, who once headed the legal strategies for Citizens Against Political Assassinations (CAPA), has assembled a team of lethal legal volunteers that has launched lawsuits against the U.S. government's Executive Branch for unlawfully failing to comply with the JFK Assassination Records Act of 1992.

Schnapf et al charge that both President's Donald Trump and Joe Biden have violated the law by not directing the National Archivist to release the remaining thousands of classified documents pertinent to the events of 11/22/63.

Almost 60 years later, Larry Schnapf is seeking justice that Oswald never got when charged as the lone assassin of JFK.

Like Trump's multiple decisions to delay release of the files in the Archives, Biden did the same on October 20, 2021, when he cited Covid as the reason to set a new date for release of December 14, 2022.

Acting swiftly, Schnapf filed a lawsuit on October 24, 2021, in the District Court of Columbia asking the judge to compel the Executive Branch to turn over underlying documents that should provide insights as to who wants the postponements and why.

"All postponements by the two Presidents did not comply with the JFK Records Act of 1992 which requires that for any single document that is postponed, there be an unclassified explanation to the American public of what the unidentifiable harm is that is the grounds for postponing the document as well as an explanation of how that harm outweighs the strong presumption of disclosure to the American public."

At the end of November 2021, Schnapf and his legal team doubled down when they filed a second lawsuit specifically targeting the CIA, FBI, State Department and President Biden for failing to comply with the JFK Records Act that was passed by Congress.

INNOCENCE PROJECT PLAN

A third legal strategy involves Schnapf's legal team executing an Innocence Project type strategy by asking a court in Dallas to expunge Oswald's arrest record.

This would require the cooperation of Oswald's widow, Marina (Oswald) Porter to file a cold case request but she has declined to get involved. Undaunted, Schnapf is considering approaching Oswald's two daughters, now of legal age, to take up the cause.

"The Innocence Project could bring a Court of Inquiry proceeding in Dallas and use the flawed forensic evidence in this case, which is often used to convict people, and apply it to this 58-year-old case to show that the evidence used to link Oswald to the assassination was either junk science, manufactured evidence or unreliable evidence," states Schnapf.

LOBBYING LARRY

Apart from his legal endeavours, Larry Schnapf is also lobbying Congress and the Senate to hold oversight hearings on the Executive Branch's breach of the law requiring all records to be released.

The legal team have written to House Committee on Oversight and Reform chairwoman Carolyn Maloney and Senate Homeland Security and Governmental Affairs

Committee co-chairs Gary Peters and Rob Portman, asking their committees to conduct hearings on why thousands of documents remain suppressed from the American public after the October 26, 2017, date established as the law by Congress.

"We want to create enough noise to get the attention of Congress to hold hearings and have representatives of the security agencies come before Congress to explain to the American people why they are still delaying documents that are 58 years old," exclaims Schnapf.

This is a call to action that you can join and put pressure on Congress to act. *"We want every representative in Congress or every Senator to get a letter from a constituent to ask that they request the appropriate committee in the House and Senate to hold an oversight hearing,"* says Schnapf.

You can participate in one of these ways:

1) If you are constituent of Oversight & Reform chairwoman Carolyn Maloney, write to her at the address in the Appendices section to ask her to hold an oversight hearing on the government's violation of the JFK Records Act of 1992.

2) If you are a constituent of Senate Homeland co-chairs Gary Peters or Rob Portman, write to them at the address in the Appendices section to ask them to hold an oversight hearing on this matter.

3) If you are a constituent of any member of the House or Senate committee members, ask your representatives to lobby the chair of their committee to hold a hearing.

4) Generally speaking, write to your Congressional or Senate representative to ask him or her to request chairperson's Maloney, Peters or Portman hold oversight hearings.

5) Write to President Joe Biden at the address in the Appendices section to ask him to immediately release all remaining sealed documents in the Archives.

To help you make a difference, Schnapf has provided a form letter which appears in the Appendices section. He encourages you to use the letter only as a guideline, adding:

"*This is a model form of letter that readers can use to send to their representative and senators requesting an oversight hearing. They should feel free to change the wording into their own voice.*

"*Writers should use the senate information in brackets when writing their senators and the House information in brackets when contacting their representative. In other words, when writing a representative, the writer should ask that the representative contact Carolyn Maloney while when writing their Senators, the writer should reference the Senate Homeland Committee,*" suggests Schnapf.

Further updates will appear on this researcher's website – ThroughTheOswaldWindow.com.

THE EXPERTS SAY...

Without having discussed these options with the panel

of top JFK assassination researchers and authors, here are the survey questions once again and their answers, presented in alphabetical order based on their last name:

NEW INVESTIGATION SURVEY

Question # 1

In your opinion, what would be the best way to formally conduct a new investigation into the JFK assassination in order to avoid another Warren Commission?

- A) Another House Select Committee on Assassinations
- B) District Attorney (New Orleans or Dallas)
- C) Special Counsel (e.g. Robert Mueller)
- D) Truth & Reconciliation Committee
- E) Other – Please specify

Question # 2

What one single area or piece of evidence would you most want a new inquiry to examine in search of the truth and why?

GARY AGUILAR, M.D.

Question 1: C - Special Counsel: who should insist the still-classified files all be released.

Question 2: Oswald's Tax returns. * Also, a forensic radiologist review of JFK's X-rays, specifically the pattern of "dust like" fragments located in the right-front quadrant of JFK's head on the lateral skull X-ray.

Biography: One of the few physicians outside the government ever allowed to see the still-restricted autopsy X-rays and photos taken during JFK's post mortem exam at Bethesda Naval Hospital.

Clinical Professor of Ophthalmology, University of California, San Francisco.

Author of numerous articles on the JFK case published in both medical/scientific journals, books, and in lay publications as well as a three lecture series on the medical/forensic evidence on C-Span.

** See links to Dr. Aguilar's work in Resources section.

JOHN BARBOUR

Question 1: There is no reason to have a new investigation. It is a cold case in The Justice Dept. Open it into a Court...along with Garrison's and the CIA's files...and every question will be answered and all the killers and abettors uncovered. It will also solve RFK, MLK and many other political murders.

Question 2: The most important evidence and proof of multiple shooters is the body of JFK. Every single x-ray and photo has to be made public!! The 26 volumes of the WR has not one!!! A total fraud!!!!

Biography: John Barbour is a Canadian actor and writer based in the United States. He is the only TV personality to win Emmys for both entertainment and news programming. John directed the film The JFK Assassination: The Jim Garrison Tapes.

WALT BROWN

Question 1: C – Special Counsel

Question 2: Eyewitnesses to LHO being in the window; because there are none that are credible.

Biography: Walt Brown has been a life-long history student, majoring in history as an undergraduate at Fordham University in the Bronx. He went back to school and earned his second M.A. and a Ph.D. in US History at Notre Dame University. His doctoral dissertation, "John Adams and the American Press" was published in 1995. Before that, however, he had read everything he could find about the broad-daylight assassination of John F. Kennedy, and after reading and re-reading, he decided to create a work that would bring closure. He hit on the idea of a trial of Lee Oswald, and the work quickly (and with luck) turned into a book, *The People v. Lee Harvey Oswald.* It met with critical and commercial success and led to additional JFK works, capped off with the 32,000 page JFK Chronology, with its Epilogue, *The Kennedy Execution.* Since 2014, Brown has left the JFK case to a younger generation and has written eight mystery novels. Brown lives in Hillsdale in the same house that he was in when JFK was killed.

JOHNNY CAIRNS

Question 1: I think an open and impartial investigative body with the help of prominent investigators that really know the case should investigate it. Men like Walt Brown, Jim DiEugenio etc. working in tandem with committee would get the truth out.

Question 2: Every single piece of it. The evidence is in utter shambles and would no way result in a conviction. That should ring alarm bells to any serious and impartial person investigating this crime. One only needs to look at the conviction reversal rate in Dallas to realize what a corrupt office (District Attorney) Wade was running.

Biography: Johnny Cairns was born and raised in Edinburgh, Scotland. His interest in the JFK presidency and assassination comes from his father Robert. Johnny is a young leader among contemporary researchers who focuses on the physical evidence in the case. Johnny's work is featured in chapters 4,5,6 and 7 of this book.

MICHAEL CHESSER, M.D.

Question 1: Another House Select Committee, as long as it included input from prominent members of the research community, with no restrictions on duration of the committee. It would be vital that all of the remaining assassination records are released, and that records from NSA and the military intel agencies are included.

Question 2: Since my primary interest is the medical evidence, I would have to say that I would like a new inquiry into the autopsy evidence. In addition, NARA should make the highest quality digital images of the autopsy photographs and x-rays available for the public (the pirated images which are widely viewed on the internet are of poor quality).

Biography: Dr. Chesser is a neurologist who was approved for three visits to view the autopsy material at NARA II. He has viewed the original and HSCA enhanced skull x-rays, and the autopsy photographs as well as the digital images of the photographs prepared by Kodak for the ARRB.

JAMES DiEUGENIO

Question 1: Special Prosecutor

Question 2: Autopsy evidence

Biography: James DiEugenio has been studying the Kennedy assassination for nearly 30 years.

He is the author of two books on the JFK case: Destiny Betrayed, and The JFK Assassination: The Evidence Today. He was the co-editor of the anthology The Assassinations, which dealt with all four assassinations of the sixties: JFK, MLK, RFK and Malcolm X.

He was the publisher of Probe Magazine for five years, 1995-2000. He was the script writer for the four-part documentary series directed by Oliver Stone, JFK: Destiny Betrayed.

DAVID MANTIK, M.D., PhD

Question 1: – Any new investigation must be done by a totally independent but fair panel. Initial members (3-5) should be chosen by respected partisans on both sides of this debate. The group's expertise must cover many disciplines. And no panel with lawyers only…that was ridiculous.

Question 2: – The metal fragments in this case would fit that bill: the fragments removed from JFK's skull, the fragments from Connally's body, CE-399, and the fragments from the limousine. A group effort could be made to list the physical and chemical studies for such comparisons. For my part, I would love to see an X-ray and photographic correlation of JFK's brain if it could be exhumed.

Biography: Dr. David Mantik is a California radiation oncologist who has examined the JFK autopsy photos and X-rays on nine occasions. He was the first specialist to apply a technology called Optical Densitometry to the X-rays, which produced findings of multiple gunmen in Dealey Plaza and evidence of the framing of Oswald as the 'lone' assassin of JFK. His work is featured in chapter 16 of this book.

JEFFERSON MORLEY

Question 1: E (Other). Congress should reconstitute and fund another Assassination Records Review Board to add new records to the JFK collection and declassify all of the still redacted documents.

As of April 15, 2021, 15,834 assassination related records still have redactions. That's 4.9 percent of the documents entire collection that are at least partially withheld from public view.

Question 2: I am seeking declassification of 44 documents about George Joannides' undercover operations in 1963 and his role as liaison to the HSCA in 1978, when he obstructed the committee's investigation into August 1963 contacts between Oswald and the Cuban Student Directorate, which he ran under the code name AMSPELL. These documents may be relevant to the framing of Oswald as the only person responsible for JFK's death.

Biography - Jefferson Morley is editor the JFK Facts blog (**jfkfacts.org**) and author of The Ghost: The Secret Life of CIA Spymaster James Jesus Angleton. His next book, forthcoming in 2022, is about the role of the CIA in the Watergate affair.

DAVE O'BRIEN

Question 1: C – Special Counsel. A Special Counsel must be given full subpoena power and needs to form specialized sub-committees involving researchers and experts from both sides of the debate to examine contentious areas of evidence such as medical/autopsy and ballistics.

Question 2: In chapters 4,5,6 & 7 in this book, contributor Johnny Cairns does a phenomenal job of debunking the very circumstantial evidence the Commission used to name Oswald as the 'lone' assassin of JFK. Much of this evidence still exists to be analyzed by a new inquiry. Also, the study of the autopsy records by Drs. Wecht, Mantik, Chesser and Aguilar (see chapter 13 & 16) destroy any notion of a single shooter.

Biography: O'Brien has studied the JFK assassination since age 13 in 1965. In 1968, he developed a pen pal relationship with Dr. Malcolm Perry (letters donated to the Sixth Floor Museum in Dealey Plaza). As a reporter, he covered the HSCA hearings and became among the few researchers granted access to the TSBD building when it was locked and sealed from the public. He is the author of Through The 'Oswald' Window and this book.

VINCE PALAMARA

Question 1: E – Other: A group of renowned authors like Jim DiEugenio, Josiah Thompson, and David Talbot (in fact, perhaps JUST these three who, coincidentally, all live close to each other) to conduct a theory-free assessment of the case. Too much time has passed and too many have passed away for A-D to matter or be realistic today, not to mention all the problems with officialdom from the past. It is too late for justice but never too late for the truth (to quote Robert Groden, who is also a possibility)

Question 2: The medical evidence - Drs. David Mantik and Gary Aguilar, perhaps augmented by Josiah Thompson, Jim DiEugenio and others.

Biography: - Vince Palamara is the leading civilian Secret Service authority and the author of 5 books: His latest book is titled Honest Answers About the Murder of President John F. Kennedy: A New Look at the JFK Assassination (2021). See Resources section chapter 17 for Vince's library of work.

Vince also appears in the DVD/BLU RAY "A COUP IN CAMELOT" (2016).

GREG PARKER

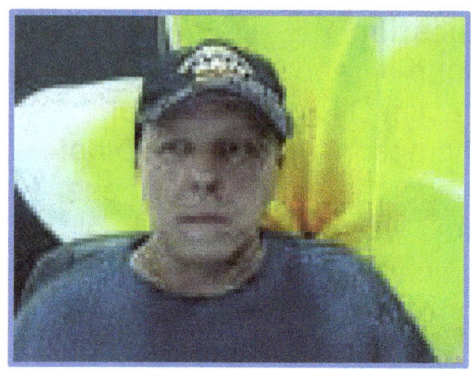

Question 1: An ARRB type set-up but with investigative ability, including the ability to call witnesses and have them sworn under oath. Also, the power to subpoena evidence from any source. It must also appoint investigators actually familiar with the case. Hearings must be open.

Question 2: - The original Darnell film, scans of which could confirm Oswald was on the steps as per his alibi.

Biography: Greg R. Parker is the Australian author of *Lee Harvey Oswald's Cold War* and is the founder of the ReopenKennedyCase forum (ROKC) website. He lives in rural New South Wales with his wife, two sons and menagerie of cats, dogs, birds, fish, snakes, echidnas and blue-tongue lizards.

LARRY SCHNAPF

Question 1: - Congress is too susceptible to political pressures. Instead, we need to focus on the courts and file a petition for a Texas Court of Inquiry to examine the forensic evidence. The petition would seek to expunge Lee Oswald's arrest on the grounds of lack of probable cause.

Question 2: - Apply what we have learned from the Innocence Project to perform state-of-the-art computerized analysis of the forensic evidence and examine chain of evidence to determine which evidence was likely inadmissible in a court of law. A technological tool that should be used is computerized scanning of the bullets and fragments to see if they truly match to the gun as well as the latent fingerprints.

Biography: Larry Schnapf is a former board member and chair of legal committee of the Citizens Against Political Assassinations (CAPA) and is presently working on a 3D animation project to definitively calculate the shots in Dealey Plaza. He has formed a group of lawyers to press for the release of the remaining JFK assassination records that were postponed by Presidents Trump and Biden in violation of the JFK Assassinations Records Review Act of 1992.

J. GARY SHAW

Question 1: Personally, I would be skeptical of doing anything that might involve Washington — no matter who's in control. Perhaps some type of litigation on behalf of Oswald's daughters might be possible. Bud Fensterwald and I were working along this line when he passed.

Question 2: In my opinion, drag ALL of the evidence that was concocted in order to convict Lee and expose it for what it really is, and isn't. Doing so will place on display the fact that the primary motive for Lee's murder was that the authorities lacked the necessary credible evidence for a conviction, which would be devastating to the plot, and the plotters. But that's just me.

Biography: J. Gary Shaw is a first generation JFK assassination researcher of the 1960's who inspired this book's author and several others to seek the truth in this case. He is a former co-director of the JFK Assassination Information Center in Dallas. After co-writing Cover-Up: The Governmental Conspiracy to Conceal the Facts About the Public Execution of John Kennedy with Larry R. Harris (1976), he co-authored three books with Charles Crenshaw, M.D. including Trauma Room One: The JFK Medical Coverup Exposed.

PAT SPEER

Question 1: I believe a large panel (10-15 members) of open-minded forensic radiology experts from around the world should be consulted on JFK's x-rays, and that their conclusions should be presented separately and independently (I.e., with each one writing a report), and not as a panel sponsored by the U.S. Govt. I, for one, am greatly curious as to what they would have to say.

Question 2: I believe a similarly-constructed panel of open-minded fingerprint experts should be granted access to all of the FBI's fingerprint evidence, and that each one should be asked to create charts demonstrating their conclusions, both as to what prints are believed to be Oswald's, and which prints are believed not to be Oswald's. I suspect the whole case against Oswald would collapse if this were to be done.

Biography: Pat Speer has been studying the JFK assassination since 2003, writing on topics such as the flawed study of the medical evidence by the HSCA medical panel, eyewitnesses to the shooting and the physical evidence tying Oswald to the crime.
He created a 4-part video series on YouTube (see Resources section) and operates his own website – patspeer.com.

CYRIL WECHT, M.D., J.D.

Question 1: B – District Attorney (New Orleans or Dallas)

Question 2: Determine what happened to JFK's brain. Where is it? Who took it? Why was it not sectioned after being fixed in formalin for two weeks? Who made the decision not to have it properly examined by a forensic neuropathologist? Why did the Clark Panel doctors in 1968 and Humes, Boswell and Finck never disclose that it was missing? Note: Not disclosed until August 24, 1972, by Dr. Wecht after he examined autopsy materials at the National Archives.

Biography: Forensic Pathology and Medicolegal Consultant Past President, American Academy of Forensic Sciences and American College of Legal Medicine Clinical Professor, School of Law, Pharmacy, and Graduate School of Public Health, Duquesne University. For his newly published book – Life and Death of Cyril Wecht: Memoirs of America's Most Controversial Forensic Pathologist, see Resources section chapter 17.

WHAT NOW?

Having presented ample evidence that was dismissed, ignored, altered or suppressed by the Warren Commission to frame Lee Harvey Oswald as a '**lone**' assassin;

And having established that subsequent 'official' investigations after the Warren Report and prior to the ARRB inquiry failed to adequately examine such evidence;

And having established reasonable doubt associated with key evidence against Oswald as would have been necessary in a court of law;

And having established that evolving technologies give us greater hope of uncovering the truth about 11/22/63 than ever before;

Historical truth demands that an impartial new investigation be undertaken.

Along with the current top researchers featured on these pages, this book challenges the next generation of JFK assassination researchers to demand an official new public inquiry into the murder of President Kennedy that operates theory free and respects the public's right to know how and why America's 35th President of the United States was assassinated on only his 1036th day in office.

APPENDICES

Letter from Dr. Malcolm Perry to this 16-Year-Old Researcher

MALCOLM O. PERRY, M. D.
5323 HARRY HINES BLVD.
DALLAS 35, TEXAS

7 May '68

Dear Mr. O'Brien,

I regret that I cannot resolve your problem. As I noted in my testimony (and verified by the transcript of the press conference) I did not know how many bullets struck him, and could not state that the neck wound was either entrance or exit. I, unfortunately, in response to questions speculated as to possible trajectory, and this was subsequently reported out of context as my opinion. The speculation was clearly preceded by qualifications indicating my lack of precise knowledge. Dr. McClelland did not see the neck wound, as I had incised it prior to his arrival, and he did not state it was an entrance wound. He also was quoted out of context in regard to a possible head wound, described to him by an emergency room attendant who only saw Mr. Kennedy being rushed into the operating room. Thus you can see that many "facts" have little basis. I hope this will shed some light on your questions.

Sincerely,
M O Perry, MD

Official Positions of the Dallas Police Department and Dallas District Attorney's Office on Formally Re-Investigating the JFK Assassination:

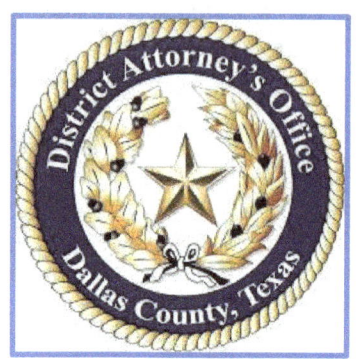

On Monday, October 26, 2020, 3:24:12 p.m. EDT, John Creuzot <john.creuzot@dallascounty.org> wrote:

Good Afternoon,

I received your letter and my responses are as follows:

Question - As the murders of John F. Kennedy, J.D. Tippit and Lee Harvey Oswald occurred in your jurisdiction, can you please confirm whether the Dallas Police Department and/or your office currently regard any or all of these crimes as officially Open or Closed?

Answer - We do not consider it open and no idea as to DPD.

Question - Specific to the murder of President John F. Kennedy and your office, I would appreciate you helping me understand the following:

Does your office have the legal jurisdiction to officially re-open this case?

Answer - Yes.

Question - If so, can you provide a hypothetical reason of what might give the District Attorney's office cause to formally re-open this case?

Answer - No.

Question - With subpoena power critical to any re-investigation, would your office have the ability to subpoena all evidence in the National Archives?

Answer - Likely not.

Question - Would your office have legal access to any still classified government agency files, subject to adhering to matters of national security?

Answer - No.

Question - Given the passage of time, do you feel your office could still effectively investigate the assassination of President Kennedy? Why or why not?

Answer - No.

Question - If the Kennedy family is successful in its effort to officially re-open the murder of President Kennedy, would your office have any formal role?

Answer - No.

Question - Finally, Mr. Creuzot, as an expert in law enforcement, please share any opinion you may have on the best way to conduct a new official investigation into the murder of John F. Kennedy that would avoid another Warren Commission.

Answer - I have no opinion.

JFK Case NOT Closed

John C. Creuzot

Dallas County Criminal District Attorney

133 N. Riverfront L.B. 19

Dallas TX 75207

The same questions were posed to Dallas police chief Renee Hall. Chief Hall referred the inquiry to Assistant Chief Avery Moore. The response received from the Dallas Police Department is as follows:

Mraz, Kimberly <kimberly.mraz@dpd.ci.dallas.tx.us>
Fri., Nov. 13, 2020 at 3:12 p.m.

Good afternoon, Mr. O'Brien -

My name is Officer Kimberly Mraz, #8077. I am Assistant Chief Avery Moore's executive officer. I hope this email finds you well.

I wanted to reach out to let you know that we did receive your letter detailing your second book, however, we will be unable to assist you with your questions because this case falls under Federal jurisdiction. We suggest you contact the Federal Bureau of Investigations or the Secret Service.

I apologize that we can not assist you with your research, however, we wish you well with your book project.
If you have any questions, please feel free to contact me.

Thank you.
Kimberly
Author's Note:

Identical letters addressed to Attorney General William Barr's Justice Department and the FBI went unanswered.

Form Letter by Larry Schnapf for you to Lobby House & Senate to Hold Oversight Hearings on Non Compliance of JFK Records Act.

YOUR ADDRESS

Hon. [ ]
[United States Senate
Dirksen Senate Office Building
Washington, DC, 20510]
or
[House of Representatives
Rayburn House Office Building
Washington, D.C. 20515]

Dear [Senator or Representative]

Re: Request for Oversight Hearing

On October 22nd, President Biden postponed the release of the remaining JFK Assassination Records for another 14 months. The President stated he was postponing the disclosure of these records because certain agencies claimed that release of 58 year old records would somehow pose a risk to national security. President Biden's memo followed a six-month postponement by President Trump in October 2017 and a 3.5 year postponement in April 2018.

Under the John F. Kennedy Assassination Records Act of 1992 (the "JFK Act"), all records identified as JFK assassination records were supposed to be disclosed by October 26, 2017 unless the release of a particular record would pose an "identifiable harm" to national security that was of such gravity that it outweighed the strong public interest in the record. Congress said that only in the *"rarest cases is there any legitimate need for continued protection of such records."* If that was true in 1992, it is certainly even more so now.

For any record proposed to be postponed, the JFK Act provides that the American people are to be provided with an unclassified explanation of the "identifiable harm" posed by the record and how that harm outweighs the public interest in the document. Neither the Biden memo nor President Trump's two memos complied with this statutory mandate.

Since it is now abundantly clear that the Executive Branch is either unable or unwilling to comply with the JFK Act, I ask that you contact the [Carolyn Maloney, chair of the House Oversight and Government Reform Committee] [Senators Gary Peters and Rob Portman, co-chairs of the Committee on Homeland Security and Governmental Affairs] and request that the committee hold an oversight hearing where the Executive Branch agencies would be forced to explain to the American people why they have refused to comply with the JFK Act.

The failure to fully comply with the JFK Act is emblematic of the national crisis of declassification. Releasing the remaining JFK assassination records would be a big step towards restoring the trust of the American people in the candor of the country's institutions.

Call on Congress and U.S. Government to Formally Re-Investigate the JFK Assassination

Contact the White House:

Contact the White House to ask President Joe Biden to release all remaining classified files on the JFK assassination and call on Congress to formally re-investigate the events of 11/22/63 – (202) 456-1414.

Written communication is better than a phone call. You can write to President Joe Biden as follows:

The White House
1600 Pennsylvania Avenue, N.W.
Washington, DC 20500

e-mail - https://www.whitehouse.gov/contact/

Contact the Department of Justice:

The Honorable Merrick Garland, Attorney General of the United States – (202) 514-2000

Contact members of Congress:

The Honorable Carolyn B Maloney – Chairwoman, House Committee on Oversight and Reform (To require government agencies to comply with the release of classified JFK files per the JFK Records Collections Act of 1992) – (202) 225-5051 or write as follows:

Personalize the form letter provided here by Larry

Schnapf and send to:

The Hon. Carolyn Maloney
Chairwoman
House Committee on Oversight and Reform
U.S. House of Representatives
Washington, D.C. 20515

Your member of Congress – To find your current representative in the U.S. House of Representatives, visit this website and simply enter your zip code:

https://www.house.gov/representatives/find-your-representative

Personalize the form letter provided here by Larry Schnapf and send to:

The Honorable (name of representative)
U.S. House of Representatives
Washington, DC 20515

To e-mail or write to your member of Congress, visit your member's website for written contact information.

Senate Representatives:

Personalize the form letter provided here by Larry Schnapf and send to:

The Hon. Gary Peters and Rob Portman
Co-Chairs
Homeland Security and Governmental Affairs Committee
U.S. Senate
Washington, D.C. 20510

To contact a particular Senator, personalize the form letter provided here by Larry Schnapf and send to:

Office of (Name of Senator)
United States Senate
Washington, D.C. 20510

How to Stay on Top of the Latest JFK Assassination Research

There are several ways to stay current with the latest research pertaining to the assassination of President John F. Kennedy as follows:

Organizations/Resources

- Sixth Floor Museum at Dealey Plaza - **https://www.jfk.org/**
- Citizens Against Political Assassinations (CAPA) - https://capa-us.org/
- JFK Assassination Records Collection - https://www.archives.gov/research/jfkhttps://www.jfk.org
- http://www.jfklancer.com/
- https://aarclibrary.org/
- https://projectjfk.com/

Websites

- **https://www.kennedysandking.com/** - Featuring leading researcher James DiEugenio
- **https://reopenkennedycase.forumotion.net/** - Operated by Greg Parker
- **www.ThroughTheOswaldWindow.com** - Operated by author of this book and Through The 'Oswald' Window
- https://www.maryferrell.org/pages/Main_Page.html
- https://jfkfacts.org/

- https://www.history-matters.com/
- https://jfkcountercoup.blogspot.com/ - Owned and operated by researcher William Kelly
- JFK Conspiracy Forum - https://jfkconspiracyforum.freeforums.net/

Radio Programs/Podcasts

- Black Op Radio - https://blackopradio.com/archives2021.html?fbclid=IwAR0xc6DyAwJEn8jD1XjpzQVGbs46RzeW9oGH9hdT-jw3TIyS7Jfd9WtiJLQ – Operated by Leonard Osanic
- Night Fright Show with Brent Holland - https://podcasts.apple.com/us/podcast/night-fright-show/id542557551
- The Conspiracy Show with Richard Syrett - https://www.audible.com/pd/The-Conspiracy-Show-with-Richard-Syrett-Podcast/B08JJNNMWX?ipRedirectOverride=true&overrideBaseCountry=true&pf_rd_p=defe5c0a-4d7a-4872-9ca0-c91016147626&pf_rd_r=X7JQ5Z898FMYBKSDR3RR
- On Target with Larry Sparano - https://www.targetsparano.com/
- The Unexplained with Howard Hughes - https://tunein.com/podcasts/Paranormal-Podcasts/The-Unexplained-With-Howard-Hughes-p412790/
- The Dallas Action Podcast – presented by Wall Street Window - https://www.facebook.com/thedallasactionjfkpodcast

Facebook Discussion Pages

Go to **www.facebook.com** and enter these groups in the Facebook search engine:

- JFK - The Continuing Inquiry
- Mice Fighting Gorillas: The Kennedy Assassinations
- The JFK Conspiracy: Critical Thought and Analysis

- Dealey Plaza and the JFK Coup
- The JFK Assassination...The Evidence
- JFK: Hands On Research
- JFK: Nothing But the Truth
- Photo and Film Analysis in the JFK Assassination
- JFK: Lone Nut or Conspiracy?
- JFK Truth Be Told
- Political Assassinations Research Group
- JFK Numbers
- Lee Harvey Oswald is Innocent
- JFK Boards

JFK Case 'NOT' Closed:

Key Evidence Dismissed, Ignored, Altered or Suppressed to Frame Lee Harvey Oswald as the 'Lone' Assassin!

Resources

Note: To access live links for these reference materials, visit the author's website (www.ThroughTheOswaldWindow.com/resources)

Introduction: Correcting History by Giving Accused JFK Assassin Lee Harvey Oswald the Defense He Never Received in Life or Death!

- Oswald asks for legal representation – November 23 The JFK Assassination YouTube channel - **https://www.youtube.com/watch?v=zPAVAjNv3fM**
- NBC News – Hoover on Oswald's guilt - **https://www.nbcnews.com/storyline/jfk-assassination-files/jfk-files-j-edgar-hoover-said-public-must-believe-lee-n814881**
- Ruby's motive to kill Oswald - **https://mcadams.posc.mu.edu/sorrow.htm**
- A CBS News Inquiry: The Warren Report (1967) - **https://www.youtube.com/watch?v=qpO0a6gRceo**
- How 8 frames of Zapruder film debunk JFK fatal head shot – Through The Oswald Window YouTube channel - **https://www.youtube.com/watch?v=qkobF6axwss&feature=youtu.be**
- Mark Lane – Rush to Judgement - **https://www.youtube.com/watch?v=TQABleerh_c**

- Geraldo Rivera first to air Zapruder film on Good Morning America - https://www.youtube.com/watch?v=4DwKK4rkeEM – courtesy of JFK Assassination History YouTube channel
- Erosion of trust in government - https://www.pewresearch.org/politics/2015/11/23/1-trust-in-government-1958-2015/
- Dr. David Mantik JFK Assassination Survey - https://themantikview.com/pdf/JFK_Survey.pdf
- List of witnesses - https://www.archives.gov/research/jfk/warren-commission-report/appendix5.html
- RFK Jr. Investigates JFK assassination - https://www.youtube.com/watch?v=V-RGk5DRuwA&t=365s – courtesy Valuetainment Short Clips YouTube channel
- Last Second in Dallas by Josiah Thompson - https://www.barnesandnoble.com/w/last-second-in-dallas-josiah-thompson/1136925320
- Online Edition of the Warren Report on the Assassination of President John F. Kennedy - https://archive.org/stream/WARREN_COMMISSION_VOLUMES/WARREN%20COMMISSION%2011#page/n425/mode/2up
- Government claims all shots came from Oswald at 6th floor window - https://www.archives.gov/research/jfk/select-committee-report/part-1a.html
- Officer Marrion Baker on confronting Oswald - https://www.youtube.com/watch?v=cclCgvkEQio
- The 'smarter' lone assassin sniper's nest - https://throughtheoswaldwindow.com/articles/oswald-window/
- The Commission denies Oswald legal representation - NY Times, Feb. 26, 1964
- Oswald's right to self-defense - Sylvia Meager - Accessories After the Fact - Forward xxix

Chapter 1: Views of Conspiracy from the 'Oswald' Window

- Author's study of the alleged 'lone' sniper's nest - https://throughtheoswaldwindow.com/ttow-lp1
- The Sixth Floor Museum at Dealey Plaza - http://www.jfk.org/
- **Robert J. Groden Website - http://www.jfkmurder.com/**
- Mark Lane's 'Rush to Judgement' on Video - http://www.imdb.com/title/tt0060920/
- Oswald Did Not Act Alone – courtesy The Fedora Chronicles - http://thefedorachronicles.com/rants/2014/2014_11_22-oswald-did-not-act-alone.html
- 1964 CBS Documentary on the Warren Report – courtesy Hidden Passage YouTube Channel - https://www.youtube.com/watch?v=rQCgQsgCyMY
- House Select Committee on Assassinations Report - http://www.maryferrell.org/showDoc.html?docId=800

Chapter 2: The Ignored Warren Commission Ballistic Tests that Disprove its Own 'Single Bullet' and 'Lone Gunman' Theories!

- The flawed 'Magic' bullet trajectory - https://www.youtube.com/watch?v=tjcLtPsOML8&fbclid=IwAR0Jw6gs5JvoH5DC_yQPpSeyD7vYIw1u7TQo3WLwww7g2o8Ak92LHNdn1Jg&app=desktop – courtesy of vydeoynkhorne YouTube video channel
- Dr. Cyril Wecht interview by Patrick Bet-David - https://www.youtube.com/watch?v=xiCxgqGB478&feature=youtu.be – courtesy Valuetainment YouTube channel
- Ballistic Tests for Warren Commission - http://22november1963.org.uk/edgewood-arsenal-bullet-tests
- Applying modern forensics to JFK murder - https://theconversation.com/what-better-forensic-science-can-reveal-about-the-jfk-assassination-88224
- Bullet chemistry analysis doesn't support one gunman in JFK case: https://www.sciencedaily.com/releases/2007/05/070517142528.htm
- What will 3D scans of JFK bullets tell us? - https://www.smithsonianmag.com/smart-news/bullets-killed-kennedy-immortalized-digital-replicas-180973714/
- Dr. Cyril Wecht testimony before HSCA - https://history-matters.com/archive/jfk/hsca/reportvols/vol1/pdf/HSCA_Vol1_0907_8_Wecht.pdf
- The not so magical bullet? - https://throughtheoswaldwindow.com/articles/single-bullet-theory/

Chapter 3: Recently Discovered Film Oddity that Indicates JFK Fatal Head Shot Fired by Second Gunman Now Backed by Modern Technologies!

- Washington Post article by Oliver Stone on the evidence - https://www.washingtonpost.com/archive/opinions/1991/12/24/the-jfk-assassination-what-about-the-evidence/9121c2b0-c625-44ce-9e5f-2a012d458d8d/
- Special Edition Zapruder Film - http://throughtheoswaldwindow.com/videos/the-zapruder-film-special-edition/
- Texas School Book Depository Building - http://mcadams.posc.mu.edu/organ4.htm
- Animation of JFK Kill Shot – https://www.youtube.com/watch?v=x7bIPzBNa60&feature=youtu.be
- Entry Wound to Rear of JFK's Skull - https://en.wikipedia.org/wiki/John_F._Kennedy_autopsy
- ABC News Study of Grassy Knoll Shot - https://abcnews.go.com/Technology/story?id=98689&page=1
- Jackie Jumps on to Trunk of Car - https://www.cbsnews.com/news/agent-who-jumped-on-jfks-limo-recounts-fateful-moments/

- Warren Commission Report on Shots from Depository Building
  http://www.aarclibrary.org/publib/jfk/wc/wr/pdf/WR_3_Shots.pdf
- Orville Nix Film - **http://throughtheoswaldwindow.com/videos/the-orville-nix-film/**

Introduction to Chapters 4,5,6 & 7

A Circumstantial Case:
A Defense of Lee Harvey Oswald by JFK Assassination Researcher Johnny Cairns

- Quorum Radio Debate – Lee Oswald guilty or Innocent? - **https://www.youtube.com/watch?v=YVa_vdo6UQM** – courtesy Best Book Network YouTube channel
- The Commission denies Oswald legal representation - NY Times, Feb. 26, 1964
- Appointment of Walter Craig - WR vol. XIV
- Oswald's right to self-defense - Sylvia Meager - Accessories After the Fact - Forward xxix
- Walter Craig on his role at WC hearings - NY Times, March 20, 1964

Chapter 4: Debunking the Circumstantial Evidence Used by the Warren Commission to Name Lee Oswald as the 'Lone' Assassin of JFK!

Part 1 – The 'Lone' Assassin Rifle

- Irregularities of PO Box issued to Oswald -http://www.jfklancer.com/Holmes.html
- Oswald monitored in Fort Worth? - FBI DeBrueys Report of 02 Dec 1963, p 135
- Oswald connected to Communist party? - Hosty Report, Dated 9/10/63, Commission Exhibit 829
- Who bought the Oswald rifle? - https://www.maryferrell.org/showDoc.html?docId=1139#relPageId=637 and http://www.whokilledjfk.net/salute_to_gil_jesus.htm
- Capability of the 'Oswald' rifle - Accessories After The Fact, page 101, by Sylvia Meagher
- Was A. Hidell named on Oswald P.O. Box? – Warren Report, page 121.
- Capability of the 'Oswald' rifle – Warren Report: CE 2974, Volume XXVI, page 455
- Oswald's proficiency as a marksman – Accessories After the Fact, page 102, by Sylvia Meagher
- Oswald's Marine Record as a Marksman – Accessories After the Fact, page 110, by Sylvia Meagher
- Oswald's Marksman Scores in Marine Corp – Rush to Judgement, page 108, by Mark Lane
- Did poor weather affect Oswald's marksman scores? – Rush to Judgement, page 109, by Mark Lane

- Marine Nelson Delgado interview with Mark Lane - https://www.youtube.com/watch?v=nS9Zi0B60lw – courtesy JFK63Conspiracy YouTube channel
- Sherman Cooley assessment of Oswald's shooting ability – Reasonable Doubt, page 99, by Henry Hurt
- Oswald's shooting ability while is Russia – The Marksmanship Ability of President Kennedy's Assassin – by Michael T. Griffin: http://michaelgriffith1.tripod.com/poor.htm
- Re-enacting the shooting by Oswald in Dealey Plaza – Accessories After the Fact, page 107, by Sylvia Meagher
- Rifle expert Hubert Hummerer on the Mannlicher weapon - http://22november1963.org.uk/mark-lane-presumption-of-innocence - courtesy of 22 November 1963 website
- Test firing Oswald's rifle by experts – Reclaiming Parkland, page 91, by James DiEugenio
- The making of an assassination rifle? – Commission Exhibit 2562, volume XXV, page 808
- Oswald latent palm print on assassination weapon – Accessories After the Fact, page 123, by Sylvia Meagher
- Commission's concern about Oswald palm print - https://www.maryferrell.org/showDoc.html?docId=59637#relPageId=8
- Was Oswald's palm print planted - https://mikegriffith.com/files/palmprint.htm
- Palm print evidence - http://22november1963.org.uk/oswald-fingerprint-palmprint-evidence
- FBI special agent Robert Frazier on condition of Oswald rifle - https://www.fbi.gov/news/stories/the-jfk-assassination-former-agent-recalls-his-role-in-the-investigation
- Assembling the JFK murder rifle – **No Case to Answer – by Ian Griggs, pages 170-171**
- Ian Griggs assembling the Mannlicher-Carcano rifle - https://www.youtube.com/watch?v=HwayY6YqeQs
- The Malcolm Blunt Archive of JFK assassination research documents - http://dealeyplazauk.com/research/collections/malcolm-blunt/documents/
- Mark Lane Interview of Lee Bowers, Rush To Judgment - https://www.youtube.com/watch?v=k8H_DaL_tQk
- A. Hiddell authorized to receive mail at Oswald PO Box? - CE 2585 - Vol. XXV, page 857-862
- Oswald prints on Hidell money order - Harvey and Lee by John Armstrong, page 449

Chapter 5: Debunking the Circumstantial Evidence Used by the Warren Commission to Name Lee Oswald as the 'Lone' Assassin of JFK!

Part 2 – The Problematic Paper Bag

- When was controversial paper bag assembled? http://22november1963.org.uk/tsbd-sixth-floor-paper-bag-genuine
- Ian Grigg demonstrates problems associated with paper bag and Oswald rifle - https://www.youtube.com/watch?v=VUh7gMA-DXs

- The Paper Bag that Never Was – Article by Ian Grigg - https://drive.google.com/file/d/1vHTMl9G3DjtF3CmyLqNz3C6UjRgOS8Ie/view
- A Sack of Lies - Article by researcher Pat Speer - http://www.patspeer.com/chapter4d%3Asackoflies
- Warren Commission testimony of Robert Studebaker of Dallas Crime Lab - https://mcadams.posc.mu.edu/russ/testimony/studebak.htm
- WC testimony of Robert Studebaker on location of paper bag - WC Vol VII, page 144
- Paper bag made in Depository - No Case to Answer, page 204 by Ian Griggs
- Warren Commission's attitude toward Buell Wesley Frazier - Steering Truth, page 55, by Buell Frazier

Chapter 6: Debunking the Circumstantial Evidence Used by the Warren Commission to Name Lee Oswald as the 'Lone' Assassin of JFK!

Part 3 – The Ammunition Linked to Oswald

- Testimony before Warren Commission of John Masen of Masen's Gun Shop – CE 2694, Vol. XXV1, Pages 62 & 63
- Reliability of 6.5 mm Mannlicher-Carcano ammunition – Accessories After the Fact, page 113, by Sylvia Meagher
- Age of assassination ammunition – Rush to Judgement, page 107, by Mark Lane
- Linking ammunition to Oswald – Accessories After the Fact, page 115, by Sylvia Meagher
- Mishandling of shell casings at 6th floor window - Connie Kritzberg's Secrets from the Sixth Floor Window, pages 39-46, with amendment's from Tom Alyea
- Testimony to Warren Commission by Richard M. Sims, detective, Dallas Police Department - http://mcadams.posc.mu.edu/russ/testimony/sims.htm
- Barry Krusch's $5000 Shell Game Challenge - http://krusch.com/jfkshell/story.html
- Photos from National Archives prove Lee Harvey Oswald was framed - https://www.youtube.com/watch?v=25QiW5K9U9c – by Barry Krusch
- The spent rifle shells - http://krusch.com/jfkshell/story_content/external_files/Shell_Game_Gil_Jesus.pdf - by Gil Jesus
- The Dented Bullet Shell: Hard Evidence of Conspiracy in the JFK Assassination – by Michael T. Griffith - https://mikegriffith.com/files/dent.htm
- **Report** – Marina Oswald Porter: Statements of a Contradictory Nature - http://iacoletti.org/jfk/marina-contradictions.pdf
- Jack Ruby lawyer Joe Tonahill interview on case against Oswald - https://www.youtube.com/watch?v=NSW9WGA8IWc
- A brief for the defense (of Oswald) - https://ratical.org/ratville/JFK/OI-ALB.html#s4 - by Mark Lane
- Dallas Police Chief Jesse Curry on Single Bullet Theory - https://www.youtube.com/watch?v=WT4Gy6_rt_o
- The Malcolm Blunt Archive for JFK assassination researchers - http://dealeyplazauk.com/research/collections/malcolm-blunt/

Chapter 7: Debunking the Circumstantial Evidence Used by the Warren Commission to Name Lee Oswald as the 'Lone' Assassin of JFK!

Part 4 – CE 399 (The Magic Bullet)

- Lawyer Joe Tonahill says Oswald would never have been convicted at trial - https://www.youtube.com/watch?v=NSW9WGA8IWc&fbclid=IwAR39jgeMKCdDPA8Mo6BlgOSGIUoBbjyf-N2OgF6BD2AX8u1qPO-mTltq6Fk – courtesy HelmerReenberg YouTube Channel
- Gary Aguilar and Josiah Thompson article on chain of custody - https://www.history-matters.com/essays/frameup/EvenMoreMagical/EvenMoreMagical.htm
- John Hunt article – The Mystery of the 7:30 Bullet - http://www.jfklancer.com/hunt/mystery.html
- O.P. Wright interview with Josiah Thompson on identifying CE 399 – Six Seconds in Dallas, page 175, by Josiah Thompson
- Neutron Activation Analysis on CE 399 - https://www.maryferrell.org/showDoc.html?docId=800#relPageId=75
- Neutron Activation Analysis on CE 399 and recovered fragments - http://22november1963.org.uk/jfk-assassination-neutron-activation-analysis
- Dr. E. Randich (Ph.D) and Dr. P. Grant (Ph.D) debunk Neutron Activation Analysis of CE 399 - https://onlinelibrary.wiley.com/doi/abs/10.1111/j.1556-4029.2006.00165.x.
- Spiegelman, Tobin, James, Sheather, Wexler & Roundhill paper on Chemical and Forensic Analysis of JFK Assassination Bullet Lots: Is a Second Shooter Possible? - https://arxiv.org/pdf/0712.2150.pdf
- Vincent Bugliosi on Neutron Activation Analysis as proof of Oswald as lone assassin - https://www.maryferrell.org/pages/Essay_-_Is_Vincent_Bugliosi_Right_that_Neutron_Activation_Analysis_Proves_Oswalds_Guilt.html
- Chain of Possession – CE 399 - http://www.jfklancer.com/hunt/phantom.htm
- CE 399 found at Parkland Hospital - WC vol VI, page 130
- O.P. Chain of Custody of bullet found at Parkland Hospital - WC vol 24, page 412
- Interview with O.P. Wright - Last Second in Dallas by Josiah Thompson, page 24 & 26
- HSCA report: "Marina Oswald Porter's Statements of a Contradictory Nature" - http://iacoletti.org/jfk/marina-contradictions.pdf, courtesy John Iacoletti
- L.H. Hitchcock's Oswald voice stress test - The Assassination Tapes - by G.J.A. O'Toole, page 129

Chapter 8 – Seeing ISN'T Believing? Putting the JFK Film and Photo Myths to Rest Once and For All

- Penn Jones Jr. Narrated Zapruder film - https://www.youtube.com/results?search_query=through+the+oswald+window+channel – with thanks to Penn Jones Jr. and Robert J. Groden

- Zapruder film alterations? - **http://jfkcountercoup2.blogspot.com/.../two-zapruder-film...**
- Zapruder's perjured testimony to Warren Commission on selling film to Life Magazine? https://mcadams.posc.mu.edu/russ/testimony/zapruder.htm?fbclid=IwAR2SuHGYtm5IXy_jseCIXTNyI1zxbDAIp4kg7xjFgCFeu-wFlfLpeRXAOiU
- Douglas Horne on the Zapruder Film mystery - https://www.youtube.com/watch?v=J_QIuu6hsAc – courtesy of e2films YouTube channel
- The Badge Man Conspiracy Theory - http://grandsubversion.com/jfkAssassination/jfk_assassination/enhanced_photos/grassy_knoll/enhspht_bm.htm
- Zapruder film enhanced - **https://www.youtube.com/watch?v=qBake6r81xc** – courtesy Chris Pittman YouTube channel
- Review of Josiah Thompson's Last Second in Dallas on KennedysandKing.com by Randy Robertson - **https://kennedysandking.com/john-f-kennedy-reviews/a-review-of-last-second-in-dallas-by-josiah-thompson?fbclid=IwAR2tAGsaB7_n3CxKpKIFA1XUDB8U_LLZHLG4POzkcXy8Jx31ESYJjs6-3pl**
- Orville Nix film - https://throughtheoswaldwindow.com/video-gallery/the-orville-nix-film/
- Twenty-Six Seconds: A Personal History of the Zapruder Film – by Alexandra Zapruder - **https://www.amazon.com/Twenty-Six-Seconds-Personal-History-Zapruder/dp/1455541699**
- Dan Rather Describes His Viewing of the Zapruder Film – courtesy of HelmerReenberg - **https://www.youtube.com/watch?v=kiSoxFHyjGY**
- Zapruder Film Shown for First Time on Good Night America – Courtesy of David Von Pein's JFK Channel - **https://www.youtube.com/watch?v=nxCH1yhGG3Q**
- The Zapruder Film: Capturing When the World Changed in 26 Seconds – courtesy of CBS.News.com - **http://www.cbsnews.com/news/the-zapruder-film-capturing-when-the-world-changed-in-26-seconds/**
- Dr. Malcolm Perry's Statement to the House Select Committee Hearings on Assassinations - **https://www.history-matters.com/archive/jfk/hsca/reportvols/vol7/pdf/HSCA_Vol7_M59If_Perry.pdf**
- Mary Ferrell Foundation Explains Single Bullet Theory - https://www.maryferrell.org/pages/Single_Bullet_Theory.html
- Governor John Connally Testimony Before House Select Committee Hearings on Assassinations – Vol. 1, Pages 11-29 - **https://www.history-matters.com/archive/jfk/hsca/reportvols/vol1/html/HSCA_Vol1_0008b.htm**
- Secret Service Agent William Greer Testimony Before the Warren Commission – Vol II, Page 112 - **http://mcadams.posc.mu.edu/russ/testimony/greer.htm**
- Jacqueline Kennedy Testimony Before the Warren Commission – June 5, 1964 - http://www.jfklancer.com/jbk_wc.html
- Sworn Statement of Secret Service Agent Clint Hill – November 30, 1963 - https://www.history-matters.com/archive/jfk/wc/wcvols/wh2/html/WC_Vol2_0070b.htm
- HD Zapruder Film - https://www.youtube.com/watch?v=2fVFO5eG8IY&fbclid=IwAR0OPZFxsPDpwCzqBIDtgAM5PLDZybFytokKCeLf4wRtsaoPRQujkUDE1LM&app=desktop – courtesy windvale YouTube channel
- Willis family on Fatal Head Shot - https://www.youtube.com/watch?v=WHvfDijnASM&feature=youtu.be&fbclid=IwAR2XHW3iWXUTRNu9Q0CtVF4IfIsOTlIDdCEqqvH55LvGmfCmaYFZkwkuFSk – courtesy of JFK63Conspiracy YouTube Channel

- Connally Talks of Shots in 1991 - https://www.youtube.com/watch?v=hSKcOoQH8bc
- The Badge Man - https://www.jfk-online.com/jfk100badge.html

Chapter 9 – The Natural, Instinctive Physical Reactions of Three Key People in Dealey Plaza that Prove a Second Gunman?

- Survey of 216 witnesses to the JFK assassination - https://www.history-matters.com/analysis/witness/index.htm
- Testimony of Bobby W. Hargis before Warren Commission - https://www.history-matters.com/archive/jfk/wc/wcvols/wh6/pdf/WH6_Hargis.pdf
- Testimony of Governor John Connally before Warren Commission - http://mcadams.posc.mu.edu/russ/testimony/conn_j.htm
- Testimony of Nellie Connally before Warren Commission – http://mcadams.posc.mu.edu/russ/testimony/conn_n.htm
- Special Edition Zapruder Film - http://throughtheoswaldwindow.com/videos/the-zapruder-film-special-edition/
- Texas School Book Depository Building - http://mcadams.posc.mu.edu/organ4.htm
- Animation of JFK Kill Shot – https://www.youtube.com/watch?v=x7blPzBNa60&feature=youtu.be
- Entry Wound to Rear of JFK's Skull - https://en.wikipedia.org/wiki/John_F._Kennedy_autopsy
- ABC News Study of Grassy Knoll Shot - https://abcnews.go.com/Technology/story?id=98689&page=1
- Jackie Jumps on to Trunk of Car - https://www.cbsnews.com/news/agent-who-jumped-on-jfks-limo-recounts-fateful-moments/
- Warren Commission Report on Shots from Depository Building http://www.aarclibrary.org/publib/jfk/wc/wr/pdf/WR_3_Shots.pdf
- Orville Nix Film - http://throughtheoswaldwindow.com/videos/the-orville-nix-film/

Chapter 10 – The 'Magic' Bullet May be Less Magical than We Thought but Still NOT Possible!

- Way beyond the Magic Bullet Theory - https://www.youtube.com/watch?v=tjcLtPsOML8&fbclid=IwAR3-UyzSIFORHy5DjDBJZ6Nsi_x6YMsXrqog07Hoy-5A1SEqeGWX0a5CzV4 – courtesy of vydeoynkhorne YouTube channel
- The Single Bullet Theory - https://throughtheoswaldwindow.com/articles/single-bullet-theory/
- Secret Service agent Clint Hill testimony before Warren Commission - https://mcadams.posc.mu.edu/russ/testimony/hill_c.htm

- Harold Rydberg duped into misrepresenting wounds on JFK - *https://throughtheoswaldwindow.com/articles/jfk-autopsy-photos/*
- Interview with Dr. Cyril Wecht – January 8, 2017
- Warren Commission Findings of Shots Fired, Origin of Shots Fired and Results of Shots Fired - http://mcadams.posc.mu.edu/russ/infojfk/jfk6/timing.htm
- Sibert and O'Neill FBI Autopsy Report - http://22november1963.org.uk/sibert-and-oneill-report
- What is the Single Bullet Theory? – courtesy of LiveScience.com - http://www.livescience.com/41369-single-bullet-theory-jfk-assassination.html
- The Magic Bullet: Even More Magical Than We Knew? – courtesy of History-Matters.com - https://www.history-matters.com/essays/frameup/EvenMoreMagical/EvenMoreMagical.htm
- Dr. Malcolm O. Perry Testimony Before the Warren Commission - https://www.history-matters.com/archive/jfk/wc/wcvols/wh6/pdf/WH6_Perry.pdf
- No Proof for Arlen Specter's 'Magic Bullet' Theory – courtesy of WND.com - http://www.wnd.com/2013/09/no-proof-for-arlen-spectors-magic-bullet-theory/
- Dr. James J. Humes Testimony Before Warren Commission – Vol. 2, Page 348 – courtesy of jfk-assassination.com - https://www.jfk-assassination.com/warren/wch/vol2/page348.php
- The Killing of a President – The Complete Photographic Record of the Assassination, the Conspiracy and the Cover-Up – by Robert J. Groden - https://www.amazon.com/Killing-President-Photographic-Assassination-Conspiracy/dp/0140240039
- Governor John Connally Testimony Before the Warren Commission – Vol 4, Page 129 - http://mcadams.posc.mu.edu/russ/testimony/conn_j.htm
- Mrs. Nellie Connally Testimony Before the Warren Commission – Vol. 4, Page 146 - http://mcadams.posc.mu.edu/russ/testimony/conn_n.htm

Chapter 11 – Altering Vital Photographic Evidence to Declare Oswald as the 'Lone' Assassin of JFK!

- Testimony of Umbrella Man Louie Steven Witt before HSCA - https://aarclibrary.org/publib/jfk/hsca/reportvols/vol4/html/HSCA_Vol4_0217a.htm
- AP Photographer James Altgens Photo - https://www.history-matters.com/archive/jfk/wc/wcvols/wh18/html/WH_Vol18_0054a.htm
- The Killing of a President by Robert J. Groden – Page 77 https://www.amazon.com/s/ref=nb_sb_noss?url=searchalias%3Daps&eld-keywords=The+Killing+of+a+President+by+Robert+Groden
- The Story of Dallas Motorcycle Cop Bobby Hargis – courtesy of the Welton Hartford YouTube Channel - https://www.youtube.com/watch?v=CfajL8aWMO8
- JFK and Governor Connally Bullet Fragments – by JFK-info.com - http://www.jfk-info.com/fragment.htm

Chapter 12 – Why the 'Military' Autopsy Alone Would Have Acquitted Lee Harvey Oswald at Trial

- Assassination Science 1998 – Experts discuss medical evidence in JFK assassination - https://books.google.ca/books?hl=en&lr=&id=yNcBAwAAQBAJ&oi=fnd&pg=PR15&dq=assassination+science+1998&ots=6iaDrpOYFw&sig=GW_qU7GRhjMwJTcmk0CKn3jgLBg&redir_esc=y#v=onepage&q=assassination%20science%201998&f=false – Recommended download by author
- Douglas Horne Webinar – Future of Freedom Foundation series – National-Security State and the Kennedy Assassination - https://www.youtube.com/watch?v=YFjuUc5C6bU
- J. Edgar Hoover Memorandum on day Oswald was murdered - https://www.nbcnews.com/storyline/jfk-assassination-files/jfk-files-j-edgar-hoover-said-public-must-believe-lee-n814881
- More than one casket on 11/22/63? - https://www.quora.com/Did-JFKs-body-arrive-at-Bethesda-in-an-aluminum-shipping-casket
- How Dr. Perry's small incision changed history - https://throughtheoswaldwindow.com/articles/dr-malcolm-perry/
- How medical illustrator Harold Rydberg was deceived into misrepresenting the wounds on JFK - https://throughtheoswaldwindow.com/articles/jfk-autopsy-photos/
- How medical illustrator Ida Dox was duped by HSCA into falsifying JFK wounds - https://throughtheoswaldwindow.com/articles/jfk-headshot/
- Q&A with Dr. David Mantik - https://throughtheoswaldwindow.com/articles/dr-david-mantik/
- FBI Autopsy Report on body of JFK - https://www.history-matters.com/archive/jfk/arrb/master_med_set/md44/html/Image0.htm
- Testimony of J. Thornton Boswell before ARRB panel – Feb. 26, 1996 - http://mcadams.posc.mu.edu/russ/testimony/boswella.htm
- Dr. Michael Chesser webinar – Future of Freedom Foundation series – National-Security State and the Kennedy Assassination - https://www.youtube.com/watch?v=YVa_vdo6UQM
- Douglas Horne webinar – Future of Freedom Foundation series – National-Security State and the Kennedy Assassination - https://www.fff.org/freedom-in-motion/video/the-jfk-medical-coverup/
- Dr. Gary Aguilar webinar – Future of Freedom Foundation series – National-Security State and the Kennedy Assassination - https://www.youtube.com/watch?v=YFjuUc5C6bU
- Dr. Gary Aguilar & Kathy Cunningham - https://www.history-matters.com/essays/jfkmed/How5Investigations/How5InvestigationsGotItWrong.htm
- Drawing of JFK wounds by FBI agent Francis O'Neill Jr. for HSCA - https://www.history-matters.com/archive/jfk/arrb/master_med_set/md86/html/md86_0011a.htm
- Drawing by mortician Tom Robinson of JFK's rear head wound for HSCA - https://www.history-matters.com/archive/jfk/arrb/master_med_set/md63/html/Image13.htm
- Statement by Clint Hill in Memorandum from Secret Service to Warren Commission - https://www.history-matters.com/archive/jfk/wc/wcvols/wh18/html/WH_Vol18_0368b.htm

Chapter 13 – Shocking Discoveries by Two Experts Who Reviewed the Sealed JFK Medical Evidence and Found Conspiracy and Cover-Up!

- Dr. Michael Chesser webinar – Future of Freedom Foundation series – National-Security State and the Kennedy Assassination - https://www.youtube.com/watch?v=YVa_vdo6UQM
- Douglas Horne webinar – Future of Freedom Foundation series – National-Security State and the Kennedy Assassination - https://www.fff.org/freedom-in-motion/video/the-jfk-medical-coverup/
- Dr. Gary Aguilar webinar – Future of Freedom Foundation series – National-Security State and the Kennedy Assassination - https://www.youtube.com/watch?v=YFjuUc5C6bU
- Black Op Radio Len Osanic interview with Doug Horne - https://shop.blackopradio.com/downloads/the-doug-horne-interviews-on-mp3/

Chapter 14 – How Two Medical Illustrators Were Duped into Falsifying Autopsy Photos in Support of a 'Lone' Assassin!

- Medical illustrator Harold Rydberg duped by lead autopsy surgeon - https://throughtheoswaldwindow.com/articles/jfk-autopsy-photos/
- Medical illustrator Ida Dox duped by HSCA - https://throughtheoswaldwindow.com/articles/jfk-headshot/
- Dr. Mantik Q&A about JFK autopsy X-rays and photos - https://throughtheoswaldwindow.com/articles/dr-david-mantik/
- Dr. Robert McClelland describes fatal JFK head wound from 9:55 to 10:47 - https://www.youtube.com/watch?v=IQ435IMaCng&t=32s – courtesy of City of Allen ACTV YouTube Channel
- Dr. Charles Crenshaw describes fatal JFK head wound on ABC News 20/20 – from 6:30 to 6:51 - https://www.youtube.com/watch?v=f6CE-WX8H8s&fbclid=IwAR1r8ajUmOx6bCwYd3V2WRD-kd05T5ZkBkrqQ10ID-yNQKbdSIWIQ6xTVYw - courtesy XJNW66B YouTube Channel

Chapter 15 – Ghosts of Witnesses Passed:

They May Be Deceased but the Many Ignored Witnesses of 11/22/63 Can Still Tell Us How JFK Was Assassinated!

- Ed Hoffman saw a man with a rifle behind the picket fence - https://www.youtube.com/watch?v=zwkzoRHBois&fbclid=IwAR06eVBOD-R8a6p_G-c3GBnxrjO-1_O5Z-b10KFbQmGW0gDQgzCgJwPhK1s – courtesy MrChrillemannen YouTube channel
- Witnesses tell Dallas Morning News reporter Earl Golz of clashes with Warren Commission interrogators during testimony - https://texashistory.unt.edu/ark:/67531/metapth339748/m1/1/
- Lee Bowers interview with Mark Lane – See 5:45 - https://www.youtube.com/watch?v=k8H_DaL_tQk – courtesy of montycombs YouTube channel
- James Tague talks spacing of shots with VOA News – See 1:55 - https://www.youtube.com/watch?app=desktop&v=MvmcV6eTfqY&fbclid=IwAR1xzcsW8bh6K72WermICP7_5aBJ60i3chK4H1WPNoS41jkNeAT1zLtkWJY
- Bill Greer testimony before Warren Commission - https://mcadams.posc.mu.edu/russ/testimony/greer.htm
- Bonnie Ray Williams testimony before Warren Commission - http://mcadams.posc.mu.edu/russ/testimony/williams.htm
- Witnesses in Dealey Plaza - www.johncostella.com/jfk
- JFK: Absolute Truth – The Killing of a President, Vol. III – by Robert Groden
- Comprehensive list of Dealey Plaza witnesses - https://tangodown63.com/d-p-witnesses/
- NBC News reporter Robert MacNeil – at 1:04 – heard two shots close together - https://www.youtube.com/watch?v=OZUsH41pU8w – courtesy BBC News YouTube channel
- Mark Lane interviews witnesses on overpass - https://www.youtube.com/watch?v=HEq63vTOwcI – courtesy of HelmerReenberg YouTube channel
- Mark Lane interview with Richard Dodd - https://www.youtube.com/watch?v=p6aTd44CIsw – courtesy of Andrew Hoff YouTube channel
- Witness statements and testimony - https://reopenkennedycase.forumotion.net/t1970-the-witnesses
- The Witnesses Speak - http://assassinationresearch.com/v5n1/v5n1costella.pdf - courtesy of John P. Costella
- Testimony of Billy Newman at trial of Clay Shaw - https://mcadams.posc.mu.edu/russ/testimony/newmwsh.htm
- Last Second in Dallas by Josiah Thompson - https://www.barnesandnoble.com/w/last-second-in-dallas-josiah-thompson/1136925320

Chapter 16 – How Advancement in Imaging Proves JFK Autopsy Photos and X-Rays Were Altered to Frame Oswald as a 'Lone' Assassin!

- Dr. David Mantik's articles and research on the JFK Assassination - https://themantikview.com/
- Q & A with Dr. David Mantik on the Medical Evidence in the assassination of JFK - https://throughtheoswaldwindow.com/articles/dr-david-mantik/
- JFK assassination Survey on the Medical Evidence in the National Archives - https://throughtheoswaldwindow.com/articles/jfk-assassination-survey-by-dr-david-mantik/
- Dr. David Mantik article on Optical Densitometry findings on JFK autopsy x-rays – Assassination Science, page 153 – edited by James H. Fetzer, PhD
- Did windshield fragment cause throat wound? – David Mantik's JFK Assassination Survey – page 58 - **https://themantikview.com/pdf/JFK_Survey.pdf**
- Autopsy photos critically altered – by Dr. David Mantik - **https://www.sott.net/article/182452-The-JFK-Autopsy-Materials-Twenty-Conclusions-after-Nine-Visits**
- Comparison of back of JFK head autopsy photo to Nov. 22/63 photo of JFK at Fort Worth - **https://themantikview.com/pdf/JFK_Survey.pdf - page 53**
- How Five Investigations into JFK's Medical Autopsy Evidence Got it Wrong – by Dr. Gary Aguilar and Kathy Cunningham for History Matters - **https://history-matters.com/essays/jfkmed/How5Investigations/How5InvestigationsGotItWrong.htm**
- Dr. David Mantik Webinar for Future of Freedom Foundation - https://www.youtube.com/watch?v=NflDau5PP18 – courtesy of Future of Freedom Foundation YouTube channel
- MANTIK, DAVID WAYNE. The John F. Kennedy X-rays: The saga of the largest "Metallic fragment". **Medical Research Archives**, [S.l.], n. 3, June 2015. ISSN 2375-1924. Available at: <https://esmed.org/MRA/mra/article/view/177>.
- Dr. David Mantik's Report on 6.5 mm metallic fragment in JFK's head not acknowledged by the Warren Report - file:///C:/Users/dobgo/AppData/Local/Temp/177-1-868-1-10-20150629.pdf
- A Demonstrable Impossibility – article on History Matters by John Hunt - https://history-matters.com/essays/jfkmed/ADemonstrableImpossibility/ADemonstrableImpossibility.htm

Chapter 17 – From Cartoons to Modern 3D Realism: These Evolving Technologies Seek to Finally Tell Us How JFK was Assassinated!

- John Orr's presentation at Houston mock trial of Lee Harvey Oswald - https://www.youtube.com/watch?v=bH_r1uDCa88 – courtesy of Citizens Against Political Assassinations YouTube channel
- John Orr's website - **http://www.mountainrivercabins.com/JFK.htm**
- DP3D Project website - **https://jfkforensics.com/index.html**

- Mark Johnson's website – www.jfkforensics.com
- Angelos Leiloglou – Owner/Operator Forensic Viz

Chapter 18 – Top Researchers Weigh In on How Best to Formally Re-Investigate the JFK Assassination and the Key Evidence that Needs to be Examined

- William Kelly – owner/operator - http://jfkcountercoup.blogspot.com/
- T&RC in South Africa model - https://www.britannica.com/topic/Truth-and-Reconciliation-Commission-South-Africa
- Objectives of a T&RC inquest - https://mettacenter.org/definitions/gloss-concepts/rehumanization-3/
- A T&RC inquest to heal the consequences of 1960's assassinations – https://www.politico.com/news/magazine/2020/08/16/does-america-need-a-truth-and-reconciliation-commission-395332
- How five investigations into JFK's Autopsy/Medical records got it wrong – by Gary Aguilar, M.D. - https://www.history-matters.com/essays/jfkmed/How5Investigations/How5InvestigationsGotItWrong.htm
- NOVA's Cold Case: JFK - the Junk Science Behind PBS's Recent Foray into the Crime of the Century – by Gary Aguilar. M.D. -Includes two lengthy rebuttals written with Cyril Wecht, MD, JD, in response to articles written by Lucien Haag in the AFTE Journal https://kennedysandking.com/john-f-kennedy-reviews/nova-s-cold-case-jfk-junk-science-pbs
- The Magic Bullet: Even More Magical Than We Knew? – by Gary Aguilar, M.D. - https://www.historymatters.com/essays/frameup/EvenMoreMagical/EvenMoreMagical.htm
- Three lectures by Gary Aguilar, M.D. on the medical/forensic evidence broadcast on C-Span - https://www.c-span.org/person/?garyaguilar
- The People V. Lee Harvey Oswald – by Walt Brown - https://www.amazon.com/People-V-Lee-Harvey-Oswald/dp/0786700815
- The Mysterious Death of Number 35 – Pat Speer YouTube series - https://www.youtube.com/results?search_query=the+mysterious+death+of+number+35+pat+speer
- Life and Death: Memoirs of America's Most Controversial Forensic Pathologist – by Cyril Wecht, M.D., J.D. - https://www.amazon.com/Life-Deaths-Cyril-Wecht-Controversial/dp/1476684243/ref=sr_1_1?crid=1V2EEUF53TCWB&dchild=1&keywords=life+and+death+of+cyril+wecht&qid=1611240530&sprefix=Life+and+Death+of+Cyril+Wecht%2Caps%2C159&sr=8-1
- Secret Service expert Vince Palamara YouTube channel - https://www.youtube.com/user/VincePalamara
- The Not So Secret Service - by Vince Palamara - https://www.amazon.ca/Not-So-Secret-Service-Agency-Kennedy-Assassination-ebook/dp/B06ZZMTYQ3/ref=sr_1_8?dchild=1&keywords=books+by+vince+palamara&qid=1619036887&sr=8-8
- Vince Palamara's five books on the Secret Service - https://www.youtube.com/user/VincePalamara
- J. Gary Shaw co-author with Charles Crenshaw, M.D. – Trauma Room One: The JFK Medical Coverup Exposed - https://www.amazon.com/Trauma-Room-One-Medical-

Coverup/dp/1931044309/ref=sr_1_6?dchild=1&keywords=j+gary+shaw+books&qid=1619218249&sr=8-6
- The JFK Assassination: The Evidence Today – by James DiEugenio - https://www.amazon.com/JFK-Assassination-James-DiEugenio/dp/1510739831/ref=sr_1_1?dchild=1&keywords=james+dieugenio+book&qid=1619219089&sr=8-1
- Re-Open JFK case - **https://reopenkennedycase.forumotion.net/**

Appendices

Resources

Index

About Johnny Cairns

About Dave O'Brien

INDEX

A

Aquilar, Dr. Gary – 10,155,156,189,197, 228,229,251-258,260,261,263,264,362,363,389,393,394,396,397
Alyea, Tom – 131,132,138,388
Altgens, James – 213-219,392
Anderson, Eugenie (Major) – 89-91
Antill, Peter – 74,141.142
Archives, National – 5,9,35,154,171,179, 181,194,196,227,229,233,238,242,243, 244,251,252,263,274,300,311,316,329, 337,349,352,368,373,379,380,384,388, 396
Arnold, Carolyn – 281,286
Assassination Records Review Board (ARRB) – 132,179,227,232,246,255, 256,257261, 305,358,361,364,369,393

B

Baker, Marrion – 280,384
Baden, Dr. Michael – 260,263,271,272, 310
Ball, Joseph – 79,136,137
Bannister, Guy - 342
Barbour, John - 355
Belin, David – 39,45,46,113,114,133-135,284,285
Biden, Joe – 2,345,349,350,352,365, 376,377
Blakey, G. Robert - 341
Boggs, Hale - 209
Bojczuk, Jeremy - 116
Boswell, Dr. J. Thornton – 206,227,246, 248,306,368,393
Bowers, Lee – 95,96,292,387,395
Brennan, Howard – 166,279-281
Brinegarn, John H. – 124,125
Bronson, Charlie - 285
Brown, Walt – 356,357,397,404
Brugioni, Dino - 179
Buckout, Dr. Robert - 166
Bugliosi, Vincent – 93,159-161,389
Burkley, Dr. George – 170,313
Bush, George W. – 339,340

C

Cabell, Earle - 292
Cadigan, James – 112,115,116,120
Cairns, Johnny – v,vii,7-9,13,38,39,49, 55,57,83,102,109,117,123,147,173,230, 233,281,334,347,357,362,386,398,403, 404
Calloway, Ted - 166
Chesser, Dr. Michael – 10,189.195-197, 228,229,234,242-251,255,263,306,307,311,316,358,362,393,394,398
Citizens Against Political Assassinations (CAPA) – 3,319,348,365,379,396
Connally, John – 11,16,40,158,190,191, 200,204,240,268,304,320,390,391,393
Connally, Nellie – 391,392
Conspiracy Theorist – 3,4,7,50,179,182, 200,204,205,228,232,332
Cooley, Sherman – 93,97
Craig, Walter E – 52,53,96,386
Crawford, James - 294
Crenshaw, Dr. Charles - 269,366,394, 397
Creuzot, John – 343,372-274
Cunningham, Cortland – 79,81,86,154, 155,343,393,396
Curry, Jesse (police Chief) – 102-104,107,170171,235,280,388

D

Darnell, James - 364
Day, Lt. J.C. – 106,132,133,138
Dealey Plaza – vi,5,8,11,15,17,23,25,29, 31,31,32,38,54,55,74,166,175,182,184-186,192,215,216,219,220,222,230,249, 251,270,277,282,284,288-290,293,297, 299,300,307,317-324,330,332-334,360, 362,365,379,380,384,387,390,391,395, 406
Delgado, Nelson – 91-93,97,98,387
DiEugenio, James – 46,98,357,359,363, 379,387,398
Doughty, Cpt. George – 135
Dox, Ida – 10,237,258,270-274,308,310, 312,313,346,394
DP3D project –
10,11,320,321,322,324,326-331,333,335, 396
Drain, Vincent T – 103,106,133,135,331
Dulles, Allen –115

E

Eisenberg, Melvin – 75,112,115,116

Ely, John - 91
Ernest, Barry – 71,404
Euins, Amos – 280

F

Fair Play for Cuba Committee – 63,64, 342
Fensterwald, Bud - 366
Ferrell, Mary – 7,379,384,386,387,389, 390
Ferrie, David - 342
Finck, Dr. Pierre – 201,227,228,240,248, 303,304,368
Fischer, Ronald – 284,285
Folsom, Allison (Lt. Colonel) – 89,91,97
Ford, Gerald – 2,39,45,46
Foreman, Percy - 105
Frazier, Buell Wesley – 82,83,117,388
Frazier, Robert – 75,76,149,154,155,157, 162,387,388
Fritz, Will (Captain) – 103,104,107,130-132,137,138,166
Fuller, Ronald – 156

G

Galanor, Stewart – 59,61
Garland, Merrick – 377
Garrison, Jim – 181,296,342,355
Golz, Earl – 284,286,395
Grant, Patrick M. – 160-162,389
Gregory - Dick – 177,333
Greer, William – 53,182,292,390,395
Griffith, Michael T. – 94,141,387,388
Griggs, Ian – 59,80,84,114,121,387,388
Groden, Robert – 7,177,178,286,287,310,333,363,384,389, 292,395
Guinn, Dr. Vincent – 158-162

H

Hall, Renee – 343,374
Hargis, Bobby – 187-189,191-193,197, 217,250,391,392
Harris, Larry – 166,366
Hathcock, Carlos - 96
Haygood, Clyde - 293
Henderson, Ruby - 285
Hickey, George - 293
Hidell, A – 57,58,60-62,66-73,386,387
Hill, Clint – 209,214,262,263,268,390, 391,394
Hitchcock, L.H. – 171,172,389
Hitler, Adolf - 222

Hoffman, Ed – 282,283,395
Holland, Brent - 380
Holland, Sam – 282,283
Holmes, Harry – 58-60,66,386
Hoover, J. Edgar – 77,143,152,170,226, 383,393
Horne, Douglas – 179,232,390,393,394
Hosty, James – 62,64,66,386
House Select Committee on Assassinations (HSCA) -25,39,165,183, 220,233,253,256,265,303,339,345,353, 358,384,390
Hughes, Howard - 380
Humes, Dr. James J. – 201,202,227,234-236,238-240,255,266,305,311-313,368,392
Hunt, John – 154-156,389,396
Hurt, Henry – 93,103,106,387

J

Jackson, Robert – 280,293
James, William D. - 160
JFK autopsy – 9.32,203,214,227,230, 233,237,243,248,251,255,260,266,274, 299,300,302,303,305,306,360,394,396
Joannides, George - 361
Johnson, Lady Bird - 292
Johnson, Lyndon – 2,170
Johnson, Mark – 320-322,324,335,397
Johnsen, Richard E – 149,153
Johnston, Carolyn - 286
Jones Jr., Penn – 5,279,389

K

Kellerman, Roy - 293
Kelly, William – 343,345,397
Kennedy, Jackie (Mrs.) – 27,40-44,47, 186-190,193,197,198
Kennedy, Joseph - 222
Kennedy, John F. – 1,12,13,25,26,51,57, 59,119,123,124,137,144,147,158,159, 170,185,199,225,317,335,338,342,347, 356,372,373,376,379,384,396,404-406
Kennedy, President – 2,3,719,22,28,29, 35,38,39,49,50,65,70,75,104,111,120, 138,140,156,163,164,171,172,175,180, 187,193,196.197,200,209,214,219,227, 228,230,231,233,234,237,238,242,249, 262,266,271,273,275,277,278,295-297,303,313,319,320,369,373,387,403, 405
Kennedy, Regis - 184
Kennedy, Robert F. (RFK) – 1,2,313,333, 338,339,347
Kennedy, Robert F. Jr. – 2,333,338,339

Killion, Charles – 154,155
King Jr., Martin Luther – 1,271,340,347, 348
King III, Martin Luther – 3

L

Lane, Mark – 5-8,13,49,52,54,90,92,95,96,127,163, 169,231,277,279,282,284,289, 383,384.386,387,388,395,404
Letona, Sebastian – 101
Law, William - 404
Lawson, Winston - 294
Lee, Vincent T. – 63,64,66
Leiloglou, Angelos – 320,324,335,397
Liebeler, Wesley – 58,59,91,92,98

M

MacNeil, Robert – 293,395
Magic Bullet – vi,55,75,147,199,200,203-205,314,385,389,391,392,397
Majewski, Steve - 155
Maloney, Carolyn – 350,351,352,376,377,378
Mannlicher-Carcano (rifle) – 29,57,73,74, 78,80,81,85,98,112,116,124,126,127,130 ,141,165,196,244,291,387.388,401
Mantik, Dr. David – 9,10,155,189,197, 228,229,233,237,245,247-249,251, 263,271,299,300-303,305,306, 308,310,311,314 316,333,360, 362,363,384,393,394,396
Marcello, Carlos - 342
Masen, John Thomas – 124,125,388
Mathieson, Olin -127
McClelland, Dr. Robert -237,256,305,309, 312,394
McKinnon, Cheryl - 283
McIntyre, William - 294
Meagher, Sylvia – 52,95,103,104,126, 128,386-388,404
Miller, Austin - 284
Mitchell, Mary - 294
Montgomery, Det. Leslie Dell -116, 118
Mooney, Luke - 294
Moore, Avery – 344,374
Moorman, Mary – 183
Morley, Jefferson – 3,361
Mueller, Robert – 339,344,353
Murphy, Thomas - 283
Murret, Charles 'Dutz' – 342

N

Neuromuscular Reaction – 45,46,181, 188,193,194,195,197
Newman, Billy & Gayle – 295,296,395
Newton's Second Law of Motion – 39,40, 178,188
Nix, Orville – 17,38,42,175,176,182,183, 186,188,192,318,386,390,391

O

O'Brien, Dave – vii,viii,ix,362,398,404,405
O'Donnell, Kenneth - 291
Odum, Bardwell D. – 150,151,155,156
Oliver, Beverly - 183
O'Neill, Francis – 238-240,392,393
Orr, John – 6,11,317-320,322,323,325, 327-335,396
Osanic, Leonard - 394
Oswald, Lee (Harvey) – v,vi,2,3,5,7,16, 22,28,38,39,49,51,52,57,58,62,65,67,,68, 71,72,93,88,94,102,104,107,113,114,117 ,124,125,140,145,149,163,169,171,172, 175,181,185,225,244,251,252,265,277-279,300,304,337,338,342,343,356,364, 365,369,372,381383,386-389,396,397,403,406.406
Oswald, Marguerite - 52
Oswald (Porter), Marina – 53,58,164,165, 388
O'Toole, George – 171

P

Palamara, Vince – 363,397,404
Parker, Greg – 364,379,404
Perry, Dr. Malcolm – 202,206,207,235, 362,371,390,392,393,405,406
Persons, James R. – 94
Peters, Gary – 351,352,376,378
Portman, Rob – 351,352,376,378
Powell, Johnny – 288

R

Randich, Erik – 160-162,389
Rankin, J. Lee – 52,64,65,77,97,143
Ray, James Earl – 340
Rea, Ralph – 59
Reid, Geraldine – 286,287
Reno, Janet – 318,319
Riggs, C.A. – 62
Rivera, Geraldo – 177,384
Roberts, Craig – 96
Robinson, Tom – 259,393

Rose, Dr. Earl – 171,226,228,303,304
Rosenstein, Rod – 344
Roundhill, D. Max – 160
Rowley, James – 153
Ruby, Jack – 8,168,176,200,346,383,388
Rydberg, Harold – 208,236,237,254,266-274,315,392-394

S

Samoluk, Tom – 132
Schnapf, Larry – 13,319,320,329,335, 348-352,365,375,378,379
Sessions, Jeff – 344
Shaw, Clay – 181,296,342,395
Shaw, J. Gary – 7,366,397
Shaw, Robert (Dr.) – 35
Sheather, Simon J. – 160,389
Sibert, James – 238-240,392
Simmons, James Leon – 283
Simmons, Ronald – 75
Simpich, Bill – 65
Sims, Det. Richard – 133,134,136-138, 388
Single Bullet Theory – 11,26,28,29,31,34, 35,159,179,193,203-205,208,235,239-241,268,273,274,304,305,315,322,325-330,388,390-392
Shankland, Gordon – 152
Sixth Floor Museum at Dealey Plaza – 32,362,379,384,390,406
Sixth Floor (Oswald) Window – 95,109, 130,167,168,285,383,388
Slack, Garland – 293
Sorrels, Forrest – 292
Sparano, Larry – 380
Specter, Arlen – 240,392
Spence, Jerry – 93
Speer, Pat – 367,388,397
Spiegelman, Cliff – 160,162,389
Springer, Pearl – 294
Stombaugh, Paul – 103
Stone, Oliver – 3,4,13,46,333,359,385
Studebaker, Robert – 110,118,388
Sucher, William – 99
Syrett, Richard – 380

T

Tague, James – 292,395
Talbot, David – 363
Thompson, Josiah – 5,7,151,152,155, 288,363,384,389,390,395
Thornton, Ruth – 294
Tippit, J.D. – 225,342,372
Tobin, William A. – 160
Todd, Elmer Lee – 149,153-155,157,163

Tomlinson, Darrell C. – 148-152,155,156, 158,162
Tonahill, Joe – 168,169,388,389
Trump, Donald – 334,349
Twain, Mark –163

U

Umbrella Man – 218-220,222,392

V

Vincente, Victor – 65

W

Wade, Henry (District Attorney) – 104
Walker, Gen. Edwin – 129
Walther, Carolyn – 285,293
Warren Commission Report – 59,83,126, 319,326,340,386,391,405
Watergate – 2,334,361
Wecht, Dr. Cyril – 12,25,29-34,189,197, 227,229,237,240,260,272,311,362,368, 385,392,397
Weisberg, Harold – 5,7,404
Weitzman, Seymour – 96,294
West, Troy – 113-115,120
Wexler, Stuart – 160
Williams, Bonnie Ray – 85,168,292,395
Willis, Linda – 294
Winborn, Walter - 283
Witt, Louie Stephen – 222,392
Wright, O.P. – 148,150,151,153,389

X

X, Malcolm – 1,347,359

Y

Yarborough, Ralph – 293

Z

Zahn, James A – 89
Zapruder, Abraham (film) – 28,37,40-42, 44,47,53,171,175-179,181,182,189,194, 204,383-385,389-391

About Johnny Cairns

JFK Assassination Researcher

Johnny Cairns lives in Edinburgh, Scotland. He first got interested in the life and death of President John Fitzgerald Kennedy from his father Robert Cairns who shared his admiration of President Kennedy with Johnny from an early age.

With regards to the murder of John Kennedy, Johnny argues that the circumstantial evidence against the accused, Lee Harvey Oswald, is seriously flawed.

With his own murder denying him a public trial, there was an almost universal rush to judgment on Oswald. This has led him to have been wrongfully branded as guilty of the murder of President Kennedy.

Johnny's focus on the circumstantial evidence against Oswald forms the basis for his contribution to this book, Case 'NOT' Closed. Much like a public trial would have done, Johnny examines key areas of evidence in Chapters 4,5,6 & 7 and exposes the flaws of the U.S. government's case against Lee Harvey Oswald.

A PERSONAL NOTE FROM JOHNNY

As one of the leaders of the next generation of JFK assassination researchers, Johnny Cairns acknowledges those who came before him.

My special thanks are reserved for Dave O'Brien for trusting me to be a part of his new project and also for his friendship. Also, to many of the other researchers who I converse with and who's time and friendship I treasurer. Thanks to Walt Brown, Greg Parker, Jim Di Eugenio, Barry Ernest, William Law, Vince Palamara, to name but a few, my respect for you is at the utmost and your time given to me is always appreciated.

To the early critics who's work on the Kennedy case was the pathway for me to understand what transpired on 11/22/63, we are all indebted to you. I raise a glass to the courage of people like Mark Lane, Harold Weisberg and Sylvia Meagher. To you, we are all indebted.

"A nation that is afraid to let its people judge the truth and falsehood in an open market is a nation that is afraid of its people."

- John F. Kennedy

About Dave O'Brien

JFK Assassination
<u>Researcher</u>

- Began studying the JFK assassination in 1965 at age 13.
- At age 13 and 14, read summary edition and 26 volumes of the Warren Commission Report.
- In grade 9, wrote a 100+ page history paper to establish reasonable doubt as would have been required at trial to find Lee Harvey Oswald not guilty as the assassin of President John F. Kennedy.
- Established a dialogue with Dr. Malcolm Perry between 1968 and 1972, the first doctor to tend to President Kennedy at Parkland Hospital. The first letter is reproduced in Chapter 4 and all three letters are displayed in the Appendices section.
- 14-part series of articles – November 1972 in The Mississauga Times.
- Covered House Select Committee on Assassinations Hearings in Washington in 1978.
- February 11, 1979 – Granted rare access to the 'Oswald' window in the Texas School Book Depository Building.
- February 21, 1979 – 15th anniversary article in The Mississauga News featuring photos taken at the infamous 'Oswald' window.

- Consultant to 1983 Canadian Broadcasting Corporation production – The Fifth Estate: Who Killed JFK? - **https://www.youtube.com/watch?v=h3xquKx4ttg**
- 1975 to Present – Gives live JFK assassination seminars in Canada to more than 200,000 people to-date.
- 2010 – Donated Dr. Malcolm Perry letters to Sixth Floor Museum at Dealey Plaza - **http://www.jfk.org/** (Readable in Museum library).
- 2019 – Authored Through the 'Oswald' Window based on extraordinary observations from the assassin's position in the Book Depository Building, as well as more than 50 years of research, writings and seminars on the assassination of President John F. Kennedy - **https://throughtheoswaldwindow.com/ttow-lp1/**
- 2022 – Authored JFK Case NOT Closed: Key Evidence Dismissed, Ignored, Altered or Suppressed to Frame Lee Harvey Oswald as the 'Lone' Assassin!

www.ingramcontent.com/pod-product-compliance
Lightning Source LLC
Chambersburg PA
CBHW062242300426
44110CB00034B/1107